HOLT SOCIAL STUDIES
AMERICA
AND ITS NEIGHBORS

JoAnn Cangemi
General Editor

HOLT, RINEHART AND WINSTON, PUBLISHERS

New York ● Toronto ● Mexico City ● London ● Sydney ● Tokyo

General Editor
JoAnn Cangemi

is Professor of Education and Director of Graduate Studies in Education at Nicholls State University, Thibodaux, Louisiana. She received her Ph.D. in elementary education from Louisiana State University. Prior to her university work, Dr. Cangemi taught in the public elementary schools for ten years. She has served as a consultant in social studies curriculum development to numerous public and private school systems. She is the author of a number of articles in professional journals. For ten summers she taught in Europe as part of a foreign exchange program. She was a 1981 recipient of the Merit Teacher Awards given by the National Council for Geographic Education.

Contributing Writers

James J. Rawls

is a native of Washington, D.C. He received a B.A. from Stanford University and a Ph.D. from the University of California, Berkeley. Since 1975, Rawls has been a history instructor at Diablo Valley College. His articles and reviews have appeared in such publications as *The Journal of American History*, *The Wilson Quarterly*, *The American West*, and *California History*. He is the author of *Indians of California: The Changing Image* and coauthor of *California: An Interpretive History* and *Land of Liberty*. Rawls has served as an historical consultant on numerous films and on a series of television programs funded by the National Endowment for the Humanities.

Pat Cuthbertson

is a writer who lives in Santa Cruz, California. She received a B.A. in English literature from the University of California at Santa Cruz, graduating with General College Honors. She has written material for Language Arts and Social Studies texts. She has two sons in whose classes she has worked as a volunteer for several years.

Tom Cuthbertson

is a writer of "how to" books who lives in Santa Cruz, California. He received a B.A. in literature from the University of California at Santa Cruz and an M.A. in writing from San Francisco State. He has written a number of technical manuals, as well as material for Language Arts and Social Studies texts. He has done volunteer work in his sons' elementary school classrooms.

James A. Harris

is an elementary principal in the D.C. Everest Area School District, Schofield, Wisconsin. He graduated from Miami University, Oxford, Ohio, and received his Master's degree in Curriculum and Instruction from the University of Wisconsin. Mr. Harris began his teaching career while a VISTA volunteer and later served in the Wisconsin Native American Teacher Corps. For ten years he taught kindergarten and primary grades in Wisconsin schools. Mr. Harris is a frequent consultant to school systems and educational corporations. He has published many articles in professional magazines and journals.

"Brooklyn Bridge," Kathy Jacobsen/Jay Johnson Gallery

Photo and art credits are on pages 477–479

ISBN: 0-03-001802-1

6789 039 9876

Teacher Consultants

Linda R. Aucoin

Teacher
Thibodaux Elementary School
Thibodaux, Louisiana

Sister Eileen Frances M. Cooke

Teacher
Saint Helena School
Philadelphia, Pennsylvania

Patricia F. Ho

Teacher
Thomas J. Watson, Sr., Elementary School
Endicott, New York

Janet A. Kaiser

Teacher
Hawthorne School—District U205
Elmhurst, Illinois

Thomas J. Ladouceur

Teacher
Stone Valley Intermediate School
Alamo, California

Dr. JoAnn B. Seghini

Director of Curriculum Development
Jordan School District
Sandy, Utah

Ramona H. Simpson, M.A.

Teacher
Saffell Elementary
Lawrenceburg, Kentucky

James Robert Warren

Teacher
Tileston School
Wilmington, North Carolina

Content Consultants

Joseph D. Baca

Social Studies Education Specialist
New Mexico Department of Education
Santa Fe, New Mexico

Sam F. Dennard, Ph.D.

Social Studies Coordinator
Clayton County Schools
Jonesboro, Georgia

Dr. George Gregory

Curriculum Consultant
Albany, New York

David M. Helgren, Ph.D.

Assistant Professor
University of Miami
Coral Gables, Florida

Betty Jo Johnson

Coordinator, Social Studies Services
Wake County Public School System
Raleigh, North Carolina

Dr. Helen E. Jones

Associate Professor of Education
Fairmont State College
Fairmont, West Virginia

Diane Lindstrom

Associate Professor of History
University of Wisconsin
Madison, Wisconsin

Eveleen Lorton

Professor of Education
University of Miami
Coral Gables, Florida

Norman McRae

Director of Social Studies Department
Detroit Public Schools
Detroit, Michigan

Thomas H. Pagenhart

Associate Professor of Geography
California State University
Hayward, California

Clyde P. Patton

Professor of Geography
University of Oregon
Eugene, Oregon

Daniel H. Ryan

Professor
College of Lake County
Grayslake, Illinois

Mary Jo Wagner

Director, Women's Studies Program
University of Oregon
Eugene, Oregon

Philip Weeks

Department of History
The University of Akron
Akron, Ohio

Susan A. White

Senior Economics Consultant
Adult Performance Level Project:
    The University of Texas at Austin
Austin, Texas

Readability Consultant

Paul Greenfield

Associate Professor
English and Humanities
Dutchess Community College
Poughkeepsie, New York

TABLE OF CONTENTS

UNIT 4

UNIT 5

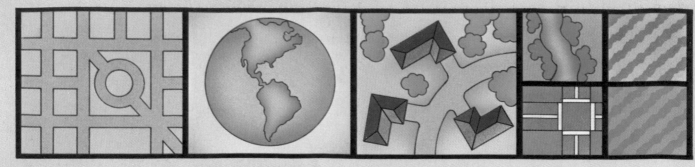

MAPS AND GLOBES

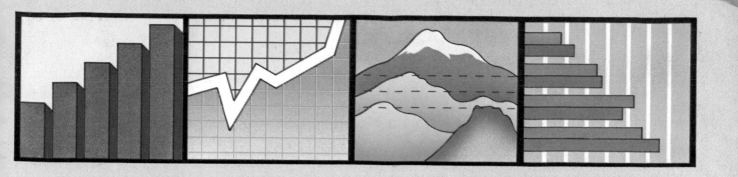

CHARTS, GRAPHS, AND DIAGRAMS

reviewing
GEOGRAPHY skills

Imagine that you are a tour guide in the United States. Some foreign visitors ask, "What is this country like?" "Where are the mountains and the rivers?" "How cold is it here?" It would be possible to answer all of these questions by showing the visitors different kinds of maps.

In this book, you will be using many kinds of maps. Some kinds you have not seen before. Others may be very familiar. All will be helpful in answering questions about your country and its history. To get the most out of maps, it is important to know how to read and use them.

Keys and Symbols

On most of the maps in this book you will find a **map key.** A map key contains the **symbols** used on the map and explains what they mean. The symbol for a railroad might look like this ++++++ . A dot is the symbol for towns and cities. The size of the dot depends on the size of the town or city. On the map at the left, the symbol ⊛ represents the capital of a nation.

Color may be a map symbol too. On the map at the left, color is used to represent countries.

Distance Scale
and Direction Finder

Another important part of a map is a **distance scale.** A distance scale tells you how much real distance is represented by the distances shown on a map. The distance scale on the page 10 map shows how much distance on a map equals 1000 kilometers and 800 miles on earth. To find the distance between two cities, you would use a ruler or paper's edge to find the distance on the map. Then you would measure this distance against the scale to find out how much the distance equals on earth.

Most maps have a **compass rose** to show the main directions of north, south, east, and west. They usually appear only as N, S, E, and W. The intermediate, or in-between directions—northeast, southeast, northwest, and southwest—may be marked as NE, SE, NW, and SW. The map on page 10 has only an arrow to indicate north. To find the other directions, you must know that south is opposite north, west is to its left, and east is to its right. As you can see on the map, Ottawa is almost directly north of Washington, D.C.

distance scale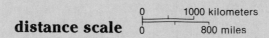

compass rose

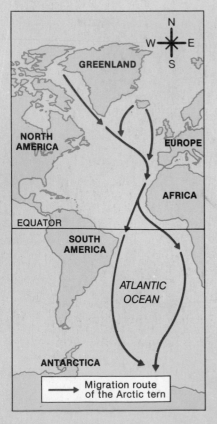

Charleston, South Carolina

Legend:
- Interstate highway
- State highway
- State road
- Bridge
- Airport

0   2 kilometers
0   2 miles

52 78
8 km.
26
7
7.5 km.
3.2 km.
Ashley River
61
5 km.
7
171
78
52
3.2 km.
17
6.6 km.

N W E S

GREENLAND
NORTH AMERICA
EUROPE
AFRICA
EQUATOR
SOUTH AMERICA
ATLANTIC OCEAN
ANTARCTICA

→ Migration route of the Arctic tern

N W E S

Maps for Special Purposes

The map of North America on page 10 is a **political map.** So is the map of the United States on pages 16–17. A political map shows how people have divided an area into nations, states, counties, or townships. A political map shows boundary lines and important cities and towns. Sometimes a political map may also show rivers, canals, railroads and the like.

A political map is only one of many kinds of maps. Throughout this book, you will study many special kinds of maps.

A **road map** is used to find the best route from one place to another. People also use road maps to measure how far one place is from another.

Look at the road map of Charleston, South Carolina. The roads are marked with numbers. State highways are marked with this symbol 17. Interstate highways which connect different states are marked like this 26. Imagine you are on Route 17, near Route 7. You want to go to the airport by the shortest route. To figure out how far the trip will be by various routes, you can add the little numbers that appear between the small red arrows like this▼. The shortest route to the airport is along Routes 7 and 26. The distance from your starting point to the intersection at Route 26 is 8.2 kilometers. The distance from this intersection to the airport is 8 kilometers. So the total distance is 16.2 kilometers.

Maps do not move, but they can show the routes followed by people, animals, wind, and rain, as they move from one place to another. The route map at the left shows how a bird, the Arctic tern, migrates, or travels, long distances every year from its breeding grounds in the north to its feeding grounds in the south. You can see the movement of the Arctic tern by following the arrows.

You will find other maps in this book showing travel routes. Some will show how people moved from one part of this country to another long ago.

The map on pages 18–19 is called an **elevation map.** It has that name because it shows the height of mountains, plateaus, plains, and other landforms. The measurement for height begins at sea level. Sea level is where the land and sea meet.

On an elevation map, each level of height is represented by a different color. You can see how high each area is by checking its color on the map and then finding the color on the elevation key. On the elevation key, find the color that represents below sea level. Then find the color that represents elevations from sea level to 200 meters.

Locate the Appalachian Mountains on the map on pages 18–19. Then study the map key. You can see that the Appalachian Mountains are not as high as the Rockies because none of the Appalachians is over 2,000 meters, or 6,562 feet.

You can learn about the climate of an area by looking at a **climate regions map.** The map below divides the United States into eight climate regions. The map key describes the climate of each region. Each kind of climate is shown with a different color. The climate regions map shows which parts of the United States are coldest, and which have milder climates.

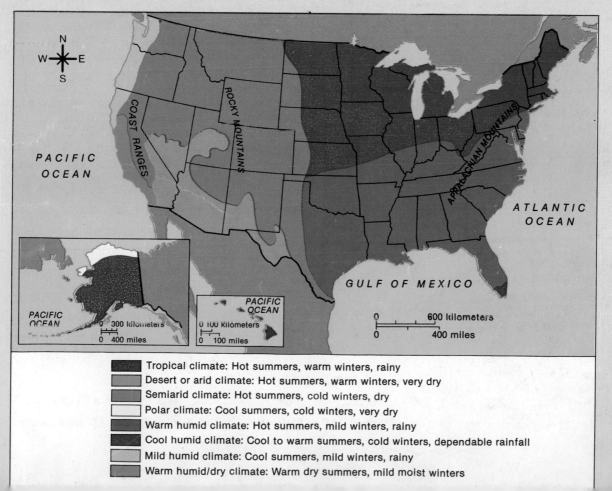

Tropical climate: Hot summers, warm winters, rainy
Desert or arid climate: Hot summers, warm winters, very dry
Semiarid climate: Hot summers, cold winters, dry
Polar climate: Cool summers, cold winters, very dry
Warm humid climate: Hot summers, mild winters, rainy
Cool humid climate: Cool to warm summers, cold winters, dependable rainfall
Mild humid climate: Cool summers, mild winters, rainy
Warm humid/dry climate: Warm dry summers, mild moist winters

Collections of Maps

When many maps are collected and put together in a book, the book is called an **atlas.** An atlas can have a special purpose. For example, a road atlas contains road maps of each area of a country.

There are many different kinds of specialized atlases. For example, there are atlases for climate, population, and products. An atlas may also be a combination of maps showing all these things and more. The atlases pictured here are only a few of the atlases you might find in your local library.

Using a Globe

As you know, a map is a flat picture of something that is not really flat. To see landmasses and oceans in a form closer to their true shape, we use a model of the earth called a **globe.** Your classroom globe probably rests in a frame like the one pictured below. The globe is tilted in its frame to show the actual tilt of the earth on its axis. Imagine the axis as a line running through the earth's center from the North Pole to the South Pole.

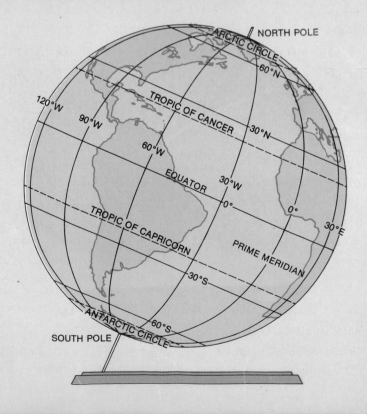

You can turn a globe in the direction of the earth's spin—west to east. The earth makes one complete turn in that direction every 24 hours. This rotation gives us day when our part of the earth faces the sun, and night when our part moves away from the sun. The earth makes 365 of these rotations every year as it moves in its orbit around the sun.

The globe is marked by a series of lines that circle it from east to west and from north to south. The east–west lines are called lines of latitude, or **parallels.** The **equator** is a parallel that circles the widest part of the earth, halfway between the North and South Poles. Two other important parallels are the Tropic of Cancer, to the north, and the Tropic of Capricorn, to the south. These two lines mark the boundaries of the warm climate zone known as the tropics. The Arctic Circle and the Antarctic Circle are two other important parallels. These lines mark the climate zones known as the polar, or frigid, zones.

The globe also has vertical—north–south—lines called lines of longitude, or **meridians.** One meridian runs from the North Pole through Great Britain, western Europe, and western Africa, to the South Pole. This is called the **Prime Meridian.** On the opposite side of the world from the Prime Meridian is the 180th meridian. These two meridians are used in dividing the world into time zones.

You can see that the parallels and meridians together form a **grid** over the globe. A grid is a pattern made when a series of lines cross. The grid of parallels and meridians can be used to describe the location of any place on the earth.

For purposes of study, the globe is often divided into **hemispheres,** or half spheres. The equator divides the globe into the Northern Hemisphere and Southern Hemisphere. The 20th west meridian is the line most often used to divide the globe into the Eastern Hemisphere and Western Hemisphere.

This book tells the story of the United States, Canada, and Latin America. Maps and globes help make the story easier to understand. By reading the chapters and studying the maps, you will learn how and why these nations and regions grew as they did.

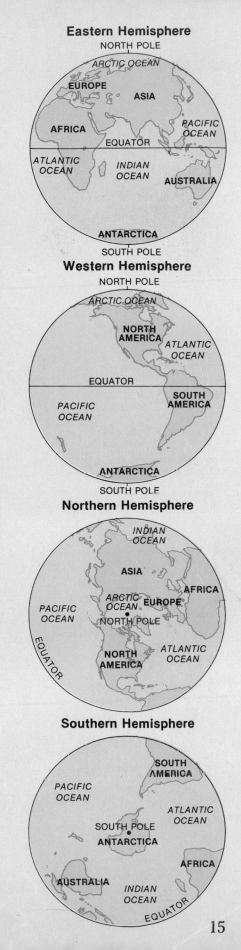

Eastern Hemisphere

Western Hemisphere

Northern Hemisphere

Southern Hemisphere

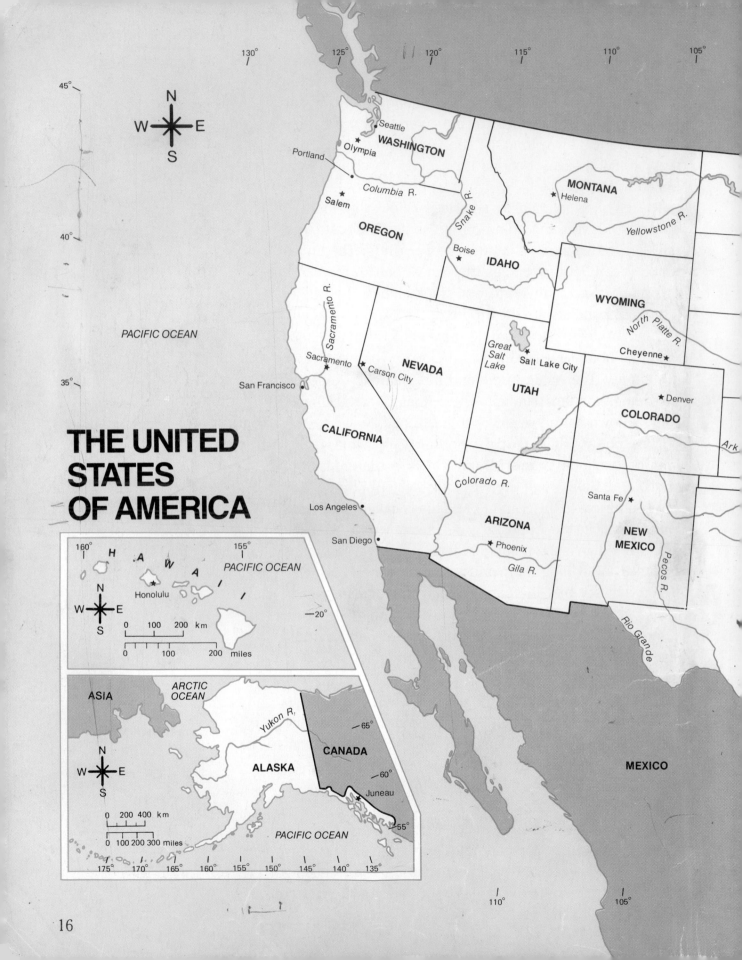

THE UNITED STATES OF AMERICA

N
W E
S

45°
130°   125°   120°   115°   110°   105°

PACIFIC OCEAN

WASHINGTON
• Seattle
★ Olympia
Portland •
Columbia R.
★ Salem
OREGON

Snake R.

MONTANA
★ Helena
Yellowstone R.

Boise ★
IDAHO

WYOMING
North Platte R.
Cheyenne ★

40°

35°

Sacramento R.
Sacramento ★
San Francisco •
Carson City •
NEVADA

Great Salt Lake
Salt Lake City ★
UTAH

★ Denver
COLORADO
Ark

CALIFORNIA

Los Angeles •

San Diego •

Colorado R.

ARIZONA
Phoenix ★
Gila R.

Santa Fe ★
NEW MEXICO

Pecos R.

Rio Grande

MEXICO

160°   155°
H A W A I I
• PACIFIC OCEAN
Honolulu ★
N
W E
S
—20°
0   100   200 km
0   100   200 miles

ASIA
ARCTIC OCEAN
Yukon R.
—65°
CANADA
—60°
N
W E
S
ALASKA
Juneau ★
—55°
PACIFIC OCEAN
0   200 400 km
0 100 200 300 miles
175° 170° 165° 160° 155° 150° 145° 140° 135°

110°   105°

CANADA

Lake Superior

St. Lawrence R.

NORTH DAKOTA
• Bismarck

MINNESOTA
St. Paul
Minneapolis

SOUTH DAKOTA
• Pierre

WISCONSIN
Madison
Milwaukee

M I C H I G A N

Lake Michigan

Lake Huron

MAINE
Augusta

45°

Montpelier

Hudson R.

NEW HAMPSHIRE
VERMONT
Concord

MASSACHUSETTS
Boston
RHODE ISLAND

NEW YORK
• Buffalo
Albany
New York City
Newark

Hartford
Providence
CONNECTICUT

Lake Ontario

NEBRASKA
• Lincoln

IOWA
★ Des Moines

Lansing
Detroit
Chicago

Lake Erie
Cleveland

PENNSYLVANIA
Pittsburgh
Harrisburg

Trenton
NEW JERSEY
Philadelphia

Kansas City
Topeka

Illinois R.
Springfield
ILLINOIS

INDIANA
Indianapolis
Columbus
Cincinnati

OHIO
Ohio R.

WEST VIRGINIA

Baltimore
Dover
DELAWARE
Annapolis
MARYLAND

KANSAS

Missouri R.
Jefferson City
St. Louis

Richmond
Charleston

Washington, D.C.

Arkansas R.

OKLAHOMA
Oklahoma City

MISSOURI

KENTUCKY
★ Frankfort

VIRGINIA

35°

Canadian R.

ARKANSAS
Little Rock

Tennessee R.

★ Nashville
TENNESSEE

★ Raleigh
NORTH CAROLINA

Red R.

Dallas

Sabine R.

MISSISSIPPI

TEXAS
★ Austin Houston

San Antonio

Baton Rouge
New Orleans
LOUISIANA

★ Jackson

Mississippi R.

ALABAMA
Montgomery

Atlanta

Savannah R.

Columbia
SOUTH CAROLINA

GEORGIA

ATLANTIC OCEAN

30°

Tallahassee

FLORIDA

GULF OF MEXICO

Miami

25°

0 100 200 300 400 500 kilometers

0 100 200 300 400 500 miles

⊛ National capital
★ State capital
• City

100° 95° 90° 85° 80° 75°

17

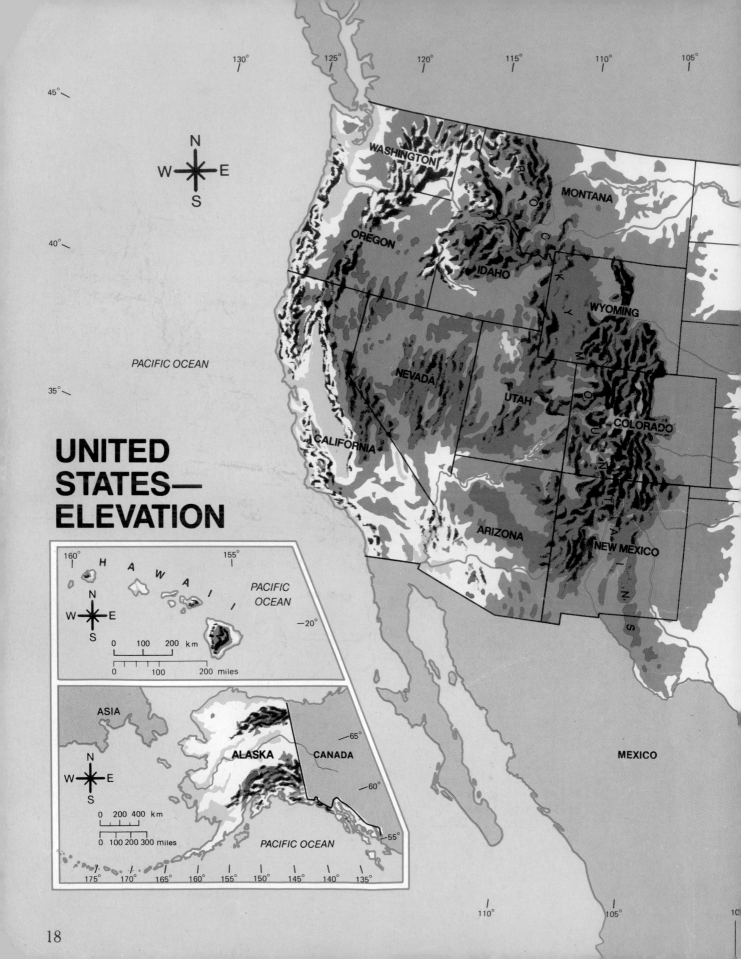

UNITED STATES— ELEVATION

PACIFIC OCEAN

WASHINGTON

OREGON

IDAHO

MONTANA

WYOMING

NEVADA

UTAH

COLORADO

CALIFORNIA

ARIZONA

NEW MEXICO

MEXICO

H A W A I I

PACIFIC OCEAN

—20°

| 0 | 100 | 200 km |
| 0 | 100 | 200 miles |

ASIA

ALASKA

CANADA

—65°

—60°

—55°

PACIFIC OCEAN

| 0 | 200 | 400 km |
| 0 | 100 200 | 300 miles |

100°   95°   90°   85°   80°   75°   70°

CANADA

NORTH DAKOTA

SOUTH DAKOTA

MINNESOTA

WISCONSIN

Lake Superior

M I C H I G A N

Lake Huron

Lake Michigan

MAINE   45°

NEW HAMPSHIRE

VERMONT

MASSACHUSETTS

RHODE ISLAND

CONNECTICUT

NEW YORK

Lake Ontario

Lake Erie

NEBRASKA

IOWA

ILLINOIS

INDIANA

OHIO

PENNSYLVANIA

40°

NEW JERSEY

DELAWARE

MARYLAND

KANSAS

MISSOURI

KENTUCKY

WEST VIRGINIA

VIRGINIA

35°

NORTH CAROLINA

ATLANTIC OCEAN

ARKANSAS

TENNESSEE

A P P A L A C H I A N   M O U N T A I N S

SOUTH CAROLINA

OKLAHOMA

MISSISSIPPI

ALABAMA

GEORGIA

30°

LOUISIANA

TEXAS

FLORIDA

25°

GULF OF MEXICO

0   100   200   300   400   500   kilometers

0   100   200   300   400   500   miles

Meters		Feet
Over 4,000		Over 13,124
2,000-4,000		6,562-13,124
1,000-2,000		3,281-6,562
200-1,000		656-3,281
Sea level-200		Sea level-656
Below sea level		Below sea level

80°   75°

19

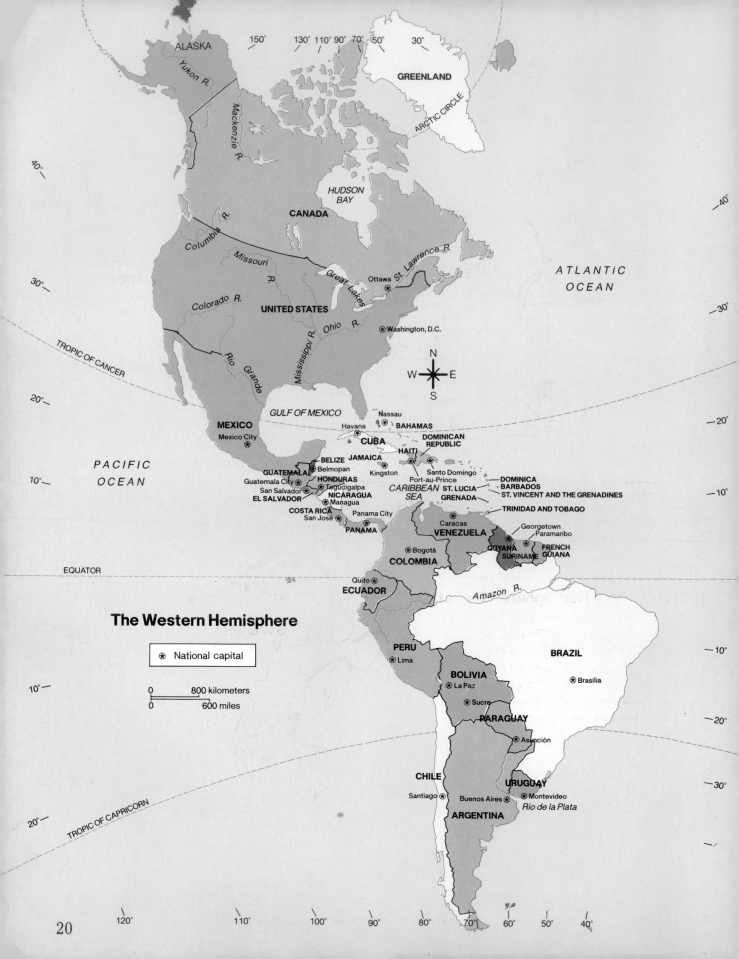

The Western Hemisphere

ALASKA

Yukon R.

GREENLAND

ARCTIC CIRCLE

CANADA

Mackenzie R.

HUDSON BAY

Columbia R.

Missouri R.

Great Lakes

St. Lawrence R.

Ottawa

ATLANTIC OCEAN

UNITED STATES

Colorado R.

Ohio R.

Mississippi R.

Washington, D.C.

TROPIC OF CANCER

Rio Grande

MEXICO

Mexico City

GULF OF MEXICO

Nassau

Havana

BAHAMAS

PACIFIC OCEAN

CUBA

DOMINICAN REPUBLIC

HAITI

BELIZE

JAMAICA

Santo Domingo

GUATEMALA

Belmopan

Guatemala City

HONDURAS

Kingston

Port-au-Prince

DOMINICA

BARBADOS

San Salvador

Tegucigalpa

CARIBBEAN SEA

ST. LUCIA

ST. VINCENT AND THE GRENADINES

EL SALVADOR

NICARAGUA

GRENADA

Managua

COSTA RICA

TRINIDAD AND TOBAGO

San José

Panama City

Caracas

PANAMA

VENEZUELA

Georgetown

Paramaribo

Bogotá

GUYANA

FRENCH GUIANA

COLOMBIA

SURINAME

Quito

ECUADOR

EQUATOR

Amazon R.

PERU

BRAZIL

Lima

BOLIVIA

Brasília

La Paz

Sucre

PARAGUAY

Asunción

CHILE

URUGUAY

Santiago

Buenos Aires

Montevideo

Rio de la Plata

ARGENTINA

TROPIC OF CAPRICORN

N W E S

⊛ National capital

0   800 kilometers
0   600 miles

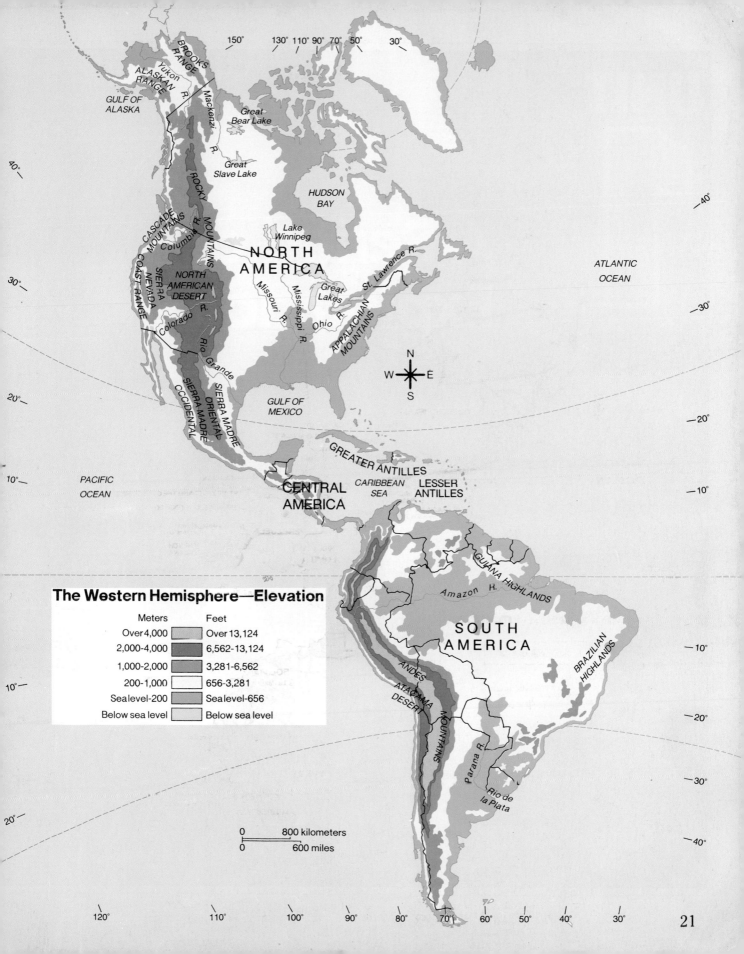

The Western Hemisphere—Elevation

Meters		Feet
Over 4,000		Over 13,124
2,000-4,000		6,562-13,124
1,000-2,000		3,281-6,562
200-1,000		656-3,281
Sea level-200		Sea level-656
Below sea level		Below sea level

BROOKS RANGE

ALASKAN RANGE

Yukon R.

GULF OF ALASKA

Mackenzi. R.

Great Bear Lake

Great Slave Lake

HUDSON BAY

ROCKY MOUNTAINS

CASCADE MOUNTAINS

Columbia R.

Lake Winnipeg

NORTH AMERICA

SIERRA NEVADA

COAST RANGE

NORTH AMERICAN DESERT

Colorado R.

Great Lakes

St. Lawrence R.

ATLANTIC OCEAN

Missouri R.

Mississippi R.

Ohio R.

APPALACHIAN MOUNTAINS

Rio Grande

SIERRA MADRE OCCIDENTAL

SIERRA MADRE ORIENTAL

N
W   E
S

GULF OF MEXICO

PACIFIC OCEAN

GREATER ANTILLES

CENTRAL AMERICA

CARIBBEAN SEA

LESSER ANTILLES

GUIANA HIGHLANDS

Amazon R.

SOUTH AMERICA

ANDES

ATACAMA DESERT

MOUNTAINS

BRAZILIAN HIGHLANDS

Parana R.

Rio de la Plata

0   800 kilometers
0   600 miles

21

A Period of Exploration

Imagine a time many thousands of years ago. A group of hunters came upon a huge, unexplored land. They were the first people in America.

Over many thousands of years, the descendants of those hunters moved farther into the new territory. Eventually, they settled in all parts of the land. Different groups developed different languages and customs.

Then one day, a new group of wanderers came to the land. They had new customs, new languages, and a very different way of life.

This tale is the history of early North and South America. In this unit, you will read about the people who first settled the land and about the people who came from Europe many years after the first settlers.

CHAPTER 1

The First Inhabitants

No one knows exactly how people first came to North America. However, many scientists believe they know what the land was like before people came. A thick sheet of ice blanketed much of the North. Large lakes covered parts of the Great Plains. In the Southwest, there were forests.

Time passed. Eventually, people came to the land. This chapter will describe how the first people may have come to North America and how they lived.

At the end of this chapter, you should be able to:

○ Trace the route of the first settlers to North America.
○ Locate where various American Indian groups lived.
● Read a map using latitude and longitude.
○ Tell how the land affected the lives of the Indians.

1 Through the Gateway

America's first settlers were probably hunters who came from Siberia, a very cold part of northern Asia. Many scientists believe these hunters followed big game animals over a land bridge into what is now Alaska. The land bridge served as the gateway to the American continents for about 10,000 years.

Bridge to America

Almost two million years ago, the weather in the northern half of the earth changed greatly. Temperatures grew colder. The snow that fell did not melt in the summer. Instead, it became icy and hard. It piled up in huge sheets of ice called **glaciers** (**glay**-sherz). Many of these glaciers moved slowly onto and across the land.

This period of time is called the **Ice Age,** because so much of the North was covered with ice. As sea water froze to form glaciers, the water level in the seas dropped. The map shows one place where this happened during the Ice

glacier
a huge sheet of slowly moving ice

Ice Age
a period of time, starting almost 2 million years ago and ending about 10,000 years ago, when much of North America was covered by glaciers

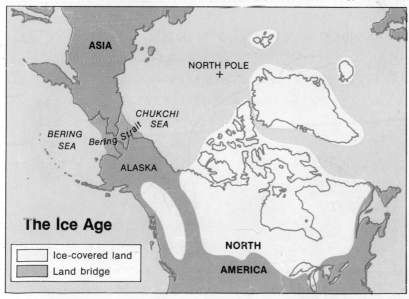

ASIA

NORTH POLE
+

CHUKCHI SEA

BERING SEA

Bering Strait

ALASKA

The Ice Age

☐ Ice-covered land
▨ Land bridge

NORTH

AMERICA

strait

a narrow waterway that connects two larger bodies of water

Age. There is a narrow waterway, or **strait,** between the Bering and Chukchi (**chook**-chee) seas. During the Ice Age, this strait probably became very shallow. In some places, it may have dried up completely. The dry places could have formed the land bridge to North America.

The scientists think the land bridge existed toward the end of the Ice Age. The people of Asia may have found it 15,000 to 40,000 years ago. Group after group moved across the bridge to the unexplored continent of North America. They passed through what is now Alaska and western Canada.

The Ice Age ended about 10,000 years ago. The weather changed again. Glaciers melted and the seas slowly rose. The land bridge was once again covered by water.

As time passed, the people explored all of the Americas. It took thousands of years to settle so much land.

Living Off the Land

North America is a land of many geographic features. There are mountains and deserts. There are forests, plains, lakes, and oceans. American Indians, descendants of the first settlers, lived in or near all these regions.

The Indians' way of life depended on the geography of the area they lived in. The Indians learned to adjust, or **adapt,** to their surroundings. They used whatever they found around them to make houses, clothing, and tools.

adapt

change in order to fit in

American Indians of the Southwest

26

Indians who settled near the ocean fished. On the Great Plains, where there were many animals, the Indians were hunters. In places with rich soil, the Indians farmed.

There were hundreds of different American Indian tribes. Each tribe had its own territory. Tribes had different languages and customs too. Tribes that lived near each other, however, often had much in common.

The American Indians can be divided into five groups, according to where they lived. The Northwest Indians lived near the forests of the Pacific Coast. The California Intermountain Indians settled between the Rockies and the California coast. The Plains Indians hunted in the central part of the continent. Tribes of Southwest Indians built their homes in the dry desert areas of what is now Nevada, Arizona, and New Mexico. The Eastern Woodlands Indians lived throughout the eastern part of the continent.

The map shows where each of these groups lived. It also lists the names of some of the tribes that lived in each region. As you read more about these groups, think about how geography affected their lives.

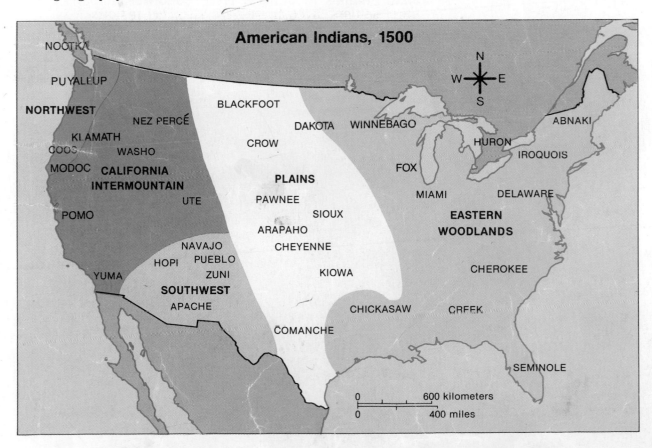

American Indians, 1500

The Northwest Indians

The Northwest Coast has thick forests and many mountains. Rather than clearing trees for settlements, the Northwest Indians lived along the seacoast. These Indians got much of their food from the sea.

The tribes used 18-meter- (60-foot-) long fishing boats, called canoes, to paddle up and down the Pacific coast. Salmon, clams, seals, and whales were plentiful.

Indians of California

Many small tribes of California Intermountain Indians lived on the land that stretches from today's California coast to the Rocky Mountains. Tribes along the coast fished. In the mountains, they hunted. And almost all of them gathered acorns and other nuts and seeds.

The Southwest Indians

Gathering food was more difficult in the Southwest. There was no ocean filled with fish. There were not many land animals to hunt. But the Southwest Indians could farm. In places with enough rainfall, tribes grew corn and beans. In drier areas, the Indians developed a way to bring water to their crops. This is called **irrigation.**

irrigation
a way of supplying water to land

American Indians of the Northwest Coast

The Plains Indians

On the Plains, there was little water for farming or fishing. However, millions of buffalo roamed the Plains. So, many Plains Indian tribes were hunters. They depended on the buffalo for food, clothing, and shelter.

The hunting tribes moved often, always following the buffalo. They built houses that they could take down easily. These houses, or tents, were called **tepees.** Plains Indians made them by stretching buffalo skins over a cone-shaped frame of poles.

tepee
a cone-shaped tent made of animal skins

Eastern Woodlands Indians

Eastern America was covered by dense woodlands. Many Eastern Woodlands Indians cleared land, built villages, and became farmers. Some fished in the Atlantic Ocean and the rivers of the region. They also hunted animals that lived around their settlements.

The Eastern Woodlands Indians used small trees to build their homes, or **wigwams.** These were bark-covered lodges with rounded roofs and wooden frames. The Iroquois (**ih**-ruh-kwoi) tribes lived in **longhouses.** These houses were long and rectangular. Some were large enough to hold 20 families.

wigwam
an Eastern Woodlands Indian dwelling with an arched frame and a bark or hide covering

longhouse
a long, wooden house shared by many families of Iroquois Indians

Section Review

Write your answers on a sheet of paper.
1. What was the Ice Age, and when did it occur?
2. How did the first American Indians reach North America?
3. What five groups can North America's early Indians be divided into?
4. Why did the Plains Indians live in tepees?
5. Do you think that people living in the United States today are as affected by where they live as were the early North American Indians? Explain.

Using Longitude and Latitude

The early Indians of North America traveled from place to place on the huge American continent without using maps. They would have had a difficult time trying to direct a person to a distant place.

Today we have maps of every place on the earth. By drawing lines across maps and globes, we can divide the surface of the earth into many sections. By numbering these lines, we can easily refer to a particular section on the earth's surface. This system lets us describe the exact location of any place. The system also tells us exactly how far one place is from another.

Lines of latitude, called parallels, identify distances north and south of the equator. Latitude is measured in degrees. There are 90 degrees of latitude north of the equator and 90 degrees of latitude south of the equator. The equator is located at 0 degrees (0°). The parallels north of the equator are numbered in degrees north. Those south of the equator are numbered in degrees south. Therefore, the North Pole is at 90 degrees north (90° N). The South Pole is at 90 degrees south (90° S). On the globe in the margin, every twentieth parallel is shown.

The distance from one degree of latitude to the next is about 111 kilometers (69 miles). To figure the distance north or south of the equator, multiply the number of degrees north or south by 111 kilometers (69 miles).

Lines of longitude, or meridians, show location and distance east or west of the Prime Meridian. The Prime Meridian is at 0°. It runs from the North Pole to the South Pole, through Europe and Africa. There are 180 degrees of longitude east of the Prime Meridian. Each meridian is numbered in degrees east. There are also 180 degrees of longitude west of the Prime Meridian. Each meridian is numbered in degrees west. Along the equator, the meridians are 111 kilometers (69 miles) apart. As you go toward

Parallels

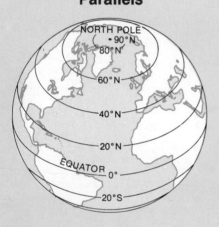

Meridians

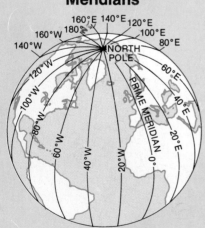

the poles, the meridians get closer together. At the poles, the meridians are zero kilometers (miles) apart.

New Orleans is located where the thirtieth parallel north meets the ninetieth meridian west. To describe the city's exact location, you must give the number, or **coordinate,** of each of these lines. We say that New Orleans is located at 30° N, 90° W.

coordinate
a number used to help pinpoint a location

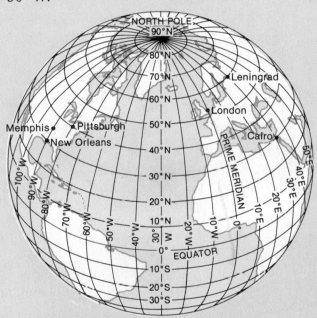

━━━━ Practice Your Skills ━━━━

1. What is located at 30° N, 31° E?
2. What are the coordinates for Memphis?
3. How many degrees north of Cairo is Leningrad? How many kilometers is this?
4. Pittsburgh is how many degrees north of New Orleans? how many degrees east?

2 Ways of Indian Life

There were many differences among the American Indian groups. Each had its own customs, language, and religious beliefs. However, they all had one thing in common. They all had a deep respect for nature. This was because the Indians relied on nature for their food, clothing, and shelter.

Nature's Role

Nature was an important part of most American Indian religions. Plants, animals, the earth, and the sun had religious importance. The Indians prayed to spirits or forces in nature whose help they needed. Often they used song and dance as part of their religious ceremonies.

Life in the Northwest

The beaver, raven, whale, salmon, and eagle were important animals in the religion of Northwest Indians. These animals were thought to bring luck, both good and bad. Therefore, it was important to keep these animals friendly.

Sandpainting was part of the Navajo Indians' religious ceremony. The painted figures represent aspects of nature.

The Northwest Indians treasured the salmon. Each year, the salmon swam upriver, against the current, to lay eggs. As the fish swam by, the Indians caught them. This yearly return of the salmon was the most important religious event in the Northwest. The Indians hoped their songs and dances would please the spirits and make the fish return.

The tribes of the Northwest placed great importance on wealth. They liked to show off their wealth. One way they did this was by giving away valuable objects. This was done at a large ceremony called a **potlatch,** which means "giving." A person who gave away much wealth could become a respected member of the tribe. Often this person became the tribe's leader.

potlatch
a Northwest Indian ceremony in which the host gives away valuables to prove her or his wealth

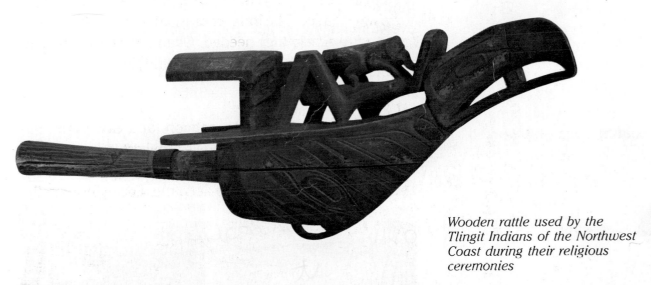

Wooden rattle used by the Tlingit Indians of the Northwest Coast during their religious ceremonies

Life in California

The California Intermountain Indians lived in small groups. In some areas, acorns and berries were plentiful. Since they did not have to work hard to find food, these Indians had time to develop many crafts. Indian tribes such as the Pomo made beautiful baskets decorated with feathers. The Indians used the baskets to collect their food.

Life in the Southwest

Indians of the Southwest lived in various kinds of houses. Some lived in dwellings that looked like modern-day apartment houses. Others lived in one-family homes.

The Pueblo (pu-**eb**-loe) families worked and lived together as a group. Usually, the Pueblo men wove cloth and farmed. The men did the heavy construction work on the houses, while the women did the lighter work. Women also made pottery.

The Navajo (**nav**-uh-hoe) people were different. The Navajos liked living in separate family groups. Each family farmed its own land.

In the Southwest, both Pueblos and Navajos depended on the coming of rain. Without rain, the crops would die. The Southwest Indians believed their religious ceremonies helped bring rain.

Life on the Plains

Because most of the Plains Indians followed the buffalo, they did not build lasting settlements. They made almost everything they owned from buffalo hides, bones, and horns.

The Plains tribes, such as the Sioux (**soo**), were divided into groups called **bands.** Each band traveled separately. Leaders were chosen because they were brave or wise. However, the leaders did not give orders. All the men in a band made decisions for the group.

band
a group formed of different American Indian families that traveled and worked together

(left) Pottery jug of the Southwest Indians

(right) Sioux shield

Eastern Woodlands Life

The tribes of the East, such as the Hurons (**hyoohr**-onz), lived in villages. The larger villages had hundreds of houses and thousands of people. A strong, high wooden fence usually surrounded each village.

Many eastern tribes farmed. The Eastern Woodlands Indians grew corn and beans in large fields outside the village. Most tribes had gardens near their homes too.

The Iroquois were a very powerful Eastern Woodlands tribe. Their tribe was divided into family groups called **clans.** Iroquois women were in charge of these clans. The women chose men to represent the clan at tribal meetings.

Like the other Indian groups, Indians of the Eastern Woodlands had a religion based on nature. They prayed to many spirits. They believed, for example, that lakes, mountains, and forests had spirits. They also believed that one spirit, the Master of Life, was most powerful.

clan
a family group in which all members had a common ancestor

American Indians of the eastern United States

Section Review

Write your answers on a sheet of paper.
1. Why was nature so important to the American Indians?
2. How did Northwest Indians show off their wealth?
3. Name one way Pueblo and Navajo Indians were different from each other.
4. In what ways do people today show their respect for nature?

CHAPTER 2
Searching for Riches

From the very first, Europeans who explored North America were looking for riches. In this chapter, you will read about those explorers. You will find out about Christopher Columbus. You will also read about some adventurers who crossed the Atlantic long before Columbus.

At the end of this chapter, you should be able to:
○ Tell who the Vikings were and where they lived.
○ Explain why explorers were searching for an all-water route to China and India.
● Use a compass to find directions.
○ Describe what lands were claimed by English, French, and Dutch explorers.
● Compare how nations are pictured on globes and maps.

1 Europe's First Explorers

It took a lot of courage to be an explorer 1,000 years ago. Every trip was a journey into the unknown. Slowly, however, explorers began to learn more about the world. With each voyage, they could draw maps more accurately. The early explorers made travel easier for those who would come later.

Viking Voyages

In the late 900's, the Vikings were the best sailors and shipbuilders in Europe. Each year, they left their homes in Scandinavia (skan-duh-**nave**-ee-uh). They sailed to foreign lands in search of food and riches.

Viking sailors also looked for land that could be used for farming. It was hard to grow food in the cold Scandinavian climate. One group of Vikings discovered and settled Iceland, an island west of Norway. Later, Eric the Red, a Viking leader, sailed farther west. He found Greenland, another large island. Eric spent three years exploring the coast of Greenland. After finding a good location for a settlement, he led 500 of his people to this new land.

The Vikings had none of the instruments or maps sailors use today. So the Vikings figured out directions by the positions of the sun and the stars—and by guesswork. On one trip, a Viking named Biarni Herjolfsson (**byahr**-nee hur-**yoohlf**-son) made a mistake. He was headed for Greenland, but he passed it and sailed all the way to North America. When he realized his error, he turned around.

When he returned to Greenland, Herjolfsson told the other Vikings about his trip. He described the thick forests he had seen. One man who listened was Leif Ericson, the son of Eric the Red. Ericson knew that the Vikings on Greenland needed wood for ships. He thought they might

Viking chess piece made of ivory

saga

story of the adventures and heroic deeds of Viking leaders

get lumber in this new land. In the summer of 1001, Leif Ericson left Greenland to see this new land.

Most of what we know about Ericson's voyage comes from stories that the Vikings told. These stories, called **sagas,** were histories of Viking leaders and their adventures. The sagas were not written down. They contained no exact geographical information. So in later years, many people did not think they were true.

But the tale of Ericson's trip was true. The sagas describe a land in which Ericson found grapes, wheat, and trees. The sagas also describe a house that Ericson built at a place he called Vinland. The descriptions match an area in what is now Newfoundland, Canada. In 1960, a scientist uncovered the remains of Ericson's settlement.

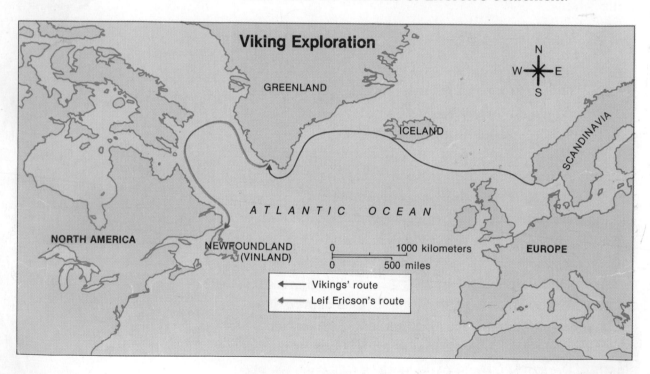

Viking Exploration

GREENLAND

ICELAND

SCANDINAVIA

ATLANTIC OCEAN

NORTH AMERICA

NEWFOUNDLAND
(VINLAND)

EUROPE

0   1000 kilometers
0   500 miles

← Vikings' route
← Leif Ericson's route

Ericson's settlement did not last long. Because of problems with the American Indians, the Vikings sailed away from Vinland.

Riches from the East

While the Vikings were sailing west, other Europeans were traveling east. Some went to the areas around the Mediterranean Sea. Others went as far east as India and China. They found these lands rich in gold, gems, and silk

They tasted new spices that could be used to flavor food and keep it from spoiling.

One traveler to the East was an Italian named Marco Polo. He went to China in 1275 and stayed for 17 years. When he returned to Italy, he wrote about his visit. In his book, Polo described the places he had visited and the customs of the people he had met. Many people first learned about China from Marco Polo's book. His descriptions of the wonders and riches that he had seen in the East made people even more eager to trade with China.

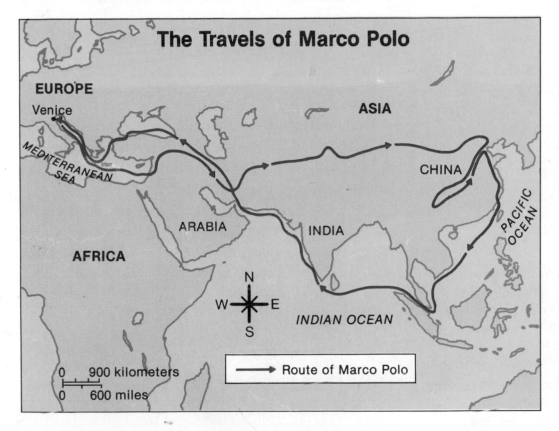

The Travels of Marco Polo

At that time, though, routes from Europe to the East crossed both land and water. Land travel was slow and often dangerous. Sometimes bandits attacked the traders. Sometimes the traders were not allowed to pass through certain lands. The traders wanted a fast and safe route to the East. European traders thought an all-water route would be better.

Prince Henry of Portugal was sure that such a route could be found. He believed that ships could reach the east by sailing around Africa. He paid for many voyages to

(left) Prince Henry the Navigator

(right) Marco Polo

navigate
to direct the course of a
ship or airplane

unexplored lands. He also set up a school for sailors. There students learned how to read maps and **navigate,** or direct the course of ships. Because of Prince Henry's school and his interest in sailing, Portugal became a center for skilled sailors during the 1400's.

In 1498, one Portuguese captain, Vasco da Gama, sailed around the southern tip of Africa. The Portuguese called the tip the Cape of Good Hope. Da Gama sailed to India and then back to Portugal. At last, an all-water route to the East had been found.

Section Review

Write your answers on a sheet of paper.
1. Why did the Vikings travel to foreign lands?
2. Why did Europeans travel east to India and China?
3. Why did Europeans seek an all-water route to the East?
4. What contributions did Prince Henry make to sailing and navigation?
5. In what ways are today's astronauts similar to the early explorers? In what ways are they different?

Using a Compass

Sailors at Prince Henry's school learned to use a tool called a **compass** that helped them keep their ships on course. A compass is an instrument that shows directions with a needle made of magnetized iron ore. The magnetized needle is attracted by the magnetic pull of the North and South poles. This attraction causes one end of the needle to point north, while the other end always points south.

To figure out directions, line up the needle with the letter **N**—for north—on the compass. Then it is easy to find the other three directions shown on the compass.

With a detailed map of an area and a compass, you can find your way in unfamiliar places. Put your compass on the map, making sure the compass needle pointing north is lined up with the arrow pointing north on the map. Then turn the map and compass together until the compass needle points to **N.** To get to a spot pictured on the map, just walk toward it.

compass

an instrument that shows directions with a needle of magnetized iron ore

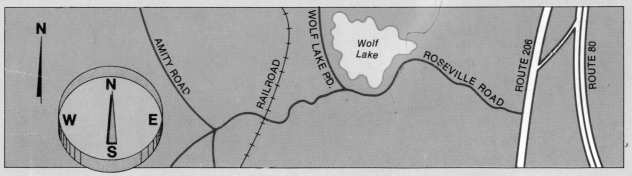

Practice Your Skills

1. To get to Route 206 from the corner of Roseville and Amity roads, in what direction would you walk?
2. If you wanted to return to Wolf Lake from Route 206, in what direction would you walk?

2 Spain and the New World

In the late 1400's, Spain began searching for another water route to the East. Instead, Spanish explorers found a continent they did not know existed. A mapmaker called it the New World—the land across the Atlantic that was not part of Asia.

The Great Explorer

Christopher Columbus grew up near the sea. His home town of Genoa, Italy, had a fine harbor filled with ships. As a boy, Columbus loved to go to the harbor and listen to the sailors' stories.

In 1476, when he was 24 years old, Columbus sailed on a ship bound for England. His ship was sunk just off the Portuguese coast, but he managed to float to shore. For Columbus, landing in Portugal was a lucky accident. No one knew more about sailing than the Portuguese.

Columbus learned Latin, geography, and shipbuilding in Portugal. He became a mapmaker and then a sea captain. Like many other Europeans, Columbus began to think that the world was round. He decided to try to find a quick route to the East by sailing west.

King John II of Portugal thought the plan was too dangerous. He refused to pay for the voyage. So in 1485, Columbus traveled to nearby Spain for help.

Queen Isabella and King Ferdinand of Spain liked Columbus's plan. Still, Columbus had to wait seven years before Isabella agreed to provide the money for sailors, ships, and supplies.

Columbus had a difficult time finding sailors. Many were fearful of making a voyage no one had tried before. Finally, Columbus found prisoners who would sail in return for their freedom.

On August 3, 1492, three ships, the *Niña,* the *Pinta,* and the *Santa María,* set out from Spain. The three small ships sailed for weeks with no sight of land. The sailors became nervous. They begged Columbus to turn back. "Sail on" was the reply.

Christopher Columbus

As time passed, the sailors grew angry. They threatened to rebel, but they finally agreed to sail on for three more days. Columbus promised that if no land was seen, they would turn back. On the morning of the third day, there was good news: Land birds were flying overhead. Then a sailor sighted land.

On October 12, 1492, Columbus stepped ashore, holding the Spanish flag high. Grateful for a safe trip, Columbus named the island San Salvador—Holy Savior.

Columbus thought he had reached a group of islands off the coast of China and India known as the Indies. For this reason, he called the people he saw on San Salvador Indians. These people welcomed Columbus and his crew.

Columbus leaving Queen Isabella and King Ferdinand, as his crew sails out to board the ships in the background

43

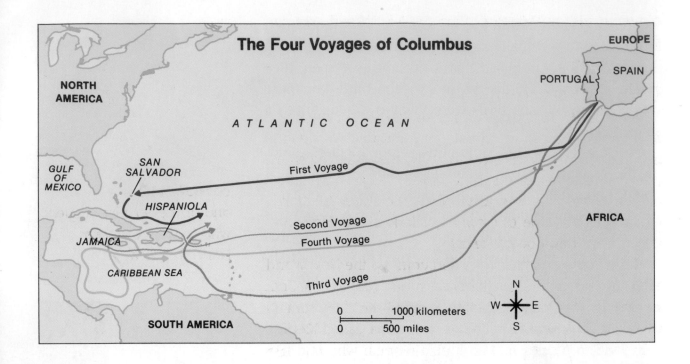

The Four Voyages of Columbus

EUROPE

PORTUGAL SPAIN

NORTH AMERICA

ATLANTIC OCEAN

GULF OF MEXICO

SAN SALVADOR

First Voyage

HISPANIOLA

AFRICA

JAMAICA

Second Voyage

Fourth Voyage

CARIBBEAN SEA

Third Voyage

SOUTH AMERICA

0   1000 kilometers
0   500 miles

N W E S

colony
a place that is governed by people from another country

Next, Columbus left San Salvador and sailed to other islands in what is now called the West Indies. He built a settlement on an island that he named Hispaniola (hihs-puhn-**yoh**-luh), or "Spanish land." This was a **colony,** a settlement governed by a distant country. It was the first European colony in America.

Columbus started back to Spain in January 1493. When he arrived two months later, the king and queen were overjoyed. Everyone thought Columbus had found an all-water route to the East. For his accomplishments, Columbus was named "admiral of the ocean sea." He was also appointed governor of all the lands he found.

Later in 1493, Columbus returned to the West Indies. Before returning to Spain, he sailed around the area, still hoping to find India. He found the islands of Jamaica and Puerto Rico instead.

Columbus made two more voyages to the New World. In 1498, he found the island of Trinidad. And in 1502, he reached the coast of Central America.

Although Columbus did not reach India, he did something even more important. He found and explored a new half of the world, or hemisphere. With his careful records, others would be able to explore the New World even further.

Cortés in Mexico

In the early 1500's, a number of Spanish soldiers and adventurers went to Hispaniola and to Cuba, an island in the West Indies. From these islands, they planned to explore other parts of the New World. These adventurers called themselves **conquistadors** (kon-**kees**-tuh-dorz), or conquerors. One of the conquistadors was Hernando Cortés (hur-**nan**-doe kor-**tezz**).

Many of the conquistadors had come to the New World after hearing rumors that there was much gold to be found. In 1519, Cortés led an expedition to find out if the rumors were true. He went to a land west of Cuba called Mexico.

In Mexico, Cortés met an Indian woman who told him about the rich and powerful Aztec (**azz**-teck) Indians. These Indians lived in Central Mexico, in a huge city, she told Cortés. They had much gold and silver.

Cortés led an army to conquer the Aztecs. The march was long and difficult. Along the way, other Indians who were willing to fight the Aztecs joined Cortés. Finally, Cortés and his army came to a land with beautiful blue lakes. On an island in one of the lakes was Tenochtitlán (tay-nawk-tee-**tlahn**), the Aztec capital city.

conquistador
one of the Spanish leaders who led the conquest of North America

Hernando Cortés

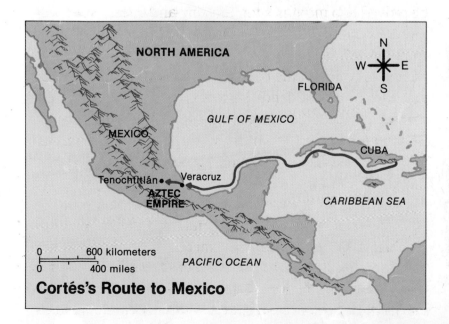

Cortés's Route to Mexico

Many explorers believed that the New World was filled with gold when they saw objects like this Aztec serpent.

Aztec pin, inlaid with turquoise and fringed with gold bells at the bottom

The Spaniards were amazed by the Aztec city and its people. The city had fine architecture and sculpture. Aztec doctors could cure many diseases. The Aztecs also had well-trained soldiers and an efficient government.

Montezuma (mon-tuh-**zoo**-muh), the Aztec leader, treated Cortés as an honored guest. He gave Cortés gold and silver. He offered Cortés a palace to stay in. Montezuma treated Cortés so well because he thought Cortés might be the great Aztec god Quetzalcoátl (ket-sahl-**kwaht**'l). Aztec holy legends had described Quetzalcoátl as fair skinned and bearded, just like Cortés.

Before long, Montezuma realized he had been wrong. Cortés was no god. The Aztec leader gave the Spaniards gifts to make them leave. Instead, the Spaniards took over Tenochtitlán. They took Montezuma prisoner.

The Aztecs tried to get their leader back. Meanwhile, fighting between conquistadors and Aztecs broke out in other parts of Mexico. It went on for months. Montezuma was killed in Tenochtitlán.

In the end, Spanish cannons, guns, and horses defeated the Aztecs. The Spaniards took over Mexico and sent shiploads of gold and silver to Spain. King Charles I of Spain was pleased. It seemed that the rumors about the New World's riches were true.

Around the World

Ferdinand Magellan (muh-**jell**-un) of Portugal had studied Columbus's maps of the South American coastline. He wanted to find a passage around South America to the Pacific Ocean. Then he could sail to the Spice Islands in what is now Indonesia and easily return to Europe. The map on the next page shows Magellan's route.

Like Columbus, Magellan asked the king of Portugal to pay for the trip. The king said no. So, like Columbus, Magellan got help from Spain.

Magellan set sail from Spain in 1519 with five ships. Near the southern tip of South America, he found the passage to the Pacific Ocean. Today this passageway is called the Strait of Magellan.

Four ships were lost on the dangerous journey. Magellan was killed by natives in what is now called the Philippine Islands.

In 1522, a single ship returned to Spain. Of the 265 men who had left, only 18 returned. They had been gone three years. But they had been able to sail around, or **circumnavigate,** the world. They proved that Columbus had been right. Ships could, indeed, reach the East by sailing west.

circumnavigate
to sail completely around something

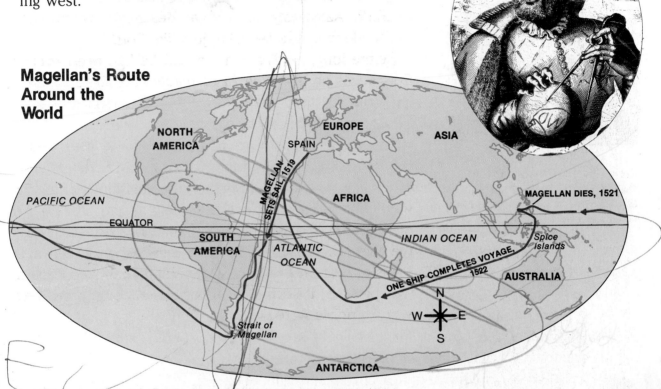

Magellan's Route Around the World

Section Review

Write your answers on a sheet of paper.

1. What did Columbus call the people he found on San Salvador? Why?
2. How did the legend of Quetzalcoátl help Cortés?
3. What did Magellan's voyage prove?
4. What voyages in this century have been as important as Magellan's?

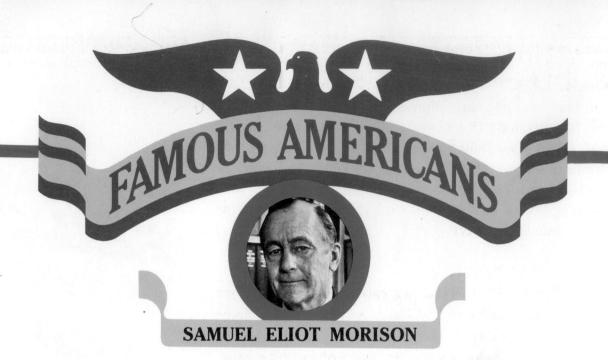

SAMUEL ELIOT MORISON

American history was Samuel Morison's first love. His second love was sailing. Morison found a way to combine both interests. He became an historian who wrote about sea battles and about explorers, such as Christopher Columbus, who were also great sailors.

Born in 1887 in Boston, Massachusetts, Samuel Morison grew up near two places that became very important in his life: Harvard University and the Atlantic Ocean. He went to Harvard as a student and later taught there. He also spent many years sailing back and forth across the Atlantic, following the routes of famous explorers.

While writing a book about Columbus, for instance, Morison sailed to the same Caribbean islands that Columbus visited. His boat was about the same size as one of Columbus's ships.

On the trip, Morison and his crew used Columbus's journal as a guide. They observed the weather, the conditions of the sea, and the location of the stars at night. Then they sailed to Spain and back again four times. Each time they checked what they saw against Columbus's records. Morison hoped this would help him to write more accurately about Columbus's voyages. Morison's book about Columbus received a famous award, the Pulitzer Prize, in 1942.

During World War II, Morison became an officer in the navy. He saw every major sea battle United States ships took part in. He then wrote 15 books about the U.S. Navy during World War II.

Samuel Morison also wrote several books about colonial life in the United States. He died in 1976. He is thought to be one of the greatest historians of the United States.

3 Other European Explorers

The first Europeans to explore North America did not come to settle the land. They came to look for a water route through it. They were trying to find an easier way to reach China and India. Spain controlled the southern parts of America. So the new explorers decided to search for this water route in the North.

English Exploration

John Cabot was an Italian sea captain who explored for England. The English hoped Cabot could reach the Spice Islands by sailing west. If the English controlled such a route, England could become the center of the spice trade.

In 1497, Cabot set sail with one small ship and 18 men. After five weeks at sea, he reached land and claimed it for England. Cabot thought he was in China.

In fact, Cabot had landed in what is now Newfoundland, Canada. Instead of spices, he found one of the richest fishing areas in the world. Today the area is called the Grand Banks.

Cabot made another trip the next year. He explored much of the northeastern coast of North America. This trip was to be Cabot's last. He and his crew were lost at sea. In the course of his voyages, Cabot had not found a water route to the East. But he had claimed England's first territory in the New World.

French Exploration

The French explorer, Jacques Cartier (zhahk kahr-**tyay**), made three voyages to the New World between 1534 and 1542. Cartier was looking for the **Northwest Passage**—a water route through North America to Asia. He found the St. Lawrence River and explored as far as present-day Montreal, Canada.

Northwest Passage
an imaginary water passage that early explorers believed would lead through North America to Asia

French explorers kept trying to find the Northwest Passage. In 1603, Samuel de Champlain (duh sham-**plane**) made the first of many voyages to North America. He explored much of what is now eastern Canada and northern New York State. He claimed land for France as far west as the present state of Wisconsin. He set up a settlement at Quebec and sailed across Lake Huron, Lake Champlain, and Lake Ontario. But he did not find the Northwest Passage.

Some French explorers thought the Mississippi River might be a passage west to the Pacific Ocean. In 1673, Louis Joliet (zhole-**yay**), a fur trader, and Jacques Marquette (mahr-**kett**), a priest, traveled down the Mississippi by raft and canoe. They passed the **mouths** of the Ohio and Arkansas rivers—the places where these smaller rivers join the Mississippi. Marquette and Joliet learned that the Mississippi flows south. It did not appear to flow toward the Pacific.

Robert La Salle (luh **sal**), another French explorer, traveled to the mouth of the Mississippi in 1682. He named the surrounding area Louisiana and claimed the entire Mississippi Valley for France.

mouth

the place where a stream or river empties into a larger body of water

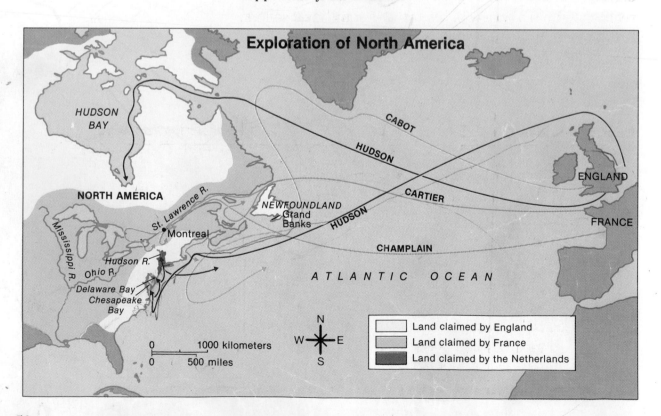

Exploration of North America

HUDSON BAY

CABOT

HUDSON

NORTH AMERICA

St. Lawrence R.

CARTIER

NEWFOUNDLAND
Grand Banks

HUDSON

ENGLAND

Montreal

Mississippi R.

Hudson R.
Ohio R.

CHAMPLAIN

FRANCE

Delaware Bay
Chesapeake Bay

ATLANTIC OCEAN

0   1000 kilometers
0   500 miles

N
W E
S

Land claimed by England
Land claimed by France
Land claimed by the Netherlands

Dutch Exploration

Henry Hudson was an English navigator who made important explorations for the Dutch and English. In 1609, spice traders in The Netherlands paid him to try a new route to the East. Hudson was to sail to the north of Europe and then, if possible, east to Asia.

Hudson set sail from The Netherlands in the *Half Moon*. Troubled by freezing weather and a crew that threatened to revolt, he changed his course and sailed southwest. Reaching North America, he explored the waterways now called Chesapeake Bay, Delaware Bay, and New York Bay. He also sailed up the river that was later named for him—the Hudson.

Hudson did not find a passage to Asia. But the land he claimed for the Dutch became New Netherland—the first Dutch colony in the New World.

The next year, a group of English merchants hired Hudson to explore northern Canada. He found what is now known as Hudson Bay and claimed all the surrounding land for England.

Hudson never returned to England. After a hard winter in Canada, his sick, starving crew turned against him. They set him adrift in a boat with his son and some loyal sailors. Hudson was never seen again.

Section Review

Write your answers on a sheet of paper.

1. What parts of North America did John Cabot explore?
2. Why did the French want to find the Northwest Passage?
3. Why were Hudson's voyages important to the Dutch?
4. In spite of the fact that early explorers could not find the Northwest Passage, much was achieved by their voyages. List some achievements.
5. Do you think water routes are as important for trade today as they once were? Explain your answer.

Comparing Maps

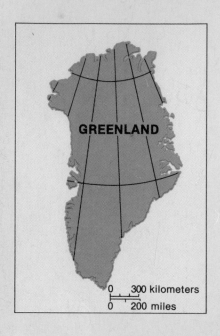

GREENLAND

0   300 kilometers

0   200 miles

John Cabot sailed from Great Britain to Newfoundland in 1497. His route passed just south of a huge island in the Atlantic that was known as Greenland. Greenland is the largest island on the earth. It is so far north that almost all of it lies within the Arctic Circle.

The drawing in the margin shows the true shape of Greenland. This is the way Greenland would look on a globe. Now look at Greenland on the maps on the next page. You will find that Greenland looks different on each one of these maps.

The reason for this difference is that it is impossible to draw every part of the round earth accurately on a flat map. Imagine peeling an orange and trying to lay out all of the pieces on a flat surface. You might be able to flatten some pieces, but others would have to be stretched or cut. Map-makers do just this when they draw the earth. In order to show some parts of the earth accurately, they have to stretch or cut other parts. Often the land areas pictured near the edges of a flat map appear to be stretched into the wrong shapes. Greenland is one land area that often appears stretched out of shape on flat maps.

Practice Your Skills

1. On which map does Greenland look wider than it is long?
2. On which map does Greenland look larger than South America?
3. On which map does Greenland appear to be larger than Australia?

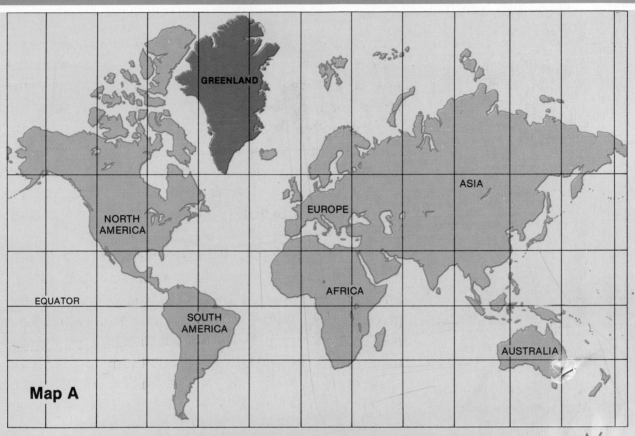

GREENLAND

NORTH
AMERICA

EQUATOR

SOUTH
AMERICA

EUROPE

ASIA

AFRICA

AUSTRALIA

Map A

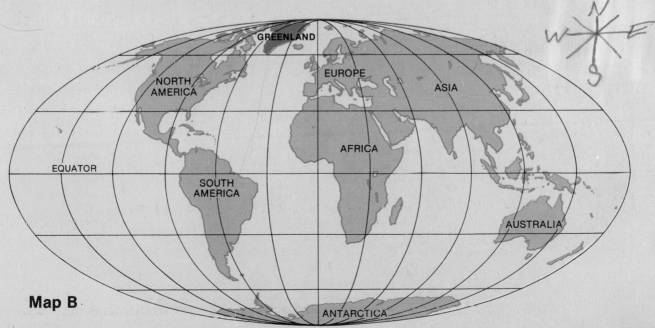

GREENLAND

NORTH
AMERICA

EUROPE

ASIA

EQUATOR

SOUTH
AMERICA

AFRICA

AUSTRALIA

ANTARCTICA

Map B

Totem Poles The Indians of the Northwest Coast were the only Indians in North America who made totem poles. Tribes such as the Chinook (shuh-**noohk**), Klikitat (**klick**-ih-tat), and Nootka had carvers who made not only totem poles but also canoes, masks, boxes, and toys out of wood. Totem poles, however, were the largest carved objects they made.

Each totem pole told a story. But unless you knew the story or someone told it to you, you could not learn the story by "reading" the totem pole.

The figures on the poles usually represented people or animals. The most commonly shown animals were beavers, seals, bears, killer whales, birds, and snakes. Often one figure on a pole might be made up of parts of different animals. A figure might have fins to show that it was a fish or that it had caught a fish. A wing might stand for a whole bird. A claw or sharp teeth might stand for a whole bear or wolf. The figure at the top of the pole was the most important. It stood for the family or tribe that owned the pole.

There were six kinds of totem poles. One kind of totem was used as a pillar to help support the roof of a building. Funeral totems were made to honor the dead. Memorial totems showed respect for a dead leader or represented the family of a new leader. These totems were the largest and most important totem poles. Some memorial poles were as much as 24 meters (80 feet) tall.

Family totems showed a family's ancestry. These poles were often part of the entrance to a family's house. A hole through the totem pole might be the door into the house. "Welcoming" totem poles greeted guests who arrived at an Indian settlement by sea or by river. These poles identified the person who owned the waterfront area. "Shame" poles showed that someone owed money or goods to the leader.

Most of the totem poles made by the Northwest Coast Indians did not last. The poles were destroyed by weather and insects. However, a few poles can still be seen today in Oregon, Washington, Alaska, and western Canada.

UNIT REVIEW

Word Work

Write the sentences below on a sheet of paper. Fill in the blanks with the correct words from the list.

mouth   bands   conquistador   sagas   glaciers

1. La Salle found the _____ of the Mississippi River.
2. During the Ice Age, much of North America was covered by _____.
3. Cortés, a _____, led the Spanish into Mexico.
4. Plains Indians traveled in groups called _____.
5. Viking _____ tell about Leif Ericson's voyage.

Knowing the Facts

Write your answers on a sheet of paper.
1. How did the American Indians arrive in America?
2. What are the five geographic groups that American Indian tribes are usually divided into?
3. In 1492, what did Columbus hope to find?
4. What was Cortés looking for in Mexico?
5. List two accomplishments of the early French explorers of North America.

Using What You Know

Choose one of the following activities. Follow the instructions given here.
1. Imagine that you were with the first hunters who crossed the land bridge into America. Write a one-page report describing the land as it might have looked then.
2. Prepare a chart listing the New World's major explorers. Include information about when and where each one explored.

Skills Practice

Use the following map of the United States to answer the questions below. Write your answers on a sheet of paper.

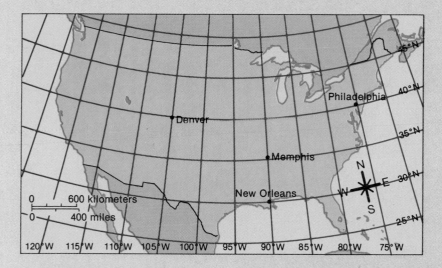

1. What major United States city lies at 40° N, 105° W?

2. What are the approximate coordinates for Memphis, a city in Tennessee?

3. What are the approximate coordinates of the southeastern tip of the United States?

Your Heritage

Find out who were the first people to live in your area. Do some research and give a short talk on the American Indians whose homes and villages were located nearby. What were the names of their tribes? What kinds of homes did they live in? What were their religious beliefs?

Perhaps you can visit a museum in your area to learn more about local American Indian tribes. Your librarian might be able to help you find out more information.

UNIT 2

A Period of Colonization

Perhaps you live near a town called New London. Today, there are nine such towns in the United States. There are also places called New Sweden and New Paris.

Many of these towns got their names from the first European settlers in the area. Often, the settlers who left Europe to come to the New World brought many European customs with them. Sometimes, they even brought the names of their home towns or countries.

In this unit, you will read about the settlers and the lives they made for themselves in the New World. You will learn how North American Indian tribes reacted to these newcomers. Also, you will see how the settlers began to set up new forms of government in their new homes.

CHAPTER 3

Early Settlements

Present-day area around Jamestown, Virginia

The first Europeans in North America were brave people. They left their homes in Spain, France, England, and The Netherlands. They left their families and friends and crossed the wide ocean in small ships. They came to the New World looking for a new life. In this chapter, you will read about the first settlements started by these courageous and hopeful people.

At the end of this chapter, you should be able to:
○ Name three areas settled by the Spanish.
○ Identify the areas settled by French and Dutch settlers.
● Use an atlas to find different kinds of map information.
○ Name the first three English settlements, and explain why these settlers came to the New World.

1 Spanish Settlements

When Christopher Columbus visited the New World, he claimed the land for Spain. Soon Spanish soldiers and settlers came to the New World. The Spaniards called their colony New Spain. Mexico City was its center, but Spanish settlers traveled far from there. They moved into areas that are now part of the United States.

Florida

A Spanish explorer named Ponce de León (ponss duh lee-**on**) reached Florida in 1513. He explored this land in the hope of finding a "Fountain of Youth." American Indians had told the explorer that such a fountain existed. According to the tale, anyone who drank from the fountain would stay young forever. Ponce de León never found the fountain, but he did claim Florida for Spain.

In time, this new land proved useful. In 1565, the Spaniards built a fort in northern Florida. From the fort, soldiers could protect Spanish ships sailing from Mexico to Spain.

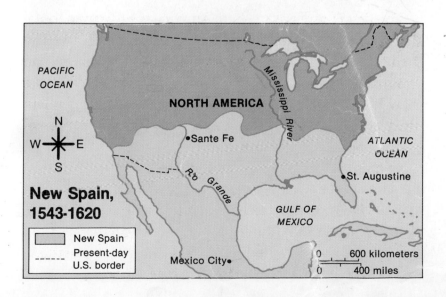

New Spain, 1543-1620

PACIFIC OCEAN

NORTH AMERICA

Mississippi River

•Sante Fe

ATLANTIC OCEAN

Rio Grande

•St. Augustine

GULF OF MEXICO

■ New Spain
- - - Present-day U.S. border

Mexico City•

0 600 kilometers
0 400 miles

These ships were often loaded with gold and silver. Pirates usually tried to attack them. The fort helped the Spanish fight against the pirates.

The Spaniards named the fort and the settlement around it St. Augustine. It was the first time Europeans settled on land that would later be part of the United States.

The Southwest

Because Spanish explorers found gold in some places, they thought it would be everywhere. In fact, many people believed a story about seven cities that were built out of gold. This story was spread by four explorers whose ship was wrecked near Texas. These men wandered in Texas and Mexico for nearly six years. During this time, they heard about the cities of gold from Indians.

Several explorers set out to find the seven cities of gold. One was Francisco Vasquéz de Coronado (frahn-siss-koe vahs-**kezz** duh koe-rah-**nah**-doe). He left Mexico in 1540 and spent three years wandering through the American Southwest. Coronado never found the golden cities. But he did explore the Great Plains and the Grand Canyon.

After Coronado's search, Spanish settlers went to the area that is now Arizona and New Mexico. Around 1609, they founded the town of Santa Fe (**san**-ta **fay**) and made it the capital of this part of New Spain.

Rock painting done by the Southwest Indians, depicting the arrival of Spanish settlers in the Southwest

California

Father Junípero Serra (hoo-**neep**-uh-roe **serr**-uh) came to the New World in 1749 to fulfill a childhood dream. His dream was to become a Catholic priest and help the Indians in North America. As a boy in Spain, he had heard many stories about these Indians.

First Father Serra spent 20 years in Mexico. Then he led the first Spanish settlers to California. At San Diego, Father Serra and other priests built a settlement called a **mission.** A mission was a small town built around a church. There priests could teach the Indians about Christianity and Spanish customs. At Father Serra's mission, the Indians learned about new ways to farm, raise cattle, and build houses.

Father Serra died in 1784. Over the course of the next 50 years, Spanish priests continued his work. They started 21 missions along the California coast. At these missions, the Indians and Spanish learned to live together as good neighbors. The missions became important centers of activity in California and other parts of New Spain.

mission
a church settlement built by priests who teach people about religion

Other Spanish settlers came to California and built ranches for raising cattle. The English word "ranch" comes from the Spanish word *rancho*, which means "farm." Many English words about cattle and cowhands come from Spanish.

San Diego Mission in California

Section Review

Write your answers on a sheet of paper.
1. Who explored Florida? What was he looking for?
2. What was the name of the first settlement built by Europeans in the United States?
3. What was Coronado really looking for when he explored the Grand Canyon?
4. Who was Father Serra?
5. Based on your reading, make up a list of the tools and supplies a Spanish explorer might have taken with him. Explain why these items are important.

2 French and Dutch Colonies

In the 1600's, other European nations also started colonies in the New World. France and The Netherlands set up colonies to obtain gold and silver, to trade, and to spread religion.

New France

In 1608, Samuel de Champlain started the first French settlement in the New World. It was located along the banks of the St. Lawrence River. Champlain called this place Quebec. The entire colony was known as New France. Today this area is part of Canada.

New France did not attract many settlers. Some people came to farm, but the weather in New France was very cold.

The fur trade was the main business of New France. In Europe, beaver hats and other clothing made of animal furs were very popular. So French settlers in New France trapped these animals and sent their skins to Europe.

French and American Indian trappers journeyed deep into the Canadian wilderness in search of animals. On

Map of Quebec as it looked in 1688

voyageur
a person who traveled by canoe in North America, buying and trading furs

these trips, the French trappers learned many Indian ways. They learned to speak Indian languages and to survive in the vast forests.

Most trappers traveled by canoe. New France was full of lakes and rivers. Men called **voyageurs** (voi-uh-**zherz**) traveled in canoes buying and trading furs. The voyageurs stopped at trading posts where they got furs from the Indians. Voyageurs' boats could carry huge loads of furs.

New Netherland

A few years after Henry Hudson's voyage in the *Half Moon,* Dutch settlers from The Netherlands came to the New World. Like the French, they planned to make money trading with the Indians for furs. Some traders sailed up the Hudson River and built a settlement called Fort Orange. There they traded for furs with the Iroquois Indians. Today the city of Albany, New York, stands on the site of this old Dutch trading post.

Trapper in New France

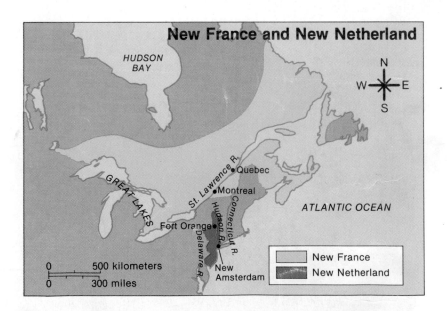

New France and New Netherland

The Dutch colony in the New World was called New Netherland. It included several scattered settlements on the Hudson, Delaware, and Connecticut rivers. Its center was New Amsterdam, on Manhattan Island. Today this island is part of New York City.

66

To manage their colony overseas, the Dutch appointed a governor. One early governor of New Netherland was Peter Minuit (**Min**-yuh-wit). In 1626, he held a meeting with the Manhottoe (man-**hah**-toe) Indians. Minuit wanted to buy Manhattan Island from them. It is said that he offered the Indians $24 worth of jewels and trinkets. The Indians accepted, and the Dutch took control of the island. Soon the settlement, called New Amsterdam, grew. The settlement's excellent harbor helped make it a center for trading with other colonies and with foreign nations.

New Amsterdam continued to grow as a Dutch colony until 1664. At that time, The Netherlands and England were at war. One day an English fleet sailed into the harbor of New Amsterdam. The commander demanded that the Dutch surrender. He said that the settlers would be able to keep their homes, schools, and churches. He also promised to allow the settlers to help make the laws for the community. He was offering the settlers more rights than they had under Dutch rule.

The governor of New Amsterdam, Peter Stuyvesant (**stive**-uh-sunt), was a strict ruler with a terrible temper. When Governor Stuyvesant ordered the settlers to open fire on the English, the settlers refused. Stuyvesant could only watch angrily as New Amsterdam surrendered to the English. The king of England then gave New Netherland and New Amsterdam to the Duke of York, his brother. The duke called them both New York.

Peter Stuyvesant

Section Review

Write your answers on a sheet of paper.
1. What was the main business of New France?
2. Why did Dutch settlers first come to the New World?
3. Why was it important for the first European settlements to be located near rivers?

Using an Atlas

atlas
a book of maps or the
map section of a book

Since the time Henry Hudson first set foot on American soil, many changes have occurred along the banks of the mighty river that Hudson explored. Suppose you wanted to find out which cities are now located along the Hudson River. What would you do?

You could begin by looking in an **atlas.** An atlas is a book of maps. To find out quickly the kinds of maps and other information included in a particular atlas, check the table of contents. The table of contents on the next page tells you where to find the political and special maps within that atlas. It also lists the special features of the atlas, such as the articles on map symbols and how maps are made.

Some atlases also list the names of all the maps found in them. The partial list of maps on the next page refers you to the page within the atlas that has a map of a particular area. The list of maps is always in alphabetical order.

Practice Your Skills

1. On which page of this atlas would you find the list of maps? On which page would you find help in reading symbols?
2. On which pages would you find maps of New York and New Jersey? Did you consult the table of contents or the list of maps for this information?
3. On which page would you find a map of the world's climates?
4. How would you find out the best land route from New York to California?

Table of Contents

Alphabetical List of Maps

3 English Settlements

People from England also started colonies. Although these first settlements were very small, they soon grew. By the 1730's, there were 13 English colonies along the eastern coast of North America.

The Lost Colony

The earliest English settlements were started on Roanoke (**roe**-uh-noke) Island, off the North Carolina coast. The first settlement, started in 1585, lasted barely a year. The settlers spent all their time looking for gold instead of planting crops. When their food ran out, they gave up and returned to England.

A second settlement was started in Roanoke in 1587. The settlers worked very hard, but the soil was poor. So the colony's governor returned to England for supplies. When he got back to America three years later, the colonists were gone. To this day, no one knows what happened to them. The only clue was the word "Croatoan," carved into a tree trunk. The Croatoans were Indians who lived near Roanoke. Today's historians call the second settlement the Lost Colony.

Map of North Carolina coast and Roanoke Island

Virginia and Jamestown

In 1606, some merchants in London, England, formed a private business called the Virginia Company. The company asked England's King James I for a grant of land to establish a colony in America. The merchants wanted to set up a trading post in America. The king agreed. The Virginia Company offered to pay the travel costs for settlers. In return, the settlers agreed to send the company a share of any crops that they grew. They also promised to send all the gold and silver they found.

More than 120 people accepted the offer and set out for Virginia, as the colony was called. They arrived in the spring of 1607. They called their settlement Jamestown, in honor of their king.

The new settlers should have planted crops and built houses. Instead, they repeated the mistake of the first colonists on Roanoke Island. They went off looking for gold.

Jamestown's settlers found no gold, and soon they began to have problems. Without new crops, food was running low. American Indians finally supplied them with food. Next, Captain John Smith took charge. He told the other settlers that if they did not work, they would not eat. He made the settlers plant crops and dig a well. John Smith also made friends with the Indians nearby.

Even so, the settlement had hard times. The settlers were not ready for the winter of 1609–1610. Colonists called it the starving time because so many people died from the lack of food and from diseases.

In 1610, the surviving settlers decided to leave the New World. As they sailed down the James River, though, they met three ships coming from England. The ships were full of supplies and new settlers sent by the Virginia Company. Jamestown was saved.

John Smith

Restoration of the Jamestown settlement

71

By 1619, there were 11 settlements in Virginia. The Virginia Company wanted Virginia to grow. To make the colony more appealing to new settlers, the company said that all men who owned land could vote. The company based its laws on English law. In England, women could not vote. So women in Virginia could not vote. Voters, or **burgesses** (**bur**-jiss-uz), elected two representatives to act for their settlement. These representatives met in a group known as the House of Burgesses. They met at Williamsburg, which was Virginia's new capital. This was the beginning of self-government in the United States.

burgess
a landowner who could vote in colonial Virginia

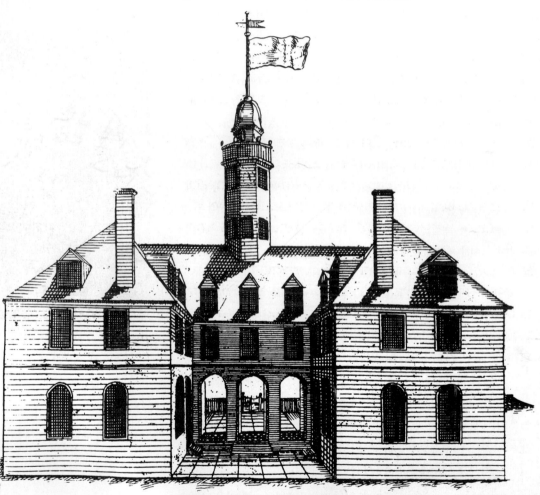

Virginia House of Burgesses

The Pilgrims

Most of the settlers you have read about so far came to the New World looking for adventure and riches. In 1620, the Pilgrims came for a very different reason. They were looking for a place where they could worship as they wished.

The Pilgrims were English people who belonged to a different church from the one supported by England's king. King James wanted everyone to belong to his church, the Church of England. People who disobeyed could be sent to jail. To escape this punishment, and to worship as they pleased, some Pilgrims left England and went to The Netherlands. Then, in 1620, a group of them got a **charter**, or document that allowed them to start a colony, from the Virginia Company. It allowed the Pilgrims to start their colony in the part of America known as Virginia.

More than 100 Pilgrims sailed for North America on a ship called the *Mayflower*. It was a long and difficult voyage. The ship drifted off course and arrived off the coast of Cape Cod, Massachusetts, in November 1620. The Pilgrims explored the coast to find a good place to build a settlement. After five weeks of scouting, they found a place with good land and a good harbor.

Before going ashore, the Pilgrims held a meeting. They agreed to be governed by a set of laws instead of the will of a ruler. This agreement was called the Mayflower Compact.

The Pilgrims called their settlement Plymouth. The Pilgrims' first winter was very hard. Many people died from the cold. Still, the colony survived.

In early 1621, an American Indian named Samoset (**sam**-uh-set) came to Plymouth and greeted the Pilgrims in English. The Pilgrims were surprised when they heard the Indian's words. Samoset explained that he had learned the language at sea, sailing with English captains. Soon

charter
a document that gave the right to establish a colony

Painting of the Pilgrim's voyage to North America

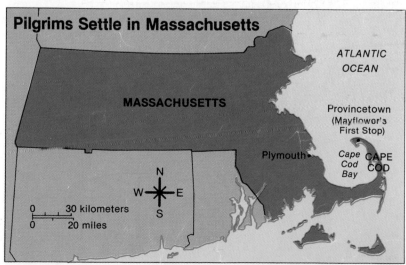

Pilgrims Settle in Massachusetts

ATLANTIC OCEAN

MASSACHUSETTS

Provincetown (Mayflower's First Stop)

Plymouth

Cape Cod Bay

CAPE COD

N
W E
S

0   30 kilometers
0   20 miles

Woman salting cod at restoration of Plimouth Plantation, Massachusetts

Samoset returned with a friend, Squanto (**skwon**-toe). Squanto stayed with the Pilgrims. He taught them how to survive in the wilderness. Squanto showed the colonists how to grow corn, how to spear fish, and where to hunt deer. He also taught them that they could keep the soil rich by burying fish in the earth.

Thanks to Squanto, the Pilgrims had a good harvest that fall. To give thanks, they invited Squanto and other Indians to a great feast. The celebration, which lasted three days, was the first Thanksgiving.

The Puritans

In England, another group of people were risking arrest because of their religious beliefs. These people were Puritans. The Puritans disagreed with the teachings of the Church of England. The Puritans thought its services had become too complicated. They wanted to make the Church of England more pure. For this reason, they were called the Puritans.

Many Puritans were wealthier than the Pilgrims. A group of them formed the Massachusetts Bay Company to direct their move to America. The company got a charter to settle in Massachusetts.

The Puritans' journey was very different from the Pilgrims' trip on the *Mayflower*. One thousand people made the crossing in 1630. They sailed in 15 ships full of supplies and tools.

Workers in the cornfields at restoration of Plimouth Plantation, Massachusetts

When they got to Massachusetts, the Puritans explored the coastline. They found an excellent harbor where the Charles River empties into the ocean. They settled there and called the place Boston.

Even with all their supplies, the Puritans found that life in Massachusetts was difficult. The winters in Boston were colder than those in England. Also, most of the Puritans were used to living in comfortable houses. Now they had to work hard to build simple homes with damp dirt floors.

Puritan mother and her child

pillory

a wooden frame with holes for head and arms, used by the Puritans to punish people

The Puritan Church was very powerful in the Massachusetts colony. The colony's political leaders were church members and followed church policies. Church leaders told people how to dress and how to act. Everyone was required to attend church on Sundays. Anyone who disobeyed these church teachings was punished. One Puritan punishment involved a wooden frame called a **pillory**. The pillory had holes for a person's head and arms. Wrongdoers would be locked into the pillory. Then they would be left out on display for a time as a lesson to the rest of the community.

The Puritans punished wrongdoers by locking them in a pillory.

Section Review

Write your answers on a sheet of paper.

1. What was the Lost Colony?
2. What was the first lasting English settlement in the New World?
3. Why did the Pilgrims come to the New World?
4. How did Squanto help the Pilgrims?
5. What are some reasons that newcomers come to settle in the United States today?

FAMOUS AMERICANS

POCAHONTAS

In 1607, a group of white people settled on land in what is now the state of Virginia. This land belonged to the Pamunkey (puh-**mun**-kee) Indians. Their leader became known to Europeans as Chief Powhatan (pou-uh-**tan**), which was also the name of one of the Indian villages.

Chief Powhatan had a young daughter named Pocahontas (poke-uh-**hahn**-tus). Her name means "the playful one." She was trusting and curious about the white people. She visited them often, and the settlers grew to know her and like her. She learned a few words of English, and Chief Powhatan and his people hoped she would be able to help keep peace with the whites. Pocahontas carried messages between the settlers and the Indians.

As more and more whites came to the settlement, however, the Pamunkey Indians became angrier. The whites were slowly taking away the Indians' land. In anger, the Indians captured Captain John Smith, the leader of the white settlement. According to a story that was told later, 12-year-old Pocahontas saved Smith's life by begging her father not to kill him. This made the English trust her even more.

When she was about 17, Pocahontas fell in love with an Englishman named John Rolfe. She became a Christian and married Rolfe in 1614. Their marriage marked the beginning of a period of peace between the colonists and the Pamunkey Indians.

Pocahontas and Rolfe later had a son. They visited England, where Pocahontas met the king and queen. Just before the family was to return to the colonies, however, Pocahontas caught smallpox. She died in 1617. Despite her short life, Pocahontas is remembered as a symbol of friendship between whites and American Indians.

CHAPTER 4

The English Colonies

View of Baltimore, Maryland, in the mid-1700's

The English settlements on the Atlantic Coast grew into 13 colonies. For purposes of study, the colonies can be divided into three regions: the New England colonies, the middle colonies, and the southern colonies. Each region had its own way of life. There were even differences among colonies in the same region. These differences came from the settlers' own backgrounds. In this chapter, you will read about what life was like in the 13 colonies.

At the end of this chapter, you should be able to:
○ Identify the three regions and tell which colonies were in each.
○ Identify Roger Williams, William Penn, and Benjamin Franklin.
● Use a time line to identify centuries.

1 New England

The New England colonies were Massachusetts, Rhode Island, Connecticut, and New Hampshire. New England has long, cold winters. The land is rocky and hard to farm. Life was not easy for the colonists, but New Englanders worked hard. By the mid-1700's, small villages had grown into towns. One town, Boston, had become a city of major importance in the colonies.

Rhode Island

Massachusetts Bay Colony had been settled by the Puritans, who had come to America for religious freedom. But no one was supposed to have any ideas that were different from those of the Puritan Church. There was no **religious toleration** in Massachusetts Bay. Yet some people did disagree with the Puritan leaders.

Roger Williams, a popular young minister in the colony, disagreed with some of the Puritan teachings. He was told to stop talking about his ideas. When he refused, he was ordered to leave the colony or face arrest. Williams set out into the wilderness.

Williams walked for four days through a terrible blizzard and freezing cold. Finally he reached a camp of friendly American Indians. Williams had learned Indian languages and had made friends with leaders of the neighboring tribes. The Indians invited Williams to spend the winter with them. In the spring, they helped him start his own settlement. He called it Providence. The new settlement grew into a separate colony called Rhode Island.

Williams proved to be a good leader. He worked out agreements for more land with the Narragansett (nar-uh-**gan**-sut) Indians, the English king, and even the Puritans. He demanded that the Indians receive fair prices

religious toleration the willingness to allow people to worship according to their own beliefs

Anne Hutchinson standing trial in Massachusetts

for their land. Rhode Island's first law was about religious toleration. It said that people would be allowed to worship as they wished.

Other people who disagreed with the Puritan leaders in Massachusetts Bay soon left for Rhode Island. One of these people was Anne Hutchinson. Like Roger Williams, Anne Hutchinson disagreed with some of the harsh teachings of the church. So she too was ordered to leave Massachusetts forever.

Anne Hutchinson lived with her large family in Rhode Island. Later she went to live among the Indians in New York. In one war in which the Indians tried to get their land back, she and 5 of her 14 children were killed.

People of other faiths also came to Rhode Island. Jews came to the colony from Holland. They built a synagogue, or Jewish house of worship, in Newport. It is one of the oldest synagogues in North America.

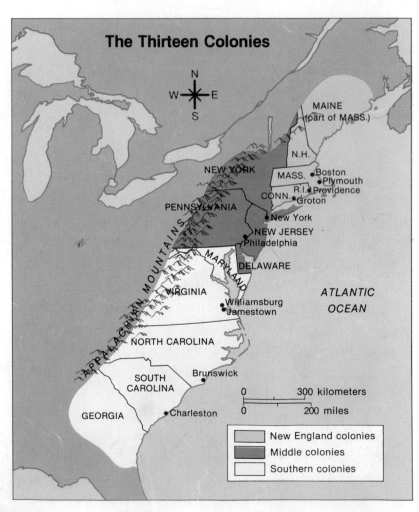

Life in New England

Religious worship was very important to most New Englanders. The church was often the center of social life. Families would spend long hours listening to sermons.

Villages usually had a large, open land area, or green, in the village center. The green belonged to the whole community. It served as an outdoor place for people to gather. The meetinghouse, usually a church, was built next to the green. Villages also had a general store. The general store sold everything from food to clothes and hardware. Money was seldom used to buy goods. Instead, people used a trading system called **barter.** They exchanged all kinds of goods. A farmer might trade maple syrup and eggs for flour or candles.

Along the Atlantic Coast, people made their living from the sea. The waters off New England were excellent fishing grounds.

barter
to trade by exchanging goods instead of money

Village green in New England in 1780

Timber from nearby forests was used to build ships. Towns along the coast, such as Groton in Connecticut, became major shipbuilding centers.

As the colonies grew, they began to trade with each other and with Great Britain. New Englanders sent pickled meat, vegetables, fish, and timber to the West Indies in exchange for sugar, molasses, and rum. Iron and tobacco were shipped to Great Britain and traded for manufactured goods, such as tools. The tools were then brought back to the colonies.

At the same time that trade was growing, the ways of life in the colonies were changing. In the early colonial years, people had to make or grow everything they needed themselves. But as the colonies grew, some people left their farms to work in the growing colonial towns and cities. They became ministers, lawyers, bankers, and merchants. There were blacksmiths, shoemakers, candlemakers, and coopers, or barrelmakers, too. These people no longer had

View of Boston, Massachusetts in 1801

to grow their own food. They could get food in exchange for the goods or services they sold.

Education was highly valued in New England. Religious leaders wanted children to be able to read the Bible, so they started schools. All towns in Massachusetts with more than 50 families were required to build elementary schools. Until 1750, only boys went to public school. These early schools were usually just one room heated by a wood-burning stove. In winter, the boys sat close together to keep warm. They learned reading, writing, and arithmetic. Larger towns built secondary schools. There they continued to study the "3 R's" as well as Latin and Greek.

In 1636, Harvard College was founded near Boston. It was the first college started in the 13 colonies. Its purpose was to train young men for the ministry.

All children were expected to work at home. Young children milked the cows and cared for the animals. Girls helped make food and clothing. Boys chopped wood and helped plow the fields.

In towns, children learned their parents' trade. Depending on what their fathers' did, boys learned how to make barrels, candles, shoes, or iron tools. Sometimes girls worked in a store. Usually, though, they cleaned, took care of younger children in the family, sewed, and cooked with their mothers at home.

Early New England hornbook, or schoolbook

Section Review

Write your answers on a sheet of paper.
1. Why did Roger Williams have to leave Massachusetts? Where did he go?
2. What is bartering? Give an example.
3. What products did New Englanders trade with the West Indies? What did they get in return?
4. How is your school different from a school in colonial New England? How are they alike?

2 The Middle Colonies

New York, New Jersey, Pennsylvania, and Delaware were called the middle colonies. The middle colonies were between New England and the southern colonies.

These colonies were settled mainly by English, French, Dutch, and German people. They developed the region into a rich farming area.

Penn's Woods

Like Roger Williams, William Penn believed in religious toleration. He founded the colony of Pennsylvania for that purpose.

Penn came from a wealthy family in England. His father was an admiral in the English navy and a friend of the king's. As a young man, Penn joined a religious group called the Society of Friends. The Friends, or Quakers, believed in the goodness of all people. They also refused to fight in any wars.

Like the Pilgrims and Puritans, the Quakers were not allowed to practice their religion in England. William Penn and other Quakers were sent to jail for their beliefs.

In 1681, Penn made an agreement with the English king. Penn's father had died in 1670, and the king had owed him a lot of money. Now he owed the money to Penn. As payment for the debt, he gave Penn a grant of land in America.

In 1681, Penn sent settlers to the land and called it Pennsylvania, which means "Penn's Woods." It was a beautiful land of thick forests, rich soil, and clean, sparkling rivers.

William Penn worked hard to build up Pennsylvania. He wrote advertisements telling people in Europe about his colony. Soon people from Germany, The Netherlands, Switzerland, and other countries came to Pennsylvania. Unlike New England, where most of the colonists were English, Pennsylvania was settled by people of many different lands.

William Penn had strong ideas about how the colony should be run. He said that Pennsylvania would be a place open to settlers of all faiths. He also believed the American

Indians should be treated well. Soon after arriving, Penn drew up an agreement with the Delaware Indians who lived in the area. He paid them a fair price for their land. He gave the Delawares his word that all disagreements would be settled peacefully. During Penn's lifetime, relations between the settlers and the Indians in Pennsylvania were very good.

Life in Philadelphia

Philadelphia was the first settlement in Pennsylvania. The name "Philadelphia" means "brotherly love" in Greek. For 300 years, Philadelphia has been known as the City of Brotherly Love.

William Penn and the Indians

View of Philadelphia's seaport

By the 1700's, more than 4,500 people lived in Philadelphia. It rivaled Boston and New York as one of the three largest and most modern cities in the colonies.

Despite being more than 160 kilometers (100 miles) from the Atlantic Ocean, Philadelphia was a busy seaport. Ships sailed from the ocean up the broad Delaware River. The city's streets were full of traffic. Workers carted wheelbarrows full of paper for the printshops and leather for the shoemakers.

Philadelphia's leading citizen was Benjamin Franklin. Franklin was a man of amazing energy and curiosity. There are few people in American history who have accomplished as much. Benjamin Franklin was an author, a scientist, an inventor, and a public servant.

Franklin was born in Boston in 1706. When he was 12, Franklin learned the printing trade from his older brother. After a quarrel with his brother, Franklin ran away to Philadelphia. He worked hard and soon became a master printer with a shop of his own. He published a newspaper, the *Pennsylvania Gazette,* which was read throughout the colonies. Franklin also published a book called *Poor Richard's Almanac.* An **almanac** is a book published every year that gives many facts, including information about the weather, stars, and tides. Franklin always included a few of his own short sayings in the almanac. Here are two:

A penny saved is a penny earned.

Little strokes fell great oaks.

Benjamin Franklin followed his own advice. He worked hard and was very successful. He also believed in helping others. The first fire department in the colonies was started by Franklin in Philadelphia. Franklin built the first library and hospital. He also built a school that later became the University of Pennsylvania.

almanac

a book of facts, which is published every year, containing information about the stars and weather

Benjamin Franklin

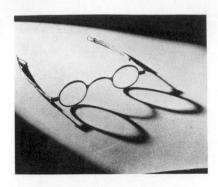

Franklin's original bifocals

Franklin was also a scientist and inventor. His Franklin stove cooked food and warmed houses better than earlier stoves. He discovered that lightning was a form of electricity. He invented bifocals, which are eyeglasses that have lenses for both reading and distance in the same frame. The Franklin stove, the lightning rod, and bifocals are all still used today.

By the 1750's, Benjamin Franklin was rich and famous. Over the next 40 years, he served the people and helped in forming a new nation—the United States of America.

Franklin's lightning rods

Franklin stove, made around 1795

Section Review

Write your answers on a sheet of paper.
1. Name the middle colonies.
2. How did William Penn get the land for his colony?
3. Why did Pennsylvania attract settlers?
4. List Benjamin Franklin's accomplishments.
5. How do you think Philadelphia's location on the Delaware River helped the city grow?

3 The Southern Colonies

The five southern colonies were Maryland, Virginia, North Carolina, South Carolina, and Georgia. These five colonies shared a warmer climate than the other colonies. Farmers had great success with crops such as tobacco and rice. However, planting and harvesting these crops required many workers. During the 1600's and 1700's, blacks from Africa were brought to the South to work on the farms.

The Carolina Experience

The first settlers in North Carolina were farmers and fur trappers. They came from Virginia in the 1650's. North Carolina had no government then. In 1663, the English king gave eight men a grant of land that included both North and South Carolina. The new landlords divided up the land into three parts and appointed a different governor for each part. This plan did not work out. In the 1690's one governor for the entire colony was appointed.

Better government helped attract more settlers to North Carolina. The settlers were soon involved in a war with the Tuscarora Indians who lived in the area. The Tuscarora fought furiously to keep their land, but in 1713 the colonists defeated them.

In 1729, the landlords sold their land back to the king. Under a governor appointed by the king, North Carolina began to grow and prosper. Tobacco grew well in the rich soil. By 1775, more than 260,000 people lived on small farms and in towns in North Carolina. The settlements stretched from the Atlantic coast all the way to the Appalachian Mountains.

Farming and Slavery

The southern colonies had a warm climate and good soil. This allowed southerners to use a different kind of farming than that found in the other colonies.

In New England and the middle colonies, farmers grew almost all their food. Any extra food was sold or traded for

cash crop

a crop raised to be sold, rather than used by the farmer

economy

the method of producing and distributing wealth

Slaves packing tobacco at a plantation in Virginia for shipment to England

other goods. Southern farmers also grew what they needed to eat. In addition, they found they could make money by raising large amounts of one crop and selling it. A crop that is raised to be sold for money instead of for the farmer's private use is called a **cash crop.** Cash crops became an important part of the southern **economy.** The economy of a place is its method of producing and distributing wealth.

Tobacco was the first cash crop in the South. The American Indians had grown tobacco for years. John Rolfe, a resident of Jamestown, Virginia, and the husband of Pocahontas, discovered a way to grow it better. Soon Virginia farmers were selling all the tobacco they could grow.

Many people were needed to work the large tobacco farms. It was not always possible to find colonists to take these jobs. Most colonists wanted their own farms. So farmers needed to find other laborers.

A TOBACCO PLANTATION

Slave women working on a plantation

In 1619, a Dutch ship full of Africans docked in Virginia. These Africans had been kidnapped and forced to come to America. Farmers eagerly paid for the Africans' passage and put them to work. These first blacks in the colonies worked as **indentured servants.** This meant that they worked for a number of years until they had paid the cost of their passage. Then they were free. The colonists had white indentured servants too.

Many colonists did not feel comfortable with these black foreigners. The blacks had different customs from the colonists and spoke different languages. For these reasons, farmers began to treat their black servants differently from their white ones. Starting in the late 1600's, some colonies passed laws saying the Africans could be bought and sold as slaves. The slaves had no rights of their own. This was the beginning of a sad part of American history.

Most southerners did not own slaves. They had small farms they worked themselves. But the large farms called **plantations** needed slaves to grow and harvest the cash crops. As the number of plantations increased in the South, slavery spread throughout the region.

indentured servant
a person who agreed to work for someone for a certain amount of time to pay off the cost of passage to the colonies

plantation
a large farm on which many workers are needed to raise crops

indigo

a plant from which a blue dye is made

Maryland had fewer plantations than the other southern colonies. Maryland was founded in the 1630's by Lord Baltimore. A Roman Catholic, he wanted a place where Catholics could worship freely. This was not possible in England at that time.

Georgia was the last of the 13 colonies to be settled. It was settled in 1733 by British people who had been in jail for not paying their debts. In a short period of time, there were many plantations in Georgia.

In the 1700's, cotton and rice became important cash crops. **Indigo,** a plant used to make blue dye, also became an important cash crop. Eliza Lucas, a South Carolina teenager, developed an indigo plant that grew well in the South.

Life in Charleston

Charleston, South Carolina, was the major city of the southern colonies. In the 1700's, more than 10,000 whites and 12,000 black slaves lived there.

Charleston had an excellent harbor. Planters from the area brought their crops to the port. There the crops were loaded on ships and sent to Great Britain, the West Indies, and other colonies.

Merchants grew rich from the busy trade. They built beautiful mansions in the city. Many of these colonial houses are still standing today.

Section Review

Write your answers on a sheet of paper.
1. Name the five southern colonies.
2. What is a cash crop? How were southern farms different from farms in the middle and New England colonies?
3. What is an indentured servant? How is an indentured servant different from a slave?
4. Why did Lord Baltimore found Maryland?
5. How do you think the climate of the South affected what people did there to earn a living?

Identifying Centuries

If the year of your birth begins with the number 19, why do people say you were born in the twentieth century? To find the answer, you have to understand how we measure time.

Just as days, weeks, months, and years represent units of time, the word "century" represents a unit of time. A century is a full 100 years.

We count time forward from the year 1, which officially marks the birth of Jesus Christ. The 100 years from 1 to 100 are called the first century. The 100 years from 101 to 200 are called the second century.

The time line below shows some important historical dates. Notice in what century each occurred.

Time line

Columbus visits America — 1401 · 1492 1500

Magellan circumnavigates world — 1501 1522 1600

Pilgrims land at Plymouth — 1601 1620 1700

America declares independence — 1701 1776 1800

Fifteenth Century · Sixteenth Century · Seventeenth Century · Eighteenth Century

Practice Your Skills

1. In what century did Columbus visit America?
2. Was Plymouth settled at the end of the sixteenth century or at the beginning of the seventeenth?
3. How many centuries passed between the time Columbus visited the New World and the year the United States declared its independence?
4. Magellan was killed a year before his crew finished its voyage around the globe. During which century did Magellan die?

Weather Vanes Have you ever seen a dancing rooster? What about a whale that spins on its belly or a prancing horse that turns around in circles? All of these curious creatures can be found on weather vanes—pointers that show the direction of the wind.

Weather vanes have been around for centuries. Farmers, sailors, and scientists around the world have used them to tell which way the wind is blowing.

Usually a weather vane is a wooden or metal figure in the shape of an animal or a person. This figure sits on top of an arrow, and the arrow fits over a rod so that it can spin as the direction of the wind changes.

A few of the earliest weather vanes made in America can still be seen today. One of them is on top of the Old North Church in Boston, Massachusetts. It is in the shape of a banner and was made in 1740. Another historic vane is on top of Boston's Faneuil (**fan**-yull) Hall. This vane, made in 1742, is shaped like a grass-

America

hopper. It is made of copper and has green glass eyes.

Thomas Jefferson created an unusual vane for his house, Monticello (mon-tuh-**chell**-oe). The rod from the vane passed down through the roof into the house. Attached to the end of the rod was a marker that showed which way the wind was blowing. So, Jefferson did not have to go outside to know the direction of the wind.

The figures on weather vanes were often symbols. They might tell something about the purpose of the building underneath or the business of the owner. For example, vanes on tops of barns often had figures of roosters, horses, or cows. A shipbuilder's home might have a vane with a ship on it. A colonial blacksmith who made metal objects might have a vane in the shape of a large key.

Hundreds of vanes are still made each year in many different shapes. Some vanes are made in the shape of cars, musical instruments, and even television sets!

UNIT REVIEW

Word Work

Write the sentences below on a sheet of paper. Fill in the blanks with the correct words from the list.

almanac   mission   burgesses   cash crop   barter

1. Landowners who voted for representatives in Virginia were known as _____.
2. Tobacco was a _____ for some farmers in the southern colonies.
3. Many farmers in New England would _____ instead of using money when they needed goods.
4. Father Serra built his first _____ in San Diego.
5. Benjamin Franklin published a famous _____.

Knowing the Facts

Write your answers on a sheet of paper.

1. How did the Dutch lose control of their colony in North America?
2. What were the first three permanent English settlements in the New World?
3. How was farming in the southern colonies different from farming in other colonies?

Using What You Know

Choose one of the following activities to do. Follow the instructions given here.

1. Write a letter to a boy or girl in one of the 13 colonies. Tell how your life differs from his or hers in at least two ways.

2. Design an advertising poster inviting people to come to the New World. Show some of the good things the country has to offer.

Skills Practice

Put the following list of events in order. Then, using these important dates, construct a horizontal time line. Use your time line to answer the questions below.

    1513 Ponce de León reaches Florida
    1497 Cabot arrives in Newfoundland
    1519 Cortés explores Mexico
    1609 Hudson sails into Hudson Bay
    1534 Cartier explores the St. Lawrence River

1. In what century did Hudson sail into Hudson Bay?
2. Did Cabot reach Newfoundland at the end of the fourteenth or the end of the fifteenth century?
3. Approximately how many centuries passed between Cabot's arrival in Newfoundland and Hudson's sail into Hudson Bay?
4. What three centuries are included in your time line?

Your Heritage

Find out about a local resident who is famous in your community's history. Perhaps a street, park, or building was named for this person. Find out when this person lived in your town, what life was like then, and why this person became famous. Give a five-minute oral report based on your research to the class. Use the library or local historical society to find the information you need.

UNIT 3

A Nation Is Established

By 1750, the 13 colonies had changed. The colonists no longer had to struggle to survive in the New World. Merchants were selling goods to other colonies and trading with other nations. This new growth made the colonists feel stronger. They wanted to have more control over their future.

In this unit, you will learn how the colonists and the British fought together to get more land in America from France. After the war with France, colonists began having trouble with Great Britain. You will read how the colonists' anger at Great Britain led to a war for independence and the birth of a new nation, the United States of America.

5 Trouble in the Colonies

A View of the Landing the New England Forces in ye Expedition against CAPE BRETON, 1745.

The New England colonial forces landing in Canada during the French and Indian War

The years from the 1750's until the mid-1770's were uneasy times in the colonies. First the colonists fought the French and American Indians to gain land. Then they argued with the British king about their rights and freedom. Colonists urged their neighbors to join the struggle and work for freedom. In this chapter, you will read about the colonists' battles and protests.

At the end of this chapter, you should be able to:
○ Identify the reasons for the French and Indian War.
○ Explain why British taxation made the colonists angry.
○ Describe the important events that led to American independence from Great Britain.

1 Trouble with France

In the 1700's, Great Britain and France were the two most powerful nations in Europe. They fought with each other to control world trade and to control the New World.

Between 1689 and 1763, the two nations fought four wars in Europe and in North America. The last and most important years of battle in America are known as the French and Indian War (1754–1763).

French and Indian War

Great Britain and France went to war in 1754 because both countries wanted to control the fur trade and control land in America. British leaders wanted to win control of the New World's fur trade from the French. Many French settlers in the New World were fur trappers. The French trappers were making large sums of money selling the valuable furs to European countries.

British colonists were not only interested in the fur trade. They were interested in land. British colonists had already settled most of the good farmland in the East. Where could they find new land? The Ohio **Territory,** an area of land west of the Appalachian Mountains, seemed like the best place. This created a problem. Both France and Great Britain claimed that land as their own.

When war broke out in 1754, the British and the French both had help from American Indian tribes. Since the French fur traders who lived in the Ohio Territory treated the Indians there fairly, many tribes helped the French fight the war. Warriors from the Shawnee (shaw-**nee**), Wyandot (**wie**-un-dot), Delaware (**dell**-uh-wair), and Abnaki (ab-**nah**-kee) tribes fought with the French. These tribes feared they would lose some of their lands if colonists came to build farms.

Voyageurs became wealthy by trapping furs in the Ohio Territory.

territory
the land and waters that belong to an area, region, state, or nation

ally
a person, nation, or group that promises support to another

Great Britain and the colonists also had some Indian supporters, or **allies,** in the war. The tribes who fought with them included the Mohawk, Oneida (oe-**nide**-uh), Onondaga (ahn-un-**daw**-guh), Seneca (**sen**-ih-kuh), Cayuga (kay-**yoo**-guh), and Tuscarora (tuss-kuh-**roar**-uh). These tribes did not want the French to settle along the Ohio and Mississippi rivers. So they helped the British, hoping that this would make the French leave.

Before the war started, the French had built forts along rivers in the Ohio Territory to protect French settlers. Rivers made it easy to transport soldiers, weapons, and furs.

In 1753, British leaders sent George Washington to the French with a message. It said the French had to leave the Ohio Territory or prepare to fight. The French refused to leave. Washington and his troops quickly built a fort south of the French Fort Duquesne (doo-**kane**). He called his fort Fort Necessity.

The war began in 1754. After losing several battles to the French, Washington was forced to surrender Fort Necessity. The French were in control of the Ohio Territory.

Great Britain did not give up. Soon more British troops sailed to America.

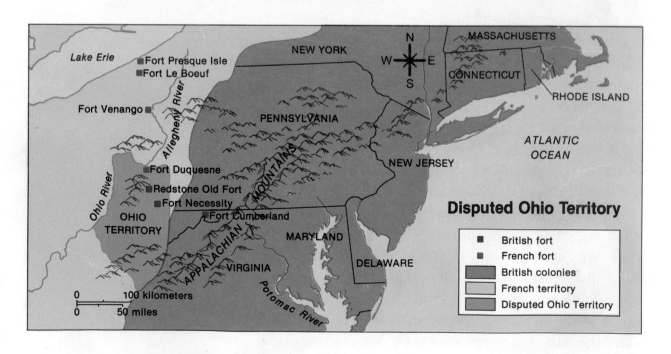

Disputed Ohio Territory

- ■ British fort
- ■ French fort
- British colonies
- French territory
- Disputed Ohio Territory

In 1755, British General Edward Braddock again tried to capture Fort Duquesne. A group of 900 French and Indians surprised the British and colonial troops who were on their way to the fort. Braddock's soldiers were not used to fighting in the woods of the Ohio Territory. And their bright red uniforms made them easy targets for the French and the Indians. The British and colonial soldiers tried to break their lines and run for cover. But Braddock forced them back. In three hours, most of the British and the colonists had been killed or wounded. The French and American Indians still controlled the land that the colonists and British wanted.

After Braddock's defeat, the war continued to go badly for Great Britain. Important battles were lost in Canada and New York. Then, in 1757, William Pitt became the new leader of the British government. He decided to send new generals, more soldiers, and more weapons to fight the war. In 1758, these troops and colonial soldiers again attacked Fort Duquesne. This time they captured the fort. The fort was renamed Fort Pitt, in honor of the British leader. The town that grew up around the fort was called Pittsburgh.

William Pitt

The Battle of Quebec

The British and colonial troops now went north to attack Quebec. Quebec was the most important French settlement in the New World. From Quebec, furs and other goods were sent down the St. Lawrence River to the Atlantic Ocean. French troops and weapons entered the New World by way of the St. Lawrence River and Quebec. If the British could capture Quebec and control the St. Lawrence River, they could win the war.

The battle for Quebec took place in September 1759. The British surprised the French by attacking from a plateau around the city rather than from the St. Lawrence River. Both the British and French generals were killed. But the British won the battle and Quebec. In 1760, the British captured Montreal as well. It was the final battle of the war.

The Treaty of Paris

treaty

a formal agreement between nations, signed by each

Most wars officially end when the enemies sign an agreement, called a **treaty.** The Treaty of Paris, signed in 1763, ended the French and Indian War. The Treaty of Paris made Great Britain the most powerful nation in North America. The British gained control of Canada and all of the lands east of the Mississippi River, including the Ohio Territory.

The colonists believed that British soldiers did not have to protect them any longer. They thought they could settle any land they wanted in the Ohio Territory.

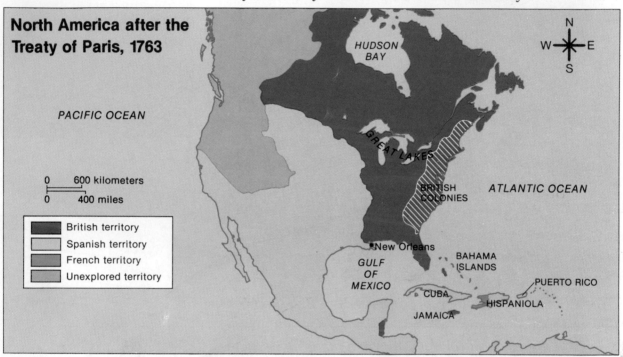

North America after the Treaty of Paris, 1763

PACIFIC OCEAN

HUDSON BAY

GREAT LAKES

BRITISH COLONIES

ATLANTIC OCEAN

0   600 kilometers
0   400 miles

- British territory
- Spanish territory
- French territory
- Unexplored territory

New Orleans

GULF OF MEXICO

CUBA

JAMAICA

BAHAMA ISLANDS

HISPANIOLA

PUERTO RICO

Section Review

Write your answers on a sheet of paper.
1. What were the causes of the French and Indian War?
2. Why did some Indian tribes support the French?
3. Why was Quebec so important to the French?
4. Indian tribes fought with either the French or British because they shared a common interest. What are some common interests or problems today that the nations of the world are working to solve?

2 Trouble with Britain

Once the war was over, Great Britain wanted to keep peace in the Ohio Territory. Its biggest worry was that the American Indians would fight with colonists who came to settle the land. Great Britain did not want to send more weapons or troops to fight. Britain had already spent too much money on its wars.

To keep peace, Britain announced that no settlers could move into the Ohio Territory. This official announcement, or **proclamation** (prock-lu-**may**-shun), was made in 1763, the same year the Treaty of Paris was signed.

proclamation
an official
announcement

The Proclamation of 1763 made many colonists upset. They had fought the French so they could settle the Ohio lands. To make matters worse, the British began to make the colonists pay taxes.

Taxing the Colonies

Great Britain taxed the colonists because it needed money to cover the cost of fighting the French and Indian War. It also wanted the colonists to pay for the support of British troops who were serving in the colonies after the war. The British said the soldiers protected the colonists from any American Indians or French settlers who were angry over losing. The British felt that the colonists should pay their fair share of these expenses.

The Sugar Act

In 1764, Britain's lawmaking body, **Parliament**, passed a law taxing the colonies. It was called the Sugar Act.

parliament
the lawmaking body
of some nations, including
Great Britain

The Sugar Act put a tax on sugar, wine, and other products that were shipped to the colonies from countries other than Great Britain. When ships landed in the colonies with these products, a tax had to be paid by the people who ordered the goods.

The colonists refused to pay the tax. They attacked British tax collectors. The colonists did not want to pay taxes that would hurt their trade with other countries. In addition, they did not want to pay taxes passed by Parliament.

The colonists felt their own lawmakers should decide whether a tax was necessary and, if so, what form the tax should take.

The Sugar Act was not Great Britain's first attempt to tax the colonies. In 1733, Parliament put a tax on molasses. Few colonists paid that tax, though, and Great Britain did not try very hard to collect it. The British were too busy fighting a war with France.

British leaders were serious about the Sugar Act, however. They sent over tax collectors from Great Britain to collect the money. These men searched all ships that came into colonial harbors. If they found a hidden item that was supposed to be taxed, they could take the ship away from its owner.

To avoid paying the tax, many ship owners became **smugglers,** people who loaded and unloaded their ships in secret. Sometimes smugglers got caught and were punished. Sometimes their ships were taken away.

The Stamp Act

In 1765, Parliament passed a new tax law—the Stamp Act. The Stamp Act put a tax on almost all printed paper goods that colonists bought. Colonists had to pay a tax for pamphlets, newspapers, and playing cards. A person who finished college had to pay a tax on the diploma. Lawyers had

smuggler
a person who brings things into, or takes things out of, a country illegally

Goods that were taxed had to be stamped by tax collectors.

to pay a tax on the wills and deeds that they wrote. To show that the tax had been paid, a stamp seller would put a stamp on the paper.

The colonists hated the Stamp Act. In Boston, crowds wrecked the offices of the stamp sellers. They poured hot tar on the sellers and then covered them with feathers. This painful punishment was called tarring and feathering.

Why did the colonists fight so strongly against the tax? The main reason was that the tax had been passed without their agreement. The colonists were used to paying taxes at home. In the colonies, they elected representatives who decided how much tax money to collect. The colonists were willing to pay these taxes because their representatives would use the tax money in ways that would help them. The tax money was used to pay for things the colonies needed, such as roads. But the Stamp Tax and other British taxes like it had been passed by Parliament.

The colonists had no representatives in Parliament. They had no say in voting for or against these taxes. The British tax laws were passed by people the colonists did not elect, and the tax money was being used for soldiers whom the colonists did not want. In the opinion of many colonists, this was taxation without representation.

A tax stamp used by the British

The colonists made their own version of a tax stamp to show how they felt about paying taxes to the British.

An angry crowd hangs a representation of a tax collector.

The Colonists Fight Back

boycott
to refuse to deal with a person, country, or business as a means of protest

repeal
to do away with; take back

In protest against the British taxes, the colonists began to **boycott,** or refuse to buy, British goods. Many British merchants had grown rich selling to the colonies. Suddenly they had very few customers. They asked Parliament to **repeal,** or do away with, the Stamp Act.

In 1766, Parliament agreed and the Stamp Act was repealed. The next year, however, Parliament passed new tax laws. They were called the Townshend (**town**-zend) Acts, after Charles Townshend, an official of the king. The acts taxed paper, glass, paint, lead, and tea that Great Britain sold to the colonies. The colonists again boycotted the goods, and British merchants again lost money.

In 1770, Parliament repealed the Townshend Acts. But it kept a tax on one item—tea. In addition, Parliament passed a law called the Quartering Act. This law made the colonists pay for the cost of housing British soldiers in America. The law said that if there were not enough buildings available for the soldiers to live in, the colonists themselves had to house, or **quarter,** the soldiers. The colonists even had to pay for food and cider that the soldiers ate and drank!

quarter
to provide housing for soldiers

These new laws made the colonists more upset than ever. Some colonists showed their anger by making fun of British soldiers and calling them names. One night, the anger led to violence.

The Boston Massacre

On the snowy night of March 5, 1770, a group of angry Bostonians began to shout and throw snowballs at eight British soldiers. The leader of the soldiers told his men not to fight back. But the soldiers opened fire. When the smoke cleared, three people lay dead. Two more were wounded and later died.

One of the dead was Crispus Attucks, a young black man. Some people believe he was not part of the teasing crowd. But Attucks has been called the first person to die for the cause of freedom in the colonies.

Paul Revere's drawing of the Boston Massacre

People all over the colonies learned about the killings. They called the event a massacre (**mass**-uh-ker), which means cruel, random killing. Most of the colonists had felt loyal to Great Britain until that time. But the Boston Massacre made many of them change their minds about Great Britain.

Organizing for Action

Some colonial leaders said that as long as Great Britain ruled the colonies, there would always be trouble. They wanted the colonists to have the freedom to govern themselves—to have their independence. One leader who spoke and wrote about independence was Samuel Adams.

Adams believed that people from different colonies should write to each other about how British laws and taxes threatened colonists' freedoms. He set up Committees of Correspondence. These were groups of people who wrote to each other about the ways colonists were protesting British laws. The colonists soon learned that anger over British taxes and soldiers was widespread. The committees helped unite the colonists.

Some committee members wanted to do more than write about their problems. They wanted to take direct action against the British. These people formed a secret organization called the Sons of Liberty. In some cities, they beat up tax collectors and destroyed papers with British stamps on them.

Another group was formed called the Daughters of Liberty. It was made up of women who secretly made goods to replace the ones that people had stopped buying from Great Britain. Their work made it easier for people to support the boycott.

The Boston Tea Party

The Sons of Liberty took their most famous action against the tax on tea. In Boston, colonists refused to unload three ships with tea on board. The British governor said that the ships would stay in the harbor until the colonists agreed to pay the taxes on the tea.

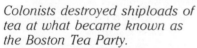

Colonists destroyed shiploads of tea at what became known as the Boston Tea Party.

On the night of December 16, 1773, colonists, dressed as American Indians, climbed aboard the British ships. They broke open hundreds of crates of tea and threw them into the water. If there was no tea, they said angrily, there would be nothing to tax. This event became known as the Boston Tea Party.

Britain's King George and Parliament were furious. British warships were sent to Boston Harbor to block any ships sailing into or out of Boston. The British said they would block the harbor until the tea was paid for. This British **blockade** ruined Boston's trade. But the colonists would not pay for the tea they had dumped.

Meeting for Action

In September 1774, 12 colonies sent representatives to the First Continental Congress, which met in Philadelphia. The Congress decided to take action on the blockade of Boston.

The members of Congress wrote to King George asking him to reopen Boston Harbor. They also told him that the colonists should be the ones to decide what their taxes should be and what the tax money should be used for. Finally, they said they would continue to boycott British goods until they got what they wanted.

King George never answered the letter. Instead, he sent more warships to the colonies.

blockade
the blocking off of a place so that no one can enter or exit without permission

Section Review

Write your answers on a sheet of paper.
1. What was the Proclamation of 1763?
2. Explain why the colonists felt Great Britain had no right to tax them.
3. How did the Committees of Correspondence help the colonies unite?
4. Why do you think the British were so angry when they heard about the Boston Tea Party?

The War for Independence

The first battle of the War for Independence at Lexington, Massachusetts

By 1775, there was much tension between the colonists and the British. On the chilly Wednesday morning of April 19, 1775, the tension led to shooting. British soldiers faced a group of armed colonists at Lexington, Massachusetts. A shot was fired. That shot was the start of the War for Independence. In this war, a brave group of colonists fought mighty Great Britain. In this chapter, you will read about the war between the British and the Americans.

At the end of this chapter, you should be able to:
○ Identify the major battles of the war.
● Read a battle map.
○ Describe how women, blacks, and Europeans helped during the War for Independence.
● Interpret a map that uses color symbols.

1 Preparing for War

In Massachusetts, people were especially upset by the blockade of Boston Harbor. Farmers in the area began organizing to practice shooting and marching. These men were called **minutemen,** because they could get ready to fight at a minute's notice.

Lexington and Concord

British leaders had discovered that the minutemen were storing extra guns and gunpowder at Lexington and Concord. On the night of April 18, 1775, 700 British soldiers marched to Lexington from Boston. The British traveled at night because they hoped to avoid fighting with the colonists. The British leaders thought they would be able to find the stored weapons and leave before the colonists knew what had happened.

But colonial spies had found out when the British planned to march. The colonists arranged a warning system. From the tower of North Church in Boston, a colonist used lanterns to signal that the British were coming. Paul Revere, William Dawes, and Samuel Prescott rode out to warn the colonists who lived nearby.

By the time the British reached Lexington, the minutemen were waiting. Suddenly someone fired. In the fighting that followed, eight minutemen were killed. Then the British marched to Concord.

At Concord, the British found more minutemen waiting for them. There was more shooting. The British began retreating to Boston. Now minutemen were waiting behind trees and stone walls. In their bright red coats, the British soldiers were easy targets for the minutemen. The colonists shot many British soldiers on the road back to Boston. The minutemen had shown they could fight the mighty British army.

minuteman
colonial soldier who could be ready to fight at a minute's notice

Paul Revere

Battle of Bunker Hill

In June 1775, the colonists tried a daring move. In the middle of the night, a large force of colonists climbed a hill near Bunker Hill, overlooking Boston Harbor. They spent all night digging trenches and putting in guns. When the British awoke in the morning, they saw colonial gunners across the harbor on a hill above them. The British decided to attack. The bloody battle that followed is known as the battle of Bunker Hill.

Thousands of British troops rowed across Boston Harbor and went up the hill. Waiting patiently at the top were the colonial soldiers. The **patriots,** colonists who wanted independence from Britain, did not have much ammunition, so they wanted to make every shot count. An officer told the men, "Don't fire until you see the whites of their eyes."

When the British soldiers were 13.7 meters (15 yards)

patriot

American colonist who wanted independence from Great Britain

The colonists fought bravely at the battle of Bunker Hill, but they were outnumbered and outarmed by the British.

away, the patriots opened fire. The British tried to take the hill three times. Finally, on the third attack, the patriots ran out of ammunition. They retreated before the British reached the top of the hill.

The British had chased the patriots off the hill, but not without losing many men. The patriots had killed or wounded more than 1,000 British troops. The colonial soldiers had lost about 450 men. Once again the colonists had shown they could fight well and bravely against the British army.

Declaring Independence

In the spring of 1775, the Second Continental Congress met in Philadelphia. They met to organize an army and navy to defend and support colonial rights. Some of the representatives wanted the colonies to declare their independence from Britain. Patrick Henry, a lawyer from Virginia, expressed their feelings when he said, "Give me liberty, or give me death!" But most of the representatives were still not ready to declare independence. Some colonists were strongly against independence. Those people who remained loyal to Great Britain during the war were called **Tories.**

In June 1775, the Congress decided to appoint George Washington the commander in chief of the colonial army. Washington left Philadelphia to take command of the army near Boston.

By the following year, more and more people had come to believe that the colonies should be independent. Colonial soldiers had died fighting for colonial rights. British leaders had shown no respect for the colonists' rights.

In the spring of 1776, the Continental Congress decided to take action. Thomas Jefferson, a young Virginian, was asked to write a statement, or declaration, explaining why the colonies should be free.

In the declaration, Jefferson described his ideas about human rights and listed the complaints colonists had against King George. Jefferson said that all people had the right to life and liberty and the right to seek happiness. No government could take these rights away. If the rulers tried

Tory
American colonist who supported the British during the war for independence

115

Delegates to the Continental Congress prepare to adopt the Declaration of Independence.

revolution

the overthrow of a government by force

to do so, the people had the right to choose a new government. Jefferson blamed the king for ignoring colonial laws, ruining trade, keeping troops in people's homes, and making people pay high taxes.

On July 4, 1776, the Congress adopted, or approved, Jefferson's Declaration of Independence. The colonies stated that they were no longer a part of Great Britain. A new nation was born! Now colonists would fight to overthrow the British government in America. It was the beginning of the American **Revolution.**

Section Review

Write your answers on a sheet of paper.
1. Who were the minutemen?
2. What was the result of the battle of Bunker Hill?
3. What important actions did the Second Continental Congress take?
4. Why are modern Americans willing to pay taxes to their government and to obey its laws?

Using a Battle Map

A battle map uses symbols to show how and where battles were fought. Often it shows who won or lost each battle and when each took place.

The battle map on this page shows the route Paul Revere followed when he rode to warn patriots in Lexington and Concord that the British troops were advancing. It also shows the route taken by William Dawes, as well as the movements of the British troops and the sites of the important battles that followed.

Read the map key to learn which symbols represent British troop movements

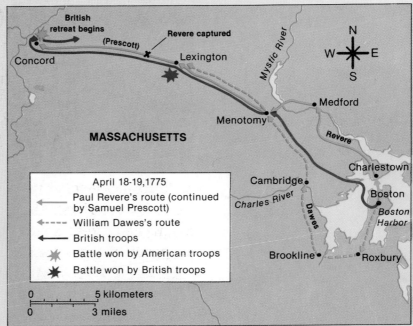

and which stand for American troop movements. The exploding star symbols show the sites of important battles and who won them.

—— Practice Your Skills ——

1. Through which towns did Paul Revere pass on his way to Lexington? Through which towns did William Dawes pass?
2. Who won the battle of Lexington? of Concord?
3. Describe the route of the British advance.
4. From what town did the British retreat begin?
5. What period of time does this map cover?

2 Defending the Nation

The Americans battled against the British for six years. It was a difficult war for both sides. The British were fighting far from their homeland. Supplies had to be sent from across the ocean. Although the Americans lacked supplies and military training, they were fighting on land they knew well. And they were fighting to protect their newly declared independence.

Washington and his troops crossed the ice-choked Delaware River to attack a British camp at Trenton, New Jersey.

Washington Retreats

In the beginning, the war did not go well for Washington's army. In 1776, the British nearly caught the Americans in a trap on Long Island, New York, but Washington and his troops managed to escape to Pennsylvania.

As winter approached, spirits were low among the colonial troops. Washington knew he needed a victory to restore hope to his troops. On Christmas night, Washington led his troops across the icy Delaware River, heading for a British camp at Trenton, New Jersey. The Americans surprised the force of 1,600 **Hessians,** German soldiers fighting for the British, and took 900 prisoners. George Washington had proven that his men could defeat a well-trained army.

Hessian
German soldier who fought for the British during the American Revolution

118

Saratoga

The American cause was helped by a great victory at Saratoga, New York, in October 1777. A British army had marched south from Canada. Two other British forces were supposed to meet this army at Albany. But the other two armies never got there. A large American army surrounded the British force at Saratoga, near Albany. The British army of more than 5,000 soldiers surrendered to the Americans.

The victory at Saratoga gave the Americans hope. It also brought help from overseas. Benjamin Franklin had been trying to get the French king to help the Americans. After the battle of Saratoga, the French king realized that the Americans had a good chance of winning. He sent soldiers and ships to help fight his enemy, the British king.

Valley Forge

But by the end of the year, hard times had returned for the Americans. The British took Philadelphia, the capital of the colonies. Washington and his army camped near Philadelphia, at Valley Forge, to keep watch on the British.

The winter of 1777 was a harsh one for Washington and his troops stationed at Valley Forge, Pennsylvania.

The bitter winter at Valley Forge was the low point of the war. One soldier described it like this: "Poor food—hard lodging—cold weather . . . nasty clothes—nasty cooking—sick half the time—Why are we here to starve and freeze?" The answer was that Americans wanted their independence, but their government had no money to pay for food or supplies for the soldiers.

The War at Sea

At the start of the war, the British navy was the most powerful in the world. The navy made it possible for the British to send supplies and troops to America from Great Britain, more than 5,500 kilometers (3,400 miles) away. There seemed little the Americans could do to stop the British navy.

But the Americans found a way to weaken the British navy. In 1779, a sea captain named John Paul Jones sailed to Great Britain. Jones raided British ports and captured several valuable merchant ships. Finally a British warship caught up with Jones. The two ships fought an intense battle. Both ships were burning and filling with water. The British captain asked Jones if he would surrender. Jones answered, "Sir, I have not yet begun to fight!" Jones's victory raised the hopes of Americans. It showed that the British navy could be defeated at sea.

John Paul Jones, captain of the Bonhomme Richard

The American ship, Bonhomme Richard, *met the British ship,* Serapis, *off the coast of England and engaged in an intense battle.*

The War Ends

In 1781, George Washington saw a chance to win a great victory. Lord Cornwallis, a British general, was camped with his army at Yorktown, Virginia. Washington knew if he acted fast enough, he could trap the British army at Yorktown. The French navy sailed to Yorktown and kept the British ships away. Washington marched his army to Yorktown. The plan worked. The British were surrounded. On October 19, 1781, Cornwallis surrendered. It was the last battle of the war.

In 1783, the British and Americans met in Paris and signed a treaty. In the Treaty of Paris, Great Britain agreed to recognize the independence of the United States. The Americans had won their revolution!

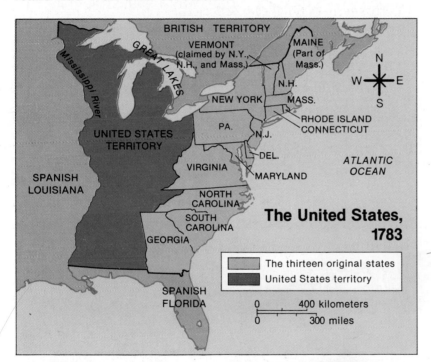

The United States, 1783

The thirteen original states
United States territory

0   400 kilometers
0   300 miles

Section Review

Write your answers on a sheet of paper.
1. Why was the American victory at Saratoga important?
2. What happened at Yorktown?
3. How can fighting a war on one's own territory be both helpful and harmful?

3 Everyone Helps

The Revolutionary War was fought in the farmyards, fields, and forests of America. Thousands of men and women helped in the fight for independence.

Women Help

During the Revolution, thousands of women followed their husbands and sons to army camps to help them. They marched, cooked, and even fought beside the men. One such woman was Mary Hays.

Mary Hays's husband, John, was a gunner in charge of firing a cannon. While he fought, she helped care for the wounded and cooked for the troops. Sometimes, in the heat of the battle, she brought cool pitchers of water to the soldiers. The soldiers called her Molly Pitcher.

During the battle of Monmouth, New Jersey, John Hays was wounded. Who would take his place at the cannon? Mary Hays stepped in and fought bravely.

Unlike Mary Hays, many more women stayed at home.

Mary Hays took over the job of loading a cannon when her husband was wounded at the battle of Monmouth.

They ran family farms and businesses. While their husbands and sons were away, these women took over men's jobs and did their own work too. In addition, some women raised money to help pay for the war.

Blacks Help

Major John Pitcairn was a popular British officer. He had led troops at Lexington and Concord. He planned to lead his soldiers into battle at Bunker Hill. Before he could, a bullet stopped him.

The bullet was Peter Salem's. Salem, a black man, had already fought at Lexington. Then he became one of 21 blacks who joined with whites to fight on Bunker Hill. Salem and two other blacks, Cuff Whitemore and Salem Poor, were honored for bravery in that battle.

During the Revolution, some blacks formed their own military units, or regiments. One Rhode Island unit was made up of 125 blacks. These soldiers fought in the battle of Rhode Island, where their unit did not give up any ground to the British. Later, one leader called the battle of Rhode Island "the best fought action of the war."

Peter Salem at the battle of Bunker Hill

Help from Overseas

Many people in Europe admired the colonies' fight for freedom. Some Europeans even came to America to help in the fighting.

The Marquis de Lafayette (mahr-**kee** duh lah-fee-**ett**) was a 20-year-old French nobleman and military officer. Lafayette hired soldiers and a ship and sailed to America. When he arrived, he offered his services to Congress. Congress made Lafayette a major general, and George Washington asked him to serve on his staff. The young officer and Washington soon became close friends.

Lafayette served bravely in the war. At one battle, he was wounded. In the final battle at Yorktown, he helped defeat the British.

Baron Friedrich von Steuben (**stoo**-ben) was a German officer who came to help the Americans. Von Steuben was good at training soldiers. During the winter at Valley Forge, he helped train American soldiers to be better fighters.

Two soldiers from Poland also came to help. Casimir Pulaski (puh-**lass**-kee) joined the Americans in 1777. He, too, became a general in the American army. Pulaski was killed in a battle in Georgia in 1779. Thaddeus Kosciuszko (koss-ee-**uss**-koe) left Poland in 1776 and came to America. He helped build forts for the American army during the war.

The Marquis de Lafayette volunteered to serve in the colonial army without pay. He fought bravely in many battles.

Section Review

Write your answers on a sheet of paper.
1. How did women help in the Revolution?
2. Name two battles in which black soldiers played an important part.
3. How did Baron von Steuben help the Americans?
4. During the American Revolution, Europeans came to help the colonists gain their independence. Can you think of any ways that Americans have helped people in other countries?

Using Colors to Interpret a Map

Colors are important map symbols. On many maps, blue represents water, for example, while green or brown represents land. The historical map on this page uses different colors to show how the United States expanded over a period of time.

On this map, each color has two meanings. First, it shows the size of a political area. Second, it represents a different period of time. For example, the yellow section shows the size of the original 13 colonies before 1781.

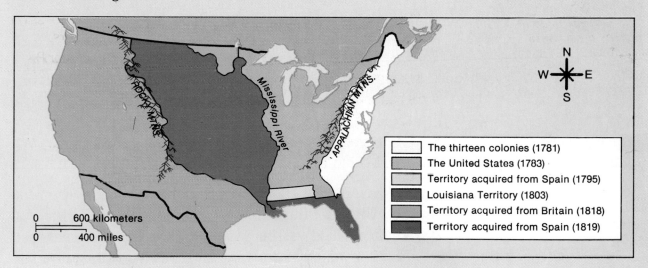

Legend:
- The thirteen colonies (1781)
- The United States (1783)
- Territory acquired from Spain (1795)
- Louisiana Territory (1803)
- Territory acquired from Britain (1818)
- Territory acquired from Spain (1819)

Scale: 0 — 600 kilometers / 0 — 400 miles

Practice Your Skills

1. Did the United States gain or lose territory after the peace treaty of 1783 was signed?
2. What natural barrier formed the westernmost border of the 13 colonies?
3. What is the territory acquired from Spain in 1819 now called?
4. What territory was acquired in 1803?

CHAPTER 7

A Nation Is Born

November 25, 1783. It was a bright morning in New York City. The last British soldiers were leaving the harbor. An American flag was being raised. The war was over, but there was much to do. Thirteen states made up a new nation. They would need a new government. In this chapter, you will learn how they formed it.

At the end of this chapter, you should be able to:

○ Explain the weaknesses in government under the Articles of Confederation.
○ Name the three branches of the national government.
○ Describe how the Constitution became the law of the United States.
● Use a chart to understand how the government of the United States is organized.
○ Describe how the United States became involved in the War of 1812.

1 Forming a Government

American colonists had fought for freedom against a powerful king. When it came time to set up a government in America, the people did not forget that fight. They did not want one strong ruler to have all the authority. Instead, they wanted the states to keep much of their power, while some power would be given to a national government. The government that was formed made this possible.

The Articles of Confederation

In the summer of 1776, Thomas Jefferson was writing the Declaration of Independence. At the same time, other members of the Second Continental Congress were planning the new nation's government. The plan they developed led to a joining together, or **confederation,** of the 13 states under the Articles of Confederation.

The Articles of Confederation called for a central law-making body to be known as Congress. Each state would send a representative to Congress. These representatives would choose a leader. Congress and its leader would make up the nation's government.

confederation
the joining together of states in order to achieve common goals

Pennsylvania State House, where the Continental Congress met

There was one major problem with the Articles of Confederation. The Articles created a Congress that did not have enough power to govern the nation effectively. The Articles of Confederation stated that Congress could pass laws, declare war, and borrow money. But the Articles did not give Congress the power to make people obey the laws it passed. Congress could not make soldiers join the army to fight the nation's wars. It did not have the power to collect taxes to pay the nation's debts.

Instead, the day-to-day affairs of the nation were handled by the individual states. Each state had its own lawmaking body, or **legislature.** The state legislatures could enforce laws and collect taxes. Each state also printed its own money, or **currency.** In many ways, the state governments were more powerful than the Congress. Many Americans felt more loyal to their states than they did to their national government.

legislature

a group of persons chosen to make the laws of a nation or state

currency

money in general use in a country

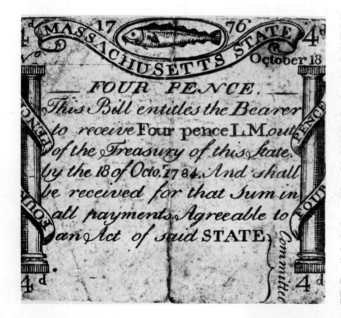

(left) Massachusetts currency

(right) Pennsylvania currency

Weaknesses of the Government

As time passed, the disadvantages of a weak Congress became clear. There was no way to solve arguments that developed among the states. The states argued over where their boundaries were. Some states would not accept money printed in other states. Some states placed fees, or

tariffs, on goods coming from other states. Congress had no power to settle these quarrels.

The new American nation also had problems with some of its neighbors. Three European nations owned territory in North America. Great Britain controlled Canadian lands to the north. France and Spain held land to the south and the west. Great Britain did not think the new country would survive as a nation because the American government was so weak. France dealt separately with each state rather than treating the United States as a single nation. This encouraged the states to ignore the national government. The king of Spain told the United States not to use the Mississippi River.

The Northwest Ordinance

Despite its weaknesses, Congress did solve some problems. One major achievement was the passage of the Northwest Ordinance of 1787. This **ordinance,** or government order, was a plan for adding new states and preventing the original states from expanding into the Northwest Territory. The Northwest Territory was the region west of Pennsylvania and north of the Ohio River.

The ordinance set up a system of self-government in the territories. Each territory had a governor and courts all ap-

tariff
money charged for permission to bring goods into a state

ordinance
an order or law made by a government

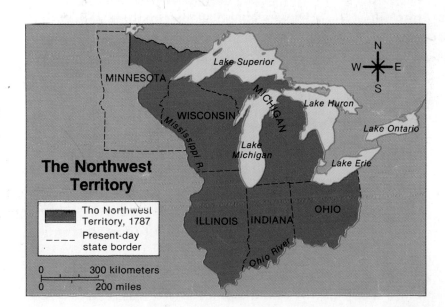

The Northwest Territory

- The Northwest Territory, 1787
- - - - Present-day state border

0   300 kilometers
0   200 miles

MINNESOTA

Lake Superior

MICHIGAN

WISCONSIN

Lake Huron

Mississippi R.

Lake Ontario

Lake Michigan

Lake Erie

ILLINOIS   INDIANA   OHIO

Ohio River

pointed by Congress. The ordinance said that five states could be formed from the Northwest Territory. When the population of any area grew to 60,000, the area could become a state and form a state legislature of its own. The citizens of the new states were guaranteed the same rights and privileges as the citizens of the original 13 states. Slavery was not permitted in any of these new states. Eventually the states of Ohio, Indiana, Illinois, Michigan, and Wisconsin were formed from the land of the Northwest Territory.

The Northwest Ordinance set an important pattern for settling new territories. New territories of the United States would not be treated as if they were colonies. As soon as their populations were large enough, the territories would become states.

The Constitutional Convention

At his home in Virginia, George Washington worried about the future of the new nation. The states were quarreling. The national government did not have enough power to settle these arguments.

What could be done? Many members of Congress realized that the national government had to be changed. They decided to call a nationwide meeting, or convention. Each state was invited to send representatives to this convention. People in Rhode Island were certain that the delegates to the convention would try to set up a stronger central government. They were opposed to this idea, so they decided not to send delegates to the meeting.

The representatives from the other 12 states met together on May 25, 1787, in Philadelphia. These 55 representatives all agreed on two things: George Washington should be president of the convention, and Congress had to be given more power. Some representatives suggested ideas for the new government. These ideas were the starting point for a new plan of government—the Constitution of the United States.

Many highly respected Americans took part in the all-important work in Philadelphia. There were lawyers, college professors, members of state legislatures, and members of Congress. Most of them were under the age of 40.

Eighty-one-year-old Benjamin Franklin was the oldest representative there. During the debates, when the delegates grew angry, Franklin's wise, well-chosen words often helped to calm the other representatives.

James Madison was a delegate from Virginia. Madison came to be known as the "Master Builder" of the Constitution, because he designed most of the plan for the new government. Before the convention, Madison had served in the Virginia State Legislature and in Congress. He used his experience in politics and his intelligence to help write the Constitution. In addition, Madison kept a journal during his weeks at the convention. Today Madison's notes are the best source of information about how our system of government was created.

Meeting of the Constitutional Convention

Conflicts and Compromises

Everyone at the convention agreed that a stronger national government was needed. The delegates, however, could not agree on how to organize representation in the new government.

The delegates had already decided that Congress would have two parts, or houses. One house was to be called the House of Representatives. The other house was to be called the Senate. But how many representatives would each state send to Congress? States with large populations wanted the number of representatives in both houses to be based on population. That way the states that had more people would have more votes in Congress.

States with small populations wanted each state to have one vote in Congress. That way they would not be outvoted by the states with larger populations.

compromise

an agreement reached when each side gives in a little

After arguing about this issue for six weeks, the delegates came up with a solution called a **compromise.** In a compromise, each side gives in a little to settle a large difference. To please the states with large populations,

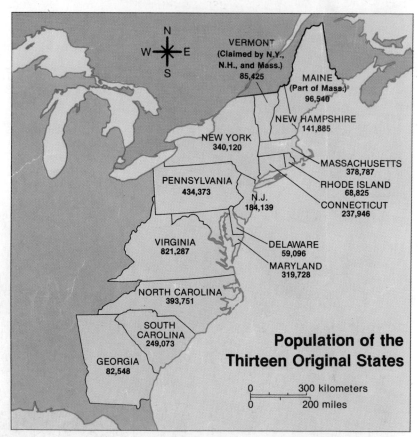

VERMONT
(Claimed by N.Y., N.H., and Mass.)
85,425

MAINE
(Part of Mass.)
96,540

NEW HAMPSHIRE
141,885

NEW YORK
340,120

MASSACHUSETTS
378,787

RHODE ISLAND
68,825

PENNSYLVANIA
434,373

N.J.
184,139

CONNECTICUT
237,946

VIRGINIA
821,287

DELAWARE
59,096

MARYLAND
319,728

NORTH CAROLINA
393,751

SOUTH CAROLINA
249,073

GEORGIA
82,548

Population of the Thirteen Original States

0   300 kilometers
0   200 miles

membership in the House of Representatives would be based on population. To please the states with small populations, each state would have two members in the Senate.

Three Branches of Government

The delegates wanted to set up a government that would be effective but not too powerful. To do this, they created a government with three divisions, or branches. Each branch would have its own powers. In addition, each branch of government could limit the power of the other two. With the power of government so divided, no single branch would become too powerful. This limiting of power is called the system of **checks and balances.**

Congress would be the lawmaking, or **legislative,** branch. Its members, in both the House of Representatives and the Senate, would make the laws. Congress would also have the power to collect taxes and regulate trade and currency. Congress could also declare war and form armies.

The President would be the law-enforcing, or **executive,** branch. The President would sign or refuse to sign the laws that Congress made. Once the laws were signed, the President would make sure they were carried out. The President would also appoint other people to help carry out the laws. Another important power of the President was to be the commander of the armed forces of the United States.

The third branch of the government would be the law-examining, or **judicial,** branch. Judges would make sure that the laws passed by Congress and signed by the President were in agreement with the Constitution, or **constitutional.** The most important of the courts was the Supreme Court.

checks and balances
a political system where different branches of government limit or check the power of the other branches

legislative
having to do with the making of laws

executive
having to do with directing a government and enforcing its laws

judicial
having to do with examining laws in a court of law

constitutional
in agreement with the laws set down in the United States Constitution

The Supreme Court building

The Capitol

The White House

The Federal System

federal
a form of government that divides power between individual states and the national government

The Constitution called for a **federal** system of government. A federal system of government sets up a union of states where power is shared between the national, or federal, government and the state governments. The federal government has some powers. The state governments have other powers.

The Constitution gave the federal government the power to coin money, make treaties with foreign countries, and make citizens join the army and navy in times of war. The state governments still had the power to make state laws and collect state taxes. The courts would judge both state and federal laws to see if they were constitutional.

Any powers not given to the federal government belonged to the state governments. Under the federal system of government set up by the Constitution, the state governments were still strong. But now they were joined together under the federal government of the United States.

Ratifying the Constitution

ratify
to approve officially

To become law, the Constitution had to be approved, or **ratified,** by at least nine of the 13 states. For many months, no one knew whether the Constitution would be ratified.

Each state held a meeting to decide whether to accept

Parade celebrating the ratification of the Constitution in New York City

the new government. Delaware was the first state to ratify the Constitution.

By 1790, all 13 states had ratified the Constitution. However, some people were uneasy. They felt that the Constitution needed additions to guarantee that the basic rights of every citizen in the United States would be protected.

The Bill of Rights

The state legislatures had passed laws that recognized and protected the basic rights of their citizens. Freedom of religion, freedom of speech, and the right to a fair trial were among these rights. But at first the Constitution said nothing about these rights. This worried many people.

Fortunately, the Constitution can be changed or added to. When something in the Constitution is changed or when new laws are added to it, this change, or addition, is called an **amendment.** The Constitution itself explains how this is to be done. By 1791, 10 amendments had been added to the Constitution. They became known as the Bill of Rights. These amendments state that the national government will protect the basic rights and freedoms of every American citizen.

amendment
a change or addition, especially a change or an addition to the United States Constitution

In writing the Constitution, the delegates set out to "form a more perfect union." By allowing for change, the delegates succeeded.

Section Review

Write your answers on a sheet of paper.
1. What powers did the national government lack under the Articles of Confederation?
2. What powers does the Constitution give to the federal government? What powers does the Constitution give to the state governments?
3. State governments also have three branches. What is the title of the person who heads the executive branch of a state?

Interpreting an Organizational Chart

On some charts, factual information is arranged in columns. That way, one kind of information can easily be compared with another. Look at the organizational chart on the next page. It shows how our government is organized into three branches. It also shows how the chief government officials are chosen and for how long a period they serve.

To read the chart, find the names of the three branches of government in the column at left. What powers are given to each branch? Look in the column labeled "Powers." As you can see, one of the powers granted the legislative branch is the power to write new laws. Who makes up the legislative branch? Look in the column labeled "Members." The legislative branch is made up of the Senate and the House of Representatives. Two senators from each state make up the Senate. Several representatives from each state make up the House of Representatives. How are these officials chosen? To find out, look in the column labeled "How chosen."

Practice Your Skills

1. What branch of government is the President of the United States a part of? What other officials make up this branch?
2. How is the President chosen? How long is the President's term of office?
3. Who makes up the judicial branch? Name their powers.
4. Who chooses the justices of the Supreme Court? How long is each justice's term of office?
5. How can the President limit the power of Congress?

Organization of the United States Government

Branch	Members	How chosen	Term	Powers
Legislative (Congress)	**Senate** Two Senators from each state	state election	6 years	Writes new laws Sets federal taxes Approves Presidential appointments Overrules Presidential vetoes Approves treaties
	House of Representatives Number of Representatives varies according to state population	state election	2 years	Declares war Impeaches a President
Executive	**President**	national election	4 years	Enforces federal laws Appoints and removes high federal officials Commands the armed forces Conducts foreign affairs Recommends laws to Congress Approves or vetoes new laws
	Executive Departments	Presidential appointment	no set term	Conducts the administration of the national government
	Independent Agencies	Presidential appointment	no set term	Oversees government regulations
Judicial	**Supreme Court** Nine justices	Presidential appointment	life	Interprets laws according to the Constitution May declare actions of the Executive and Legislative branches unconstitutional
	Lower Federal Courts	Presidential appointment	life	Decides cases that involve the Constitution and federal laws

2 The New Nation

The Constitution was a plan for a new government. No one knew how well it would work. Many pieces had to be put in place to form the new government. It was necessary to elect a President. Representatives and senators had to be chosen for Congress. Supreme Court justices had to be appointed.

The First President

On April 30, 1789, George Washington promised to "preserve, protect, and defend the Constitution of the United States." With that promise, Washington was placed in office, or **inaugurated,** as the first President of the United States.

Washington had commanded the troops that won America's freedom. He had served as president of the Constitu-

inaugurate

to install in office with a formal ceremony

Washington's arrival in New York City for his inauguration

138

tional Convention. In electing Washington to the Presidency, the people seemed to have chosen well.

President Washington worked long and hard to make the right decisions for the new nation. To help him make these decisions, he wanted advice from experienced people. The helpers, or advisers, formed a group that eventually became known as the **Cabinet.** Each member of the President's Cabinet was head, or **secretary,** of certain areas of the government.

Washington's Cabinet

Washington appointed a New York lawyer to head the Department of the Treasury. As secretary of the treasury, Alexander Hamilton made decisions about taxes, banks, and the debts of the nation.

Thomas Jefferson was placed in charge of the nation's affairs with other countries. Jefferson became the first secretary of state.

From the beginning, Hamilton and Jefferson argued about what was best for the United States. Hamilton wanted to see the country become a nation of great cities and large industries. Jefferson wanted the nation to remain a country of small communities and farms. Hamilton supported laws that would make the national government stronger. Jefferson urged that more power be left to the states.

Each man had supporters among the people. In time, those who followed Hamilton called themselves Federalists. Jefferson and his supporters were called Democratic-Republicans. The split between the two groups grew. Eventually the Federalists and the Democratic-Republicans became the first two political parties in the United States.

A Capital City

During the 1790's, work started on the construction of a new capital city for the United States. Virginia and Maryland each donated land along the banks of the Potomac River. This land was called the District of Columbia. The

Alexander Hamilton

Benjamin Banneker

new city was named Washington, in honor of the first President. While the city was being built, New York City, and then Philadelphia, served as the capital of the United States.

Pierre L'Enfant (**pyair** lahn-**fahn**), a French-born engineer, was hired to plan the new city. Helping with this work was Benjamin Banneker, a black surveyor, astronomer, and inventor. These two men and others selected sites for the United States Capitol, the White House, and other important buildings.

L'Enfant and Congress could not agree about the plans, however. L'Enfant was fired. Taking the only copies of his plans with him, he returned to France. But work on the capital continued. Luckily, the brilliant Banneker had memorized the plans.

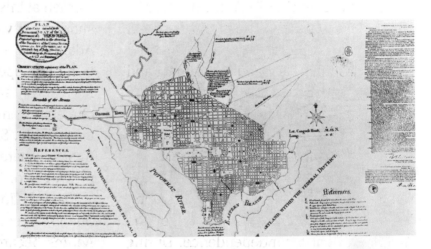

Plan for Washington, D.C.

Section Review

Write your answers on a sheet of paper.
1. What is the President's Cabinet? Name two famous Americans who served in Washington's Cabinet.
2. Who were the Federalists and the Democratic-Republicans? List the differences between them.
3. As you look at the United States today, has the Federalist or the Democratic-Republican idea of the future come true? Explain your answer.

FAMOUS AMERICANS

ABIGAIL SMITH ADAMS

One of the new nation's most capable, hard-working people was Abigail Smith Adams. She was a woman who cared deeply about her husband, her family, and the birth and growth of her country, the United States of America.

Like many other women during the Revolution, Abigail Adams took care of the family business while her husband, John, was away. John Adams traveled around the colonies, working in support of the American fight for independence. During that time, Abigail Adams stayed home in Massachusetts. There she managed a large farm and cared for their four young children.

Abigail stayed in touch with John during his long absences by writing letters. She helped keep her husband informed of events in Massachusetts.

Although she never attended a real school, Abigail Adams was a smart, well-informed woman. Unlike many other women at this time, she was not shy about sharing her views with others. While John Adams was helping to write the Declaration of Independence, Abigail Adams told him what she thought should be included. "Remember the ladies . . ." she once wrote. She meant that women had a right to share in the responsibilities and privileges of forming a new nation.

In 1797, John Adams became the second President of the United States. Abigail Adams became First Lady, the title given to the President's wife.

Twenty-seven years later, Abigail and John Adams's son, John Quincy Adams, was elected President of the United States. Abigail Adams is the only woman in the history of the United States to be the wife of one President and the mother of another.

Abigail Adams had raised a family, managed a farm, and still found time to be concerned for the future of her country.

3 The War of 1812

Overseas, wars in Europe continued to affect the United States. Great Britain and France were still enemies. Because the United States had ties to both countries, it tried to stay out of the fighting. By not supporting either side, though, the United States was often caught in the middle.

Causes of the War

After winning independence, the United States became an important shipping nation. American trading ships sailed to China, Africa, and Europe. Foreign trade created jobs for many American shipbuilders, sailors, business people, and shopkeepers.

neutral

not supporting one side or the other in a conflict

While Great Britain and France fought, the United States remained uninvolved, or **neutral.** American ships continued trading with both countries. Great Britain, however, did not want France to get supplies from the United States. So Great Britain attacked American ships sailing to France. The French also tried to prevent other nations from trading with Great Britain. The French navy attacked American ships that were on their way to British ports.

American ship arriving at a French port

Between 1804 and 1807, the United States lost more than 700 trading, or merchant, ships because of British attacks. About 200 American ships were lost to the French. In addition, thousands of sailors were kidnapped from American ships by the British. Great Britain claimed that these sailors had run away from, or deserted, the British navy. These sailors were forced to serve in the British navy. Many of the sailors were American citizens. This practice angered Americans. Some called for war with Great Britain.

American settlers in the Northwest Territory also wanted war with Great Britain. They feared the British and their American Indian allies to the north in Canada. The settlers hoped that a war with Great Britain would give them the chance to claim land in Canada for the United States.

American leaders tried to find peaceful solutions. But none of them worked. In 1812, the President, James Madison, asked Congress to declare war against Great Britain. Congress supported him and the United States went to war.

War in the Northwest

In the Northwest Territory, the war went badly for the United States. The British captured Detroit. They were ready to cross into the United States from Canada and the Northwest. The only hope for the United States was its small navy. Captain Oliver Perry was sent to the Great Lakes. His orders were to keep the British forces out of the United States.

Sailing in homemade boats, Perry's crews of newly trained Kentuckians defeated the British fleet on Lake Erie. The Northwest Territory would remain American.

Painting depicting the battle of Lake Erie by Nathaniel Currier

British troops burning Washington, D.C.

Dolley Madison

The British Strike Back

After their defeat in the Northwest, the British attacked from the south. Landing in Maryland, 4,500 British soldiers marched on Washington, D.C. Their goal was to burn the capital.

The British made a surprise attack on Washington. Alone in the President's home, First Lady Dolley Madison heard the cannons. Fire and smoke were pouring out of the Capitol Building. The Madisons' home would be next. Dolley Madison only had time to rescue her husband's papers and a portrait of George Washington before making her escape. When the British arrived, they removed all the furniture from the Madisons' home, stacked it on the lawn, and burned it.

The President's home was not badly damaged. After the war was over, it was repaired and repainted white to cover the burned places. It has remained the White House ever since.

The shelling of Fort McHenry

After burning Washington, the British army marched to Baltimore. Meanwhile, British ships shelled Fort McHenry in Baltimore Harbor. Francis Scott Key was a young American lawyer. He was on board one of the British ships arranging for the freedom of an American prisoner. All night Key watched the fort being attacked. Later he wrote a poem, "The Star Spangled Banner," describing the battle. Key's poem was later set to music and became the national song, or anthem, of our country.

By 1814, both Great Britain and the United States were ready for peace. The war had no clear winner. But the United States had shown that it could defend itself on land and sea. Foreign nations realized that the young United States was a country that was going to last.

Section Review

Write your answers on a sheet of paper.
1. What were the causes of the War of 1812?
2. What did the War of 1812 demonstrate about the United States?
3. Why would warring nations want to attack each other's capital cities?

The First Flag Who created the design for the first American flag? No one is certain, but there are several stories about the flag's beginnings.

According to one tale, several men, led by George Washington, designed the flag. They decided to have a sample of it made. So they asked an expert seamstress, or woman who sews, to make it. They chose Betsy Ross of Philadelphia. It is said that they planned to use a star with six points. Instead, Ross showed them how to cut a five-pointed star. This star is used in the flag today. Many people doubt this story.

However, it is true that Betsy Ross made many flags and banners.

Another story gives credit for the design to Francis Hopkinson. He was a signer of the Declaration of Independence. In fact, Hopkinson sent a bill to Congress asking to be paid for designs he made of "the flag of the U.S." But he was never paid. Congress said Hopkinson was not the only person who helped design the flag. But Congress did not say who these other designers were.

One thing is certain: On June 14, 1777, Congress met in Philadelphia to carry on

the business of government. Many matters were discussed that day. One was a resolution about a flag for the new country. The resolution read:

> RESOLVED, That the flag of the thirteen United States be thirteen stripes, alternate red and white; that the union be thirteen stars, white in a blue field . . .

The resolution passed. By law, the United States now had an official flag of its own. But the law did not say how big the field of blue should be or how wide the stripes should be. It did not say how to arrange the stars. So flagmakers came up with all sorts of flags. Some had wide stripes with stars in rows. Some had a large field of blue with stars in a circle. Some flags even had vertical stripes. However, all of these were American flags. This is because they all had the 13 stars and 13 stripes—one star and stripe for each original colony. The flag as we know it was designed by Congress in 1818. There are 13 stripes for the original colonies and one star for each state. In time, the American flag became known as the Stars and Stripes.

UNIT REVIEW

Word Work

Write the sentences below on a sheet of paper. Fill in the blanks with the correct words from the list.

Tory   legislature   smuggler   Cabinet   treaty

1. An American colonist who sided with the British during the American Revolution was called a _____.
2. The Congress, or _____, is a lawmaking body.
3. President Washington formed a _____, or a group of advisers to help him govern the new nation.
4. France and Great Britain signed a _____ to end the French and Indian War.
5. Someone who brought sugar into the country secretly to avoid paying a tax was a _____.

Knowing the Facts

Write your answers on a sheet of paper.
1. What were the causes of the French and Indian War?
2. How did the American colonies respond when Great Britain tried to tax them?
3. What were the weaknesses of the national government under the Articles of Confederation?

Using What You Know

Choose one of the following activities to do. Follow the instructions given here.
1. This unit described many patriots, soldiers, and political leaders who helped form our nation. Choose three of these people, and write several sentences explaining why the person was important in American history.
2. Dozens of land and sea battles were fought during the American Revolution. Write a brief description of a battle, describing who took part, why and how it was fought, what its importance was, and who won.

Skills Practice

Use the map and the map key shown here to answer the questions below. Write your answers on a sheet of paper.

1. What kind of map is this? What does it show?
2. Which battle was fought first? Which was fought last?
3. Who won the battle of Savannah? of Saratoga?
4. List each battle in order. Then place each one on a time line. Indicate who won the battle with an A or B, A standing for the American colonies and B standing for Great Britain.

Your Heritage

Each state has two senators in the Senate. Find out who the two senators from your state are. How often are they elected to the Senate? Each state also has a certain number of representatives in the House of Representatives. How many representatives to Congress come from your state? Which representative represents you?

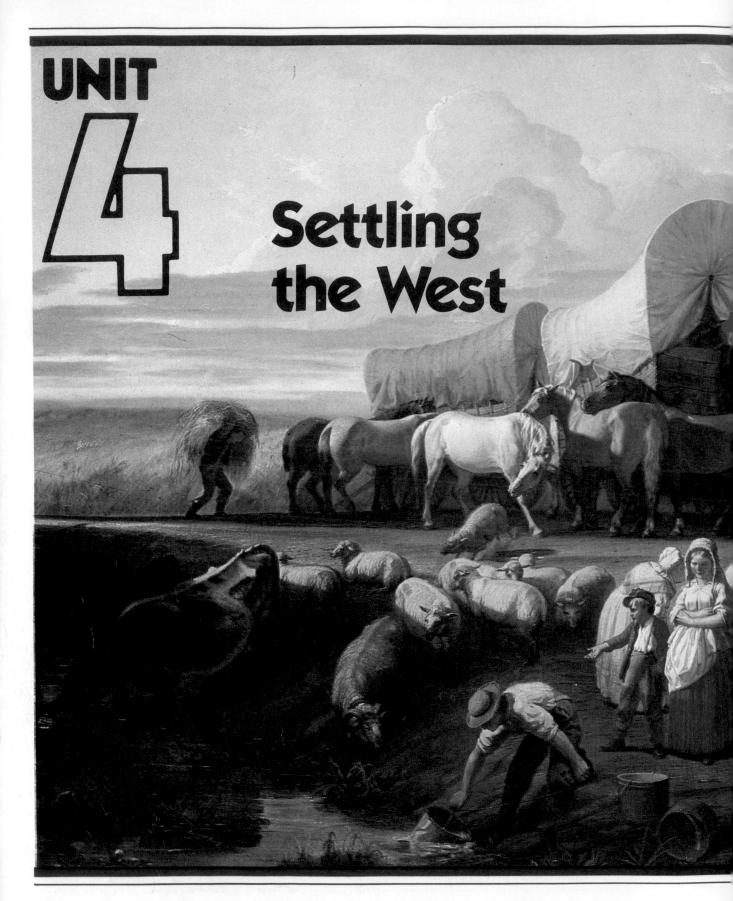

UNIT 4

Settling the West

Many of the early Americans were adventurous people. They crossed mountains and made homes in the wilderness. In 1790, the United States was a small country of 13 states on the Atlantic coast. By 1850, the nation had grown until it stretched all the way to the Pacific Ocean.

As the nation expanded, Americans kept looking for better ways to get things done. New inventions changed the way Americans worked, traveled, and lived. In this unit, you will read about the first Americans to settle in the West. You will learn how the United States grew in size. And you will find out how the nation changed as it grew.

CHAPTER 8

The Pioneers

The year is 1793. An American family heads into the Kentucky wilderness. They carry few belongings—some grain, tools, a horse, and a cow. Their trip through the wilderness will be hard and dangerous.

In the years after the American Revolution, thousands of Americans headed west. In this chapter, you will learn about these people.

At the end of this chapter, you should be able to:
○ Describe the building of the Wilderness Road and explain its importance.
● Identify and measure routes.
○ Describe how people lived on the frontier.
○ Discuss the importance of the Louisiana Purchase, the journey of Lewis and Clark, and the settling of Florida.

152

1 Settling the Frontier

In the middle of the 1700's, much of the land west of the Appalachian Mountains was a rich wilderness. It was a hunting ground for the Cherokee, Shawnee, and other American Indians. Bear, buffalo, deer, and wild turkey were plentiful. Many colonists were eager to claim some of this land for themselves.

Daniel Boone

One person who helped open the way west was Daniel Boone. He was a scout, a hunter, and a settler of the wilderness, or a **pioneer.**

Daniel Boone grew up in Pennsylvania. Later his family moved to North Carolina on the **frontier.** A frontier is the very edge of a settled area that borders on an unsettled area.

As a young man, Boone heard stories about the Kentucky wilderness beyond the Appalachians. In 1769, Boone and a few friends decided to explore Kentucky.

They spent months on the trail. They followed paths that eventually led to an opening between the mountains called Cumberland Gap. When Boone finally saw Kentucky for the first time, he thought it looked like paradise. Much of the land was covered with trees. Buffalo, bears, and deer ran through the fields.

Daniel Boone spent more than two years in Kentucky exploring the beautiful land and hunting. He returned to the East with tales of the beauty of the land he had seen.

In 1775, Richard Henderson, a businessman, hired Boone to build a road through the Cumberland Gap to Kentucky. With a group of strong men armed with axes and guns, Boone headed west again.

The road Boone and his men built was called the Wilderness Road. It cut through the mountains, leaving the way to the Southwest open for settlement.

pioneer
one of the first settlers in a new area who opens the way for others

frontier
an area at the very edge of a settlement that borders on an unsettled area

Daniel Boone

Daniel Boone leading pioneers into the Kentucky wilderness

The Way West

The Wilderness Road was steep and narrow. In places, it was barely wide enough for a single horse and rider. The trip to Kentucky was difficult. People loaded their goods onto farm animals. Most people walked alongside the animals as they made their way up and down the steep mountain road.

Walking was not the only way of getting over the mountains, however. Thousands of pioneers traveled overland to Pittsburgh. There they could buy or build boats, load their belongings, and sail down the Ohio River to the Ohio Territory. Boat travel was easier and quicker than overland travel. And settlers could bring more belongings with them on a boat than they could carry over the Wilderness Road.

But river travel also had its problems. In spring, the rivers flooded. Dangerous rapids and waterfalls could break a boat apart. In addition, pioneer boats were frequently attacked. Bandits and pirates often sank the boats and stole the pioneers' goods. American Indians, hoping to discourage new settlers on their lands, fought with many pioneers as they sailed along the river.

Flatboats and Keelboats

The pioneers used many different kinds of boats. The most popular was the flatboat. It was built out of wood, and it had a large deck, with a small cabin at one end. The pioneer family stayed in the small cabin. Livestock and most of the family's belongings were kept on the deck. The boat's flat bottom allowed it to travel in shallow parts of the river. Many of the boats were steered by long oars from the roof of the cabin.

Flatboats had one disadvantage. They could travel in only one direction—downstream. When pioneer families reached their destination, they usually took their boats apart and used the timber to build houses.

Keelboats were smaller than flatboats, but they could travel upstream as well as downstream. On each side of the keelboat was a narrow walkway called a running board. Keelboat workers walked along the running board carrying long poles, which they used to push the boat upstream.

By the 1790's, many boats sailed along the Ohio and Mississippi rivers carrying pioneers and their belongings. From Pittsburgh, the boats followed the Ohio River west to where it joined the Mississippi River. On the Mississippi, boats could sail south as far as New Orleans.

A flatboat on the Ohio River

A keelboat on the Ohio River

New States

In 1791, Vermont became the fourteenth state in the United States. Kentucky became the fifteenth state in 1792. A few years later, in 1796, Tennessee became a state. The frontier was quickly becoming settled.

Section Review

Write your answers on a sheet of paper.
1. Who was Daniel Boone? Why was he important?
2. Describe the Wilderness Road. Explain why wagons could not travel on it.
3. What were some dangers of river travel?
4. What was the main disadvantage of flatboats?
5. New types of boats were developed to suit different people's needs. What other methods of transportation have changed over the years as people's needs have changed? Explain your answer.

Identifying and Measuring Routes

Daniel Boone had to consider the natural hazards of the Kentucky wilderness when he worked on the Wilderness Road. The road would have to cross steep mountains, deep valleys, and wide rivers. Boone wanted to make the Wilderness Road as easy to travel on as possible. He carefully plotted the road, curving it over only the most gradual slopes of each mountain it crossed. Boone also angled the road sharply to take advantage of the natural openings through the mountains. Where he could, he avoided crossing rivers.

Because the Wilderness Road twists and turns as it rises and falls over the mountains, it cannot be measured with a straight ruler. Instead, to measure the route on the map, take something flexible, such as a piece of string. Then use the distance scale on the map to calculate the road's length.

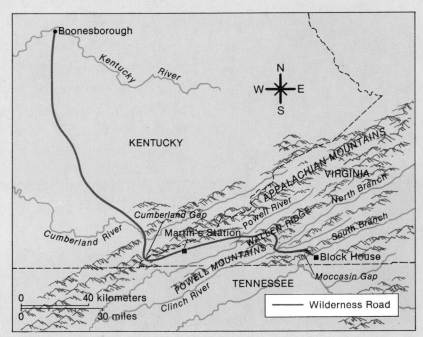

Practice Your Skills

1. In which two places did Boone curve the road so it would pass through natural openings in the mountains?
2. Where did the Wilderness Road make a sharp turn west?
3. Approximately how long is the Wilderness Road? If Boone had been able to build this road in a straight line, about how long would it have been?

2 Pioneer Life

Pioneer life was hard for everyone. Men, women, and children all braved danger. Families left their friends, neighbors, and often many of their belongings when they moved west. But they all brought two things with them: their courage and their dreams of a better life.

Help on the Frontier

When pioneers found a place to settle down, they faced a great challenge. The land was covered with forests and thick brush.

The family's first need was shelter. Often the pioneers built a rough, three-sided shelter that could be put together quickly. Sometimes a new family could count on help in building a home. Neighbors would spread the word that there were newcomers in the area. Then a house-raising was planned to build the new settlers a cabin.

Pioneers burned trees to clear land for the planting of crops.

Everyone was involved in a house-raising. The women prepared lots of food. The men chopped down trees and rolled them to the place where the cabin would stand. Next they cleared the trees of branches. Then the men notched the trees at the ends so that they would fit together.

Four of the logs were put together to form a base, or foundation. The rest were placed on top of each other to form the walls. Women and children put mud between the cracks in the logs to keep out wind, rain, and snow.

When the work was finished, everyone sat down to the big feast the women had cooked. Usually someone took out a fiddle to play. Even after working all day, the pioneers still had enough energy for square dancing.

Pioneers helped each other in many ways. In areas such as Kentucky and Tennessee, most farmers grew corn. After the corn was harvested in the fall, the pioneers had to remove the outer leaves, or husk, the corn. This was a hard job for one family to do alone. To make husking easier, families gathered in someone's barn and divided into two teams. The teams competed to see who could husk the most corn. Husks seemed to fly as people ripped at the ears of corn. When all the corn was husked, the people ate dinner and danced until late at night.

Pioneer women helped each other make quilts. At a quilting bee, women sewed patches of material together and passed the time telling stories.

Quilting bees made work more pleasant because pioneers had a chance to see and talk to their neighbors.

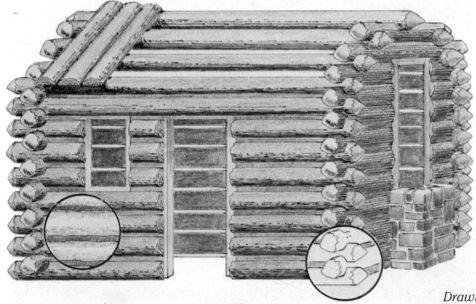

Drawing of a frontier cabin

Everyone helped when it came time to plow the fields and plant corn in the spring.

One of the many tasks of pioneer women was spinning wool for clothing.

Though pioneers helped each other as often as possible, most of the time pioneer life was hard and lonely. Families often lived far apart from one another. In the wilderness, there were no stores. Each family had to fill its own needs. Building a log cabin and clearing the land was only the first step. Pioneers had to make their own clothes and grow their own food. When they needed furniture, tools, soap, or candles, they had to make them too.

Getting enough food was not usually a problem for the pioneers. The woods were full of animals, and the streams were full of fish.

In order to survive, each member of a pioneer family, except the very small children, had to work hard. The work was divided up. The men and older boys would cut down trees, clear stumps, and chop wood. They did almost all the hunting, fishing, and trapping of animals.

The women and older girls did the housework, nursed the sick, spun wool for cloth, made clothing, and cared for the children. There were few schools on the frontier. With all their chores, few children had time for school. Some studied at home.

Even small children could be put to work grinding corn, pulling weeds, or gathering pine needles. These pine needles would be used as stuffing for mattresses made from cloth sacks.

Everyone helped plant crops in the spring and harvest them in the fall. The men tended the large fields, while the women and small children cared for the vegetable garden near the house. Usually the women would take care of chickens and milk the cows.

Pioneers had little time to rest. Even in winter, the family was kept busy. The fat from animals, called tallow, was used to make candles. Wood was cut and shaped to be used for fences.

The pioneer house was more than a home. It was also a workshop. Each family member became skilled at different tasks. Without these skills and hard work, the family could not survive in the wilderness.

The Pioneer Spirit

A new feeling developed among those who lived in the wilderness. It was the pioneer spirit. People had to depend on themselves to survive. But part of the pioneer spirit was pitching in and helping others too. It mattered little where people came from. The frontier struggle made people accept one another. Anyone who could survive on the frontier was respected.

Section Review

Write your answers on a sheet of paper.
1. How did pioneers help each other?
2. What was the first and most important task a frontier family faced?
3. List the chores of each member of a frontier family.
4. A frontier is an area that has just begun to be explored or settled. Can you think of any places today that are frontiers? Where are they?

3 Expanding the Nation

For the pioneers, the Mississippi River was a great water highway. The river was given its name by the Ojibway (oe-**jib**-way) Indians. It means "Great Water." The Mississippi flows south for more than 3,200 kilometers (2,000 miles) from its source in Minnesota to its mouth near New Orleans, on the Gulf of Mexico.

Flatboats and keelboats traveled the river. River ports, such as New Orleans, Baton Rouge, and St. Louis, grew as river travel increased. From these ports, pioneers moved westward to settle the new lands of the Louisiana Purchase.

The Louisiana Purchase

In 1803, France owned the important port of New Orleans. President Thomas Jefferson was worried about a European power so close to the United States. With the French in control of New Orleans, they could close the Mississippi River to American ships at any time. Goods from the western terri-

New Orleans in 1803 was a busy port and an important outlet for products from the frontier.

UNDER MY WINGS EVERY THING PROSPERS

tories would not be able to reach the East. Travel and settlement would be difficult, too, if the Mississippi River were closed to American water traffic.

Jefferson believed that the United States had to gain control of New Orleans in order to be truly independent. So in 1803, he sent James Monroe to France to buy the port city of New Orleans.

The leader of France then was Napoleon Bonaparte (nuh-**pole**-ee-un **bone**-uh-pahrt). Napoleon was involved in a war in Europe. He needed money to pay for the war. So Napoleon decided to sell the entire Louisiana Territory.

Napoleon wanted to make the sale quickly. When Monroe arrived in France, he found that the French wanted to sell all of Louisiana! Monroe quickly agreed to the offer.

For about $15 million, the United States received nearly 2,150,000 square kilometers (830,000 square miles) of land. Bounded by the Mississippi on the east and the Rocky Mountains on the west, the area was almost the size of the original 13 colonies. For a few pennies per hectare (acre) the Louisiana Purchase, as the deal was called, was one of the greatest bargains in United States history.

When Jefferson heard about the Louisiana Purchase, he was delighted. Now there was room for the United States to grow. But little was known about the land. What was out there beyond the Mississippi?

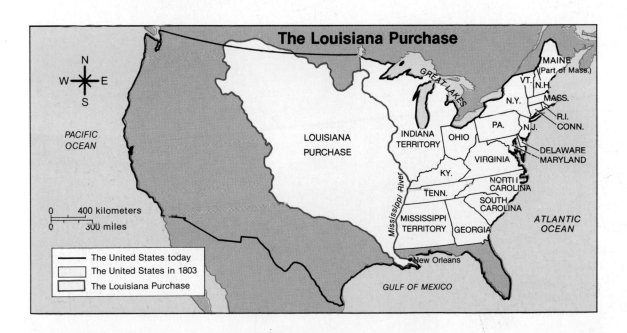

The Louisiana Purchase

Lewis and Clark

President Jefferson sent Meriwether Lewis and William Clark, two army captains, to lead the exploration of Louisiana. On May 14, 1804, Lewis and Clark began their journey, or **expedition.** Starting from St. Louis, Missouri, the men traveled up the Missouri River. They crossed the Great Plains, passing areas where herds of buffalo grazed.

The men spent the winter in what is now North Dakota. There they were joined by a French-Canadian fur trapper and his Indian wife, Sacajawea (sack-uh-juh-**wee**-uh). Sixteen-year-old Sacajawea was a Shoshone (shuh-**shone**-ee) Indian by birth. Lewis and Clark planned to travel in Sioux and Shoshone country, so they asked Sacajawea to serve as their interpreter.

expedition

a journey for a special purpose

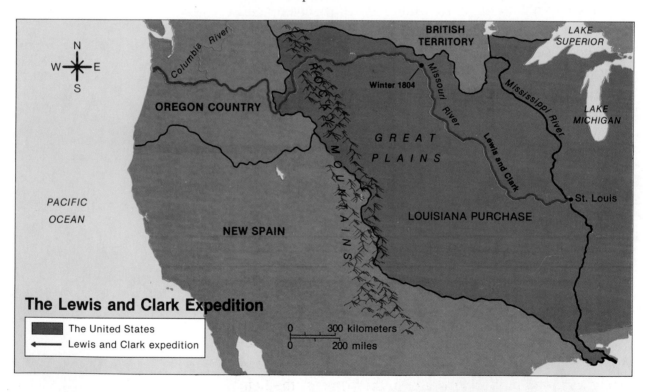

The Lewis and Clark Expedition

- The United States
- ← Lewis and Clark expedition

0   300 kilometers

0   200 miles

Sacajawea sits nearby while another Indian acts as an interpreter between Lewis and Clark and the Shoshone Indians.

In the spring, the group reached the Rocky Mountains. The men hoped to buy horses from the Shoshones to travel across the Rockies. They wanted to go beyond the boundaries of the Louisiana Purchase, to the Pacific Ocean. But the Indians living there did not want white people on their lands.

Lewis and Clark were concerned about their safety. Then the young Shoshone leader, Cameahwait (kuh-**may**-uh-wate), heard that the group had a Shoshone interpreter. When he saw Sacajawea, he embraced her. Sacajawea was his sister, whom he had not seen in years.

Because of Sacajawea, the Shoshones sold the explorers the horses they needed and helped guide them through the mountains. On November 7, 1805, Lewis and Clark sighted the Pacific Ocean.

The party returned to St. Louis on September 23, 1806. They had been gone so long that people thought they were dead. When they later reported to President Jefferson in Washington, they described a rich, beautiful land of broad plains, tall mountains, and mighty rivers.

Lewis and Clark had shown that Americans could travel overland to the West. As a result, more pioneers began the move westward to the Pacific coast.

Florida

Americans were also interested in settling Florida. At the time of the Revolution, Florida had been a colony of Spain for more than 250 years.

In the 1800's, Florida was the home of many runaway slaves from Georgia plantations. Since Florida was under Spanish control, the slaves thought they were safe from being recaptured. Florida was also the home of the Seminole Indians who had been driven out of Georgia by settlers. In anger, these Indians made raids into Georgia, killing people and burning farms. Farmers and plantation owners in Tennessee and Georgia wanted to stop slaves from escaping to Florida, and they wanted to put an end to raids by Seminole Indians.

In 1818, General Andrew Jackson took an army into Florida to fight the Seminoles. Jackson captured Spanish forts.

Hiding out in one of these forts were two Seminole chiefs. When Jackson found them, he ordered them to be hanged. He also killed two British traders who had sold guns to the Seminoles. Great Britain was furious. The Seminoles were furious. Even some members of Congress were furious. Jackson had made war without the permission of Congress or the President.

Jackson's actions were very popular with most Americans, however. He had brought all of eastern Florida under the control of the United States. Spain realized it could not defend its territory. So in 1819, Spain sold all of Florida and its Gulf Coast lands to the United States for $5 million.

The Trail of Tears

Settlers soon rushed to Florida. They settled on land where the Seminole, Apalachee, and Calusa Indians had lived for generations. In Tennessee, Georgia, and North Carolina, people moved onto Indian land too. Often there was trouble between the settlers and the Indians, as the Indians fought to defend their homes.

The Cherokee Indians of Georgia were a settled people. Cherokee land owners had built large plantations. A Cherokee named Sequoya (sih-**kwoi**-uh) had invented an alphabet for the Cherokee language. The Cherokees had their own schools and a newspaper. They had their own government and a constitution.

In 1830, Congress passed a law taking away the Cherokee

Sequoya holding a copy of the Cherokee alphabet he invented

land and the land of all other American Indians living east of the Mississippi River. The law required the eastern Indians to move west of the Mississippi and live on the lands of the western Indians.

The Cherokee resisted the move. Finally, American soldiers forced them off their land. In the cold winter of 1838–1839, the Indians had to march more than 1,600 kilometers (1,000 miles) to their new home in the barren Oklahoma Territory. More than one quarter of the Cherokee froze or starved to death on the way. For the Cherokee, this tragic trip became known as the Trail of Tears.

Cherokee Indians being forced to move west in what became known as the Trail of Tears

Section Review

Write your answers on a sheet of paper.
1. Why did President Jefferson want to buy New Orleans?
2. What did the United States gain as a result of the Louisiana Purchase?
3. How did Sacajawea help Lewis and Clark?
4. Why was the Cherokee march to Oklahoma called the Trail of Tears?
5. Lewis and Clark had little idea of what they would find in the unexplored Louisiana Territory. Are there any people today who are exploring new places or new areas of study? Explain your answer.

To the Pacific

In the early 1800's, the land west of the Mississippi River was very thinly populated. Some American Indian tribes lived there. Spain, and later Mexico, claimed most of the Southwest.

American Indian and Spanish land claims did not stop American pioneers. They kept moving west. There seemed to be no claims, challenges, or dangers that could stop the pioneer families of the United States.

At the end of this chapter, you should be able to:

○ Describe how the Southwest became part of the United States.

○ Describe how Oregon and Utah were settled.

○ Explain how the gold rush helped California become a state.

1 Mexico

The mountains, plains, and deserts of the American Southwest were controlled by Spain for almost 300 years. Few Spaniards ever lived in this vast land, however. American Indians had been living there for 10,000 years, but their settlements were far apart.

In 1820, Americans started going to the Southwest. Some of the Americans went to trade. Others went to settle.

The Santa Fe Trail

Santa Fe, an important town in the Spanish territory, was far from Mexico City, New Spain's capital. For years, Santa Fe depended on supplies brought in from Mexico City, more than 2,300 kilometers (1,445 miles) away. Santa Fe was much closer to the edge of the American frontier in Missouri. But the Spanish governor would not allow Americans

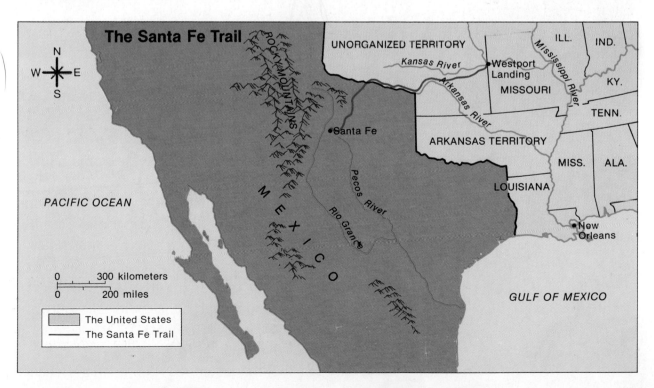

The Santa Fe Trail

N W E S

ROCKY MOUNTAINS

UNORGANIZED TERRITORY

Kansas River

Westport Landing

MISSOURI

ILL.

IND.

Mississippi River

KY.

Arkansas River

TENN.

Santa Fe

ARKANSAS TERRITORY

MISS.

ALA.

Pecos River

LOUISIANA

MEXICO

Rio Grande

PACIFIC OCEAN

New Orleans

GULF OF MEXICO

0   300 kilometers
0   200 miles

◻ The United States
— The Santa Fe Trail

A church in Santa Fe, built in 1795, that still stands today

to trade in Santa Fe. He wanted the people of New Spain to trade only with the Spanish. Any Americans found there were arrested.

In 1821, Mexico won its independence from Spain, and Santa Fe became a Mexican city. The Mexicans allowed Americans to trade in Santa Fe.

William Becknell was the first American trader in Santa Fe. Becknell loaded a wagon train full of goods. He hired scouts and men to drive the wagons across the desert to Santa Fe. The wagons left from Westport Landing, a town on the Missouri River. Westport Landing grew into two cities on both sides of the Missouri River: Kansas City, Missouri, and Kansas City, Kansas. The route the wagons took to Santa Fe became known as the Santa Fe Trail.

In return for the manufactured goods that Becknell

brought, people in Santa Fe gave him furs, and silver from the nearby mines.

Soon other wagon trains went to Santa Fe. Many of the Americans who went were frontier people who had never seen a real city. They were amazed at the beauty of Santa Fe. There they found elegant Spanish houses and many friendly people who were educated and dignified.

Texas

In the early 1800's, Texas was a wide-open area with scattered settlements. In 1820, the Spanish government made an agreement with Moses Austin, a banker from Missouri. In return for a grant of land, Austin would bring 300 families to settle in Texas.

But Austin died before he could build his settlement. When Mexico won its independence from Spain, the new government made the same offer to Austin's son, Stephen. In exchange for land, Austin promised that the first settlers from America would become Mexican citizens and obey Mexican laws. Stephen Austin arranged for people to go to east Texas. Other Americans settled in different areas of Texas, as well. By the 1830's, there were more than 20,000 Americans in Texas. The newcomers far outnumbered the Mexicans who lived there. The ever-growing American population brought a new culture, new religions, and a new language with them.

Many of the newcomers did not want to obey Mexican laws. Mexican laws were strict, detailed, and hard to change. In addition, many Americans were slave owners. Mexico did not allow slavery. Before long, there was trouble between the Texans and the Mexican government.

In 1835, the trouble turned into war. Texans in the city of San Antonio forced Mexican soldiers out of the town. General Santa Anna, the leader of Mexico, decided to teach the Texans a lesson. With an army of more than 4,000 men, he marched north from Mexico City.

Texan leaders decided that they would have to fight the Mexicans for their freedom. They wrote a constitution and formed a government. Quickly, they organized an army and chose Sam Houston (**hyoo**-stun) to lead it. On March 2, 1836, Texas declared its independence from Mexico.

Stephen Austin

"Remember the Alamo!"

Santa Anna and his army headed for San Antonio. There, the Alamo, a mission-fort, was defended by a small group of Texans.

The Mexican army camped outside the walls, ready to attack. Inside the Alamo were about 180 Texan fighting men, and some women and children.

The men inside were mostly frontiersmen. They were skilled hunters, used to handling rifles. Their leader was Colonel William Travis. Jim Bowie was a famous frontiersman at the Alamo. He had invented the Bowie knife, which became a popular tool on the frontier. Davy Crockett was the most famous of the Alamo heroes. Crockett was a fron-

A small force of Texans tried to defend the Alamo even after Mexican troops broke through the walls of the fort.

tiersman from Tennessee who loved to boast and tell tall tales. He liked to tell people that he once killed a bear by grinning at it and making it laugh. Before going to Texas, Davy Crockett had served in the United States Congress.

Santa Anna's army attacked the Alamo for 10 days. The Texans fought fiercely and kept the Mexican troops away from the Alamo. But the Texans were running out of ammunition. On March 6, 1836, the Mexican troops broke through the walls of the Alamo. When the shooting ended, almost everyone inside the fort had been killed.

Santa Anna now thought that it would be easy to finish off Houston's small army. At the town of Goliad, Santa Anna's army surrounded a small group of Texans and forced them to surrender. Santa Anna had them killed. Elsewhere, Houston kept retreating, using the time to get his small army organized.

On April 21, at the San Jacinto (san huh-**sin**-toe) River, Houston saw his chance. He caught Santa Anna in a trap. His 800 Texans attacked, yelling "Remember the Alamo!" and "Remember Goliad!" They killed 600 Mexican soldiers and wounded others. Santa Anna, disguised as an ordinary soldier, tried to escape. But he was recognized by one of the Texans.

Houston took the Mexican leader prisoner. Santa Anna promised that his country would recognize Texas' independence. He signed a treaty, making good his promise.

The Lone Star Republic

Texas was now an independent country. Sam Houston was elected the first president of the new Republic of Texas. A **republic** is a country that is governed by elected representatives. Texans called their land the Lone Star Republic because their flag had only a single star.

Since most Texans were originally from the United States, many wanted Texas to become part of the United States. But Mexico was still angry about losing Texas. It did not want the Texas republic to become part of the powerful United States. If Texas became a state, it could mean war between Mexico and the United States. American leaders decided they did not want to risk war and refused to accept Texas as a state.

republic
a country that is governed by elected representatives

The Lone Star flag

173

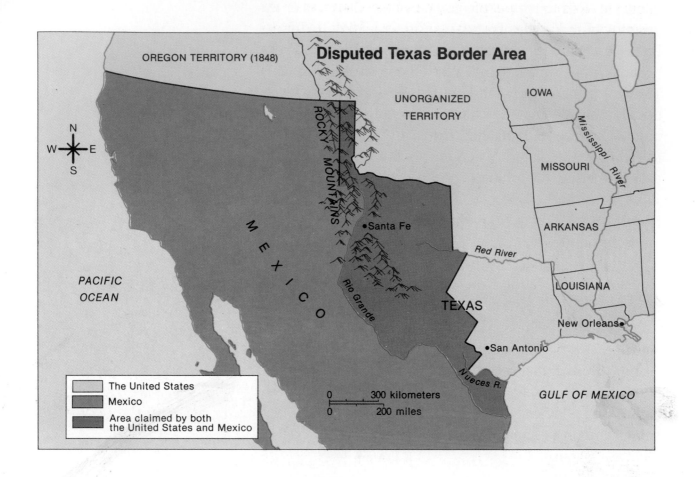

OREGON TERRITORY (1848)

Disputed Texas Border Area

UNORGANIZED
TERRITORY

IOWA

Mississippi River

ROCKY MOUNTAINS

MISSOURI

•Santa Fe

ARKANSAS

Red River

MEXICO

Rio Grande

LOUISIANA

TEXAS

PACIFIC
OCEAN

New Orleans•

•San Antonio

Nueces R.

The United States
Mexico
Area claimed by both
the United States and Mexico

0   300 kilometers
0   200 miles

GULF OF MEXICO

James K. Polk

War with Mexico

James K. Polk was elected President of the United States in 1844. Polk was not afraid of Mexico's threats of war. In 1845, Texas joined the United States as the Lone Star State.

There was a disagreement about the border of the new state. The United States claimed that the Rio Grande (**ree**-oe **grand**-ay), a river, was the southern border of Texas. Mexico said the border was farther north at the Nueces (noo-**ay**-sace) River. There was also a disagreement over the territory in the Southwest and in California. Mexico owned those lands. The United States had tried to buy the lands a number of times. Mexico had refused to sell them. President Polk thought that the United States should try to buy them once more. Again, Mexico seemed unwilling to discuss the sale.

In 1846, President Polk sent an army to the Rio Grande.

This angered Mexico. Shots were fired. When President Polk received the news of this, he asked Congress to declare war on Mexico. The war lasted until 1848. The Mexicans fought bravely, but in the end, the United States won.

In 1848, the United States and Mexico signed the Treaty of Guadalupe Hidalgo (**gwah**-duh-**loop**-ay hih-**dal**-goe), ending the war. Mexico gave up all claims to Texas and sold the rest of the Southwest to the United States for $15 million.

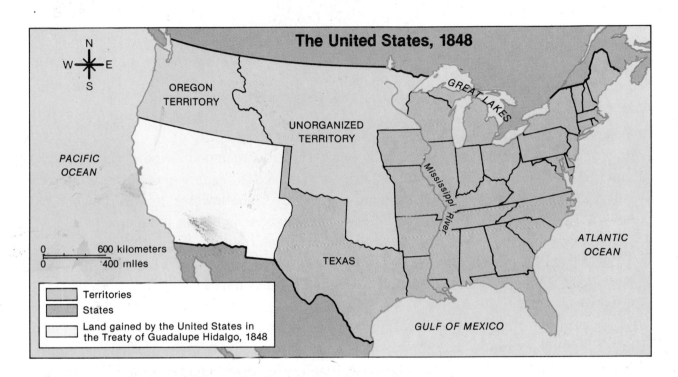

The United States, 1848

Legend:
- Territories
- States
- Land gained by the United States in the Treaty of Guadalupe Hidalgo, 1848

Section Review

Write your answers on a sheet of paper.

1. Why did the Spanish governor forbid Americans to trade in Santa Fe?
2. What was the result of the war between Mexico and the United States?
3. In the early 1800's, Spain helped its economy by regulating who could trade with the people of New Spain. What are some ways in which the United States regulates trade today to help the American economy?

FAMOUS AMERICANS

SAMUEL HOUSTON

Samuel Houston was a man of many talents and experiences. He was a frontiersman, trader, teacher, friend of the American Indians, congressman, senator, governor of two states, general, and president of a country!

Sam Houston was born in Virginia in 1793. As a teenager, he moved to the Tennessee frontier with his family.

Houston left home at 15. He lived with the Cherokee Indians for three years. Houston fought for Cherokee rights all his life. At one time, he represented the Cherokees in their dealings with the United States Government.

When he returned to Tennessee, Houston became a teacher in a country school. He joined the army during the War of 1812 and fought bravely. After the war ended, Houston became a lawyer and entered Tennessee politics. He served in Congress and later became governor of Tennessee in 1827.

Houston resigned as governor in 1829 and moved to Texas, where he ran a trading post. By 1835, however, he was drawn into the Texans' fight for independence. He formed and led the Texas army.

In 1836, Houston commanded the Texans against the Mexicans at the battle of San Jacinto. There the Texans defeated the Mexican army and gained their independence. Houston became the first president of the Republic of Texas. In 1845, when Texas became a state, he was one of its first senators.

As a senator, he spoke up for American Indian rights and spoke out against slavery.

Sam Houston devoted the last part of his life to Texas. After serving as senator, he was elected governor of the state. Today he is remembered as one of the heroes of Texas. The city of Houston, Texas, is named after this founder of the Lone Star State.

2 Oregon and Utah

When Lewis and Clark traveled to the Pacific coast, they went far beyond the boundary of the Louisiana Purchase. At that time, the Pacific Northwest was known to Americans as the Oregon Territory. Today the states of Washington, Oregon, and Idaho occupy this area. Farther to the south lies Utah. In the early 1800's, few white people had explored this land.

After Lewis and Clark, the first whites to cross west of the Rocky Mountains were people called mountain men. They often lived alone for years at a time trapping furs and trading for supplies they needed.

Jedediah Smith

Early Settlers

The most famous mountain man of all was a man named Jedediah Smith. In 1830, he discovered an opening through the Rocky Mountains called South Pass. It was a broad valley in southern Wyoming that led through the mountains. Until Smith's discovery, few people thought that pioneers would be able to get across the steep peaks of the Rockies. The discovery of South Pass opened up the Oregon Territory for settlement.

One of the first white settlers in the Oregon Territory was a **missionary** named Marcus Whitman. A missionary is a person who tries to convert people to his or her religion. Whitman went to Oregon to bring Christianity to the Cayuse (**kie**-yoos) Indians. Once there, he saw the beauty of the land: its rich soil, mild climate, broad rivers, and majestic mountains.

missionary
a person who tries to convert people to his or her religion

Whitman returned to the East to tell people about the beautiful land. He married and returned with his wife, Narcissa, to the Oregon Territory. She was the first white woman to cross the Rocky Mountains. Together, the Whitmans set up a mission near what is today Walla Walla, Washington.

The Oregon Trail

In the late 1830's many businesses were not doing well in the United States. Banks had loaned businesses a lot of money. When people could not repay their loans, they were forced to go out of business. Many people lost their jobs. Some of these people decided to go to Oregon to make a new start.

Beginning in 1842, wagon trains of settlers traveled from Independence, Missouri, to Oregon. The route they followed was called the Oregon Trail. The trail was more than 3,200 kilometers (2,000 miles) long. It wound through prairies, deserts, and mountains. So many wagons traveled the Oregon Trail that today you can still see places where wagon wheels cut deep ruts in the trail.

Wagon Trains

The trip west took six months. The pioneers needed courage, determination, and the ability to cooperate to make the dangerous journey.

Families traveling to Oregon gathered at Independence, Missouri, in the spring. There they waited for others who wanted to go west. Independence was a bustling town where merchants sold supplies to the pioneers.

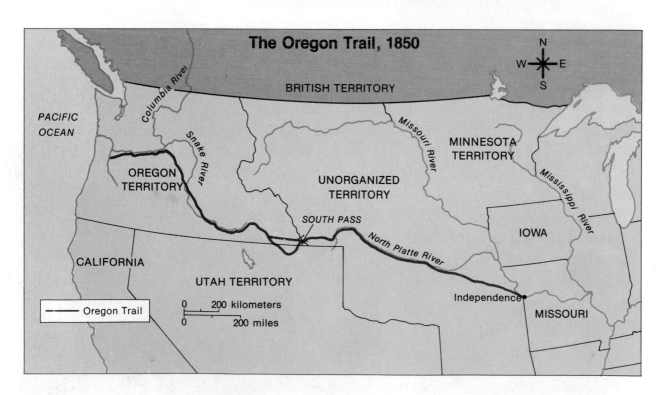

The Oregon Trail, 1850

On the prairie outside town, pioneers waited in their wagons and tents. When enough families gathered, they would form a wagon train. The pioneers hired a scout who knew the way. They also elected one person to be the leader of the wagon train. On the trail, the scout and the leader made all the important decisions for the wagon train.

Early on spring mornings the cry "Wagons ho!" could be heard across the prairie. Then the long line of covered wagons would move out across the land.

Wagon trains had one rule that everyone learned to obey. That rule was "Keep the wagons moving!" Every day wagons started moving out just after dawn. They stopped only at noon and in the evening. They traveled seven days a week. Traveling this way, a wagon train could cover 24 to 32 kilometers (15 to 20 miles) a day. At night, the pioneers brought their wagons into a circle for protection. American Indians, who did not want settlers crossing their lands, often attacked the wagon trains. Weather was also a threat to the pioneers. Any weather delays on the trail could mean that the pioneers might be trapped in the mountain snowstorms.

Still, the settlers came. Each year more and more pioneers braved the dangers of the Oregon Trail to settle in the Far West.

Part of the trail west required pioneers to cross wide rivers. Here pioneers cross the North Platte River on a raft.

Wagon trains were brought into a circle at night for protection.

Utah

Utah was settled in 1847 by Mormons. The Mormons were a religious group that had started in New York. They later moved to Ohio and then to Illinois. In each place they lived, the Mormons were treated with hostility by people who disliked some of the Mormon beliefs.

The Mormon leader, Brigham Young, decided the Mormons would be better off out west, far away from other Americans. In 1847, Young and a group of Mormons traveled on the Oregon Trail. After going through South Pass, they left the trail and headed southwest. Near the valley of the Great Salt Lake, Brigham Young stopped, looked around, and is quoted as saying, "This is the place."

In the years that followed, the Mormons built their settlement into Salt Lake City. In the first year, more than 12,000 people went to the Mormon settlement. The first building they began was a huge stone temple to worship in. They cut huge blocks of stone and carried them on sleds pulled by oxen to the place where they were building their temple. It took 40 years to complete.

The land outside the city was desert. But the Mormons built irrigation ditches to bring fresh water to the land. They raised their own crops and made whatever else they needed. They had found a place where they could support themselves and practice their religion freely.

Mormons moving west

Section Review

Write your answers on a sheet of paper.
1. Who was Marcus Whitman?
2. What were some of the dangers faced by pioneers on the Oregon Trail?
3. Who was Brigham Young?
4. Why was it important for the Mormons to be able to produce all they needed to live in Utah?
5. The leader was an important person in a wagon train. How are leaders important in groups you belong to?

3 California

The famous mountain man Jedediah Smith was one of the first Americans to travel over the mountains to California. Other Americans traveled by ship to this land of Spanish missions and ranches. By 1846, a few thousand Americans were living in California.

One American, John Sutter, received a large grant of land in the foothills of the Sierra Nevada Mountains from the Mexican government. There he built a fort that served as a trading post. In January 1848, one of Sutter's workmen, James Marshall, saw something shiny lying on the bottom of a shallow stream.

The Gold Rush

What James Marshall saw in the stream was gold. He and John Sutter tried to keep their discovery a secret, but soon the word was out.

Suddenly people in California got "gold fever." In 1848, San Francisco was a town of 800 people. When people heard about the discovery of gold, half the population of San Francisco left what they were doing to look for gold.

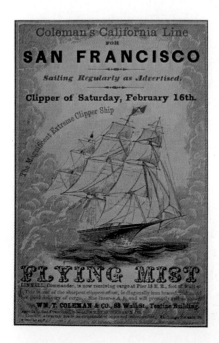 

Ads for ship transport to California

Thousands of Chinese came to California to work in the gold mines.

In the rush for gold, sailors deserted their ships when they arrived in San Francisco. Soon there were empty ships lying at anchor in San Francisco Bay. There were stories about ships where the only thing left on board was the captain's cat!

Gold fever soon spread to the East. People quit their jobs, left their homes, and headed for California. The journey to California took five months by ship. Ships had to go all the way around the tip of South America and then up the Pacific coast to California.

Others tried a short cut. They got off ships in the Central American land of Panama and walked through the jungle to the Pacific Ocean. Many got sick and died.

Most people came by wagon train. Thousands of wagons moved west across American Indian lands in the spring of 1849. The gold rush brought more than 80,000 people to California in 1849 alone. These people were called forty-niners, and they all dreamed of making their fortune. They came from all over. Some came from South America and Mexico. More than 25,000 Chinese came in the years just after the discovery of gold. Most of them worked for other miners in the gold fields. The forty-niners turned California into a bustling place.

Get Rich or Go Bust

The forty-niners came to California expecting to find gold everywhere. A few people did find fortunes. But most miners went bust, or broke, before long.

Mining towns with such names as Hangtown and Rattlesnake Diggings came into being overnight. Miners had a rough life with few comforts. They lived in huts and tents. There was not much law and order in the mining towns either. To protect themselves from thieves, most miners slept with their guns beside them.

Some people got rich selling goods to the miners. One person who made his fortune was a German businessman named Levi Strauss. Strauss had bought strong denim canvas that he planned to use in making tents. Other people were selling tents, though, so Strauss turned his denim canvas into sturdy overalls. He called them Levis. Today, more than a century later, these blue denim pants are worn all over the world.

Statehood

The gold rush helped change California from a frontier area into a state. In 1849, Californians wrote a constitution and asked to be admitted to the United States. In 1850, California became the thirty-first state. In the years ahead, many forty-niners gave up mining. They found California a rich land for ranching and farming.

Section Review

Write your answers on a sheet of paper.
1. Who was John Sutter?
2. Who were the forty-niners?
3. What was life like in the early mining towns?
4. Who was Levi Strauss?
5. Like California in 1849, certain areas of the United States are growing rapidly in population. Where are these areas? What are the reasons for this growth?

10 New Ways in the New Nation

As the United States began to grow, it began to change. At election time, more people had the right to vote. More people were traveling around the country, often using new forms of transportation. And as they traveled, they discovered that different sections of the country were developing in different ways. In this chapter, you will learn about these changes.

At the end of this chapter, you should be able to:

○ Explain the Age of the Common Man.

○ Explain the importance of the Seneca Falls Convention.

○ Describe changes in transportation in the early 1800's.

○ Name the three sections of the United States and describe how various ways of life developed in each.

● Use a pie graph to describe the occupations of Americans in 1850.

1 Democracy Grows

The United States was a bustling, growing nation in the first half of the 1800's. People seemed to be forever on the move. Many moved to the West. Newcomers came from Europe and Asia to settle the land. As the country grew, so did the spirit of **democracy.** In a democracy, all adult citizens have the right to vote in elections.

In colonial times, and during the first years of the nation, only white men who owned property were allowed to vote. This meant that all women, blacks, American Indians, and poor white men had no say in government.

The opening of the frontier for settlement brought a new spirit to the United States. On the frontier, people's abilities mattered more than how much money they had, how much property they owned, or how important they were. Each new state that came into the union after 1800 gave the vote to all white men, rich and poor alike. Gradually, the older states in the East changed their laws and let all white men vote. By the 1850's, all eastern states had done this. However, women, blacks, and American Indians still could not vote.

democracy
a type of government where all adult citizens have the right to vote in elections

"Old Hickory"

In 1828, American voters chose Andrew Jackson of Tennessee to be the seventh President of the United States. Jackson was the first President to come from the West. Until then, all United States Presidents had come from either Virginia or Massachusetts.

Jackson was born in a log cabin and grew up on the North Carolina frontier. He became a famous soldier. The soldiers called him Old Hickory. They said he was tough and stubborn, just like the tough, hard hickory tree of the Appalachian Mountains. The nickname stuck with Jackson

Andrew Jackson

"The County Election" by George Caleb Bingham shows the role of the common people in government.

even after he became a wealthy lawyer and later, when he became President.

After his election, Jackson invited everyone who voted for him to come to Washington, D.C., for his inauguration. At the inauguration, rough frontiersmen with coonskin caps stood on the furniture of the White House to get a better view of their hero. People in Washington were shocked by the frontiersmen's manners as well as by their clothes. Jackson's election was important to these people from the frontier. Like them, he had lived on the western frontier. Like them, he judged people by their abilities, not by their wealth. When he became President, Jackson proved that a frontiersman could fill the most important office in the land. And now frontiersmen and other common, or ordinary, American men could vote. For these reasons, the period of Jackson's presidency was called the Age of the Common Man.

Rights for Women

American women had almost no rights at the time of Jackson's presidency. No woman could vote or serve on a jury. In most states, married women could not sell the property they owned, sue in a court of law, or keep the wages they earned. And it was not thought proper for a married woman to have a job.

Elizabeth Cady Stanton and Lucretia Mott were two women who dedicated their lives to working for women's rights. For years, they spoke out and wrote articles to attract supporters. Finally they organized a convention to discuss women's rights. On July 19, 1848, more than 300 people met in Seneca Falls, New York. Most of the people who came were women, but 40 men also attended.

The Seneca Falls Convention voted to adopt a list of women's rights drawn up by Elizabeth Cady Stanton. These rights included the right to vote, to own property, and to go to school—all rights that men enjoyed. Stanton had used the Declaration of Independence as her model.

News of the Seneca Falls Convention soon spread. Some people were angry. They thought that women should forget about rights and simply obey their fathers or husbands. They did not want women to vote either. Others thought the idea of a woman voting, holding a job, or going to school was very odd. In the past, only men had done these things.

Women slowly gained more rights. In some states, married women won the right to own property. More women began working as teachers. A teacher from Massachusetts named Mary Lyon started Mount Holyoke College in 1837. It was the first college for women. Lyon believed that women should have the same opportunities to learn that men had.

(left) Lucretia Mott

(right) Elizabeth Cady Stanton

Mary Lyon

Mary Lyon's idea about education for women was still not widely accepted. But during these years, other colleges for women were started. Some men's colleges began accepting women students. A few women began to do jobs that only men had done before. In 1849, Elizabeth Blackwell became the first woman to graduate from medical school.

Not all the goals of the women's rights movement were achieved, but some progress was made. The struggle for full equality continued over the years that followed.

Elizabeth Blackwell

Section Review

Write your answers on a sheet of paper.
1. Why was the period of Jackson's presidency called the Age of the Common Man?
2. What rights were denied to women in the early 1800's?
3. Why were Elizabeth Cady Stanton and Lucretia Mott important?
4. What jobs are women doing today that used to be done only by men?

2 New Transportation

In 1800, people traveled much as they had for centuries. Boats were powered by sails or oars. The best way to get around on land was by horse.

The United States was a big country, and methods of travel were slow in the early 1800's. It took days for eastern farmers to get to city markets. It took weeks to cross the Appalachians. A trip to the Rockies could take six months or more. The country needed better transportation and communication to reach all its citizens and markets. Americans started using both old and new ideas to move people, goods, and news faster.

New Way of Powering Boats

An American artist and inventor named Robert Fulton offered one solution to the transportation problem of the United States. During a visit to Great Britain, Fulton had learned about a new invention called the steam engine. Fulton thought a steam engine would be a good way to power a boat upstream against the river current. His first attempt at building a steamboat, though, was a failure. The engine was so heavy it fell through the boat and sank.

In 1807, Fulton built another steamboat. He called it the *Clermont.* Most people called it *Fulton's Folly* because they did not expect it to work.

The Clermont

On August 17, 1807, a surprised crowd cheered as the *Clermont* steamed away from a New York City pier. The steamboat was heading toward Albany, 240 kilometers (150 miles) away. About 30 hours later, the *Clermont* arrived in Albany. Fulton's steamboat was a success! Steamboats were soon traveling on many rivers and lakes in the United States.

New Transportation Routes

The National Road was an important improvement in transportation. It made travel between the East and the West easier. The road went from Cumberland, Maryland, to Wheeling, in what later became West Virginia. Later the National Road was lengthened to reach St. Louis, Missouri. Before the road was built, it took several weeks to get from Baltimore, Maryland, to Wheeling. By using the National Road, travelers could make the same trip in a few days. The road was called the National Road because federal taxes supplied the money to build it.

Most of the roads built at this time were unpaved. When it rained, they became rivers of mud. In summer, the horses kicked up clouds of dust. Because the roads were

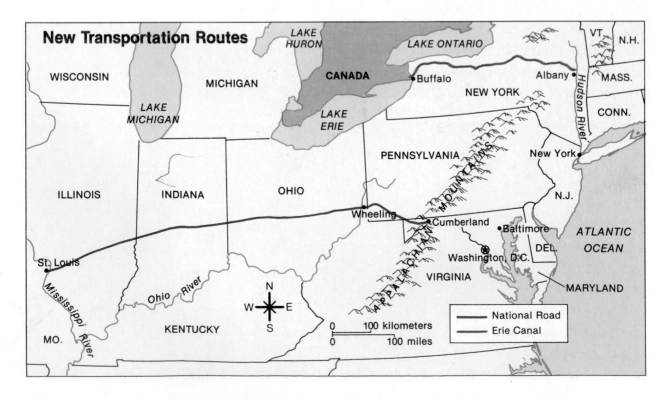

poor, most people who traveled long distances went by steamboat, canalboat, and railroad.

The construction of canals also improved transportation. In 1817, people in New York began construction of a canal connecting Albany, on the Hudson River, to Buffalo, on Lake Erie. The 580-kilometer (360-mile) Erie Canal was completed in 1825. The canalboats were pulled up by mules on a path alongside the canal, called a towpath. Even though the boats went only about 3 or 4 kilometers (2 or 2½ miles) per hour, canal transportation was still faster and cheaper than hauling goods over the mountains.

The Erie Canal was a great success. The canal opened up trade between New York and the West. It was now possible to go from the Atlantic coast to the Great Lakes area entirely by water. Buffalo became a center of western trade. New York City became the transportation center of the country. The success of the Erie Canal encouraged the building of other canals in the United States.

The Erie Canal

Railroads

Railroads were not yet the most popular way to transport people and goods. The first train engines were frightening. Noisy and smoky, they terrified horses and scared cows so much that they would not give milk.

These iron horses, as they were called, traveled at the unheard-of speed of 25 to 32 kilometers (15 to 20 miles) per hour! They moved people and goods much faster than

Samuel Morse

steamboats or canalboats. But the first trains of the 1830's were not very comfortable. Passengers traveled in open carriages, where engine sparks and soot fell on them. The noise and rough ride made train travel an adventure. Like steamboats, railroads changed the way Americans traveled and transported goods.

The Talking Wire

Improvements in communication were being made during this time period too. For some time, several different inventors had been working on ways to use electricity for sending messages. A man named Samuel Morse perfected a way to make news travel faster. This idea was called the telegraph. To send messages, Morse invented a code. In Morse Code, each letter of the alphabet is a series of dots and dashes.

People laughed at Morse's idea at first. In 1843, though, Congress gave Morse money to build a telegraph line between Baltimore and Washington, D.C. On May 24, 1844, with senators and congressmen looking on, Morse showed that the telegraph worked. Morse's telegraph was a great improvement in communication. News that once took weeks to reach distant places could now be sent in just a few hours.

Section Review

Write your answers on a sheet of paper.

1. Who used steam to improve American transportation? What did people call his invention at first? Why?
2. During the early and middle 1800's, why did people prefer to travel long distances by boat or railroad rather than by road?
3. Why was the Erie Canal so important?
4. What was the purpose of the telegraph?
5. What other inventions are based on the same idea as the telegraph?

192

3 The Nation's Sections

In the early 1800's, sections of the country were growing and changing in different ways. Each section had a different style of life. In the North, people began moving to the cities and working in new industries. In the South, new ways of producing cotton made owning and using slaves a part of everyday life. In the West, most people were busy farming and settling the frontier.

Factories in the North

Until 1800, most goods were made by hand. But in the late 1700's, a new way of producing goods by machine was developed in Great Britain. **Factories** were built to house the machines. Soon factories replaced the small workshop, where goods were made by hand. The machines in the factories could produce goods more quickly and therefore more cheaply.

factory

a place where goods are made by machines

The first American factory, Slater's mill in Rhode Island

The first factory machines in Great Britain were used to produce cloth, or textiles. The owners of British textile factories became very rich. They wanted to keep the designs for their machines a secret. To protect their designs, a law was passed saying that no one who knew anything about these machines could leave Great Britain. It was illegal to take the machines or their designs out of the country too.

That did not stop a young man named Samuel Slater. First Slater memorized everything he needed to know about the machines. Then, he used a disguise so that he was able to leave Great Britain for the United States. Slater set up the first textile factory in this country at Pawtucket, Rhode Island, in 1790. Other factories were built soon after this.

New England was a good place for the first factories. There were plenty of rivers and streams to provide the waterpower needed to run the machines.

Lowell, Massachusetts, became a well-known factory town in the 1800's. Factory owners hired New England farm girls as workers. The young women lived in boardinghouses near the mills, as the factories were called. They worked from sunup to sundown, six days a week. Sunday was their only day off.

Factory life began to change as time went on. By the middle of the 1800's, many Europeans left their homes to come to the United States. They came hoping to find jobs and a better life. With so many people around who were looking for work, factory owners found that they could hire the newcomers for less pay than the American farm girls.

Most factories were not as clean or as safe as the first Lowell mills. People worked long hours in dark, dirty places. Workers were often injured by dangerous machines. Because the pay was low, factory workers lived in poor housing near the factories. Many became sick from the unhealthy working and living conditions.

The number of factories in the United States continued to grow. The factory system changed the way people worked and lived so completely that it was called a revolution—the Industrial Revolution.

The revolution had the biggest effect in New England.

The cover of a book containing articles written by Lowell factory girls

People left their farms to work for others in factories. Towns grew into cities as they became factory centers. Railroads, canalboats, and steamboats carried goods from the factories to customers in other cities.

The factory system changed the lives of many Americans. It changed the places where they lived and worked. It changed the type of work they did. And it gave Americans many more goods to buy and sell.

King Cotton

Before 1800, tobacco, corn, and rice were the main cash crops of the South. Cotton was also grown, but it took a long time to harvest. Once the cotton was picked, the seeds had to be separated from the cotton fibers by hand. It could take 8 or 10 hours to clean just about 0.5 kilogram (1 pound) of cotton.

In 1793, Eli Whitney invented the cotton gin. This machine cleaned cotton by combing the seeds away from the fibers. The cotton gin could clean 50 times as much cotton as one person could clean by hand.

Eli Whitney's cotton gin

Whitney's cotton gin changed farming in the South. Cotton became the new cash crop. It was in great demand in northern textile mills, so southern planters sowed thousands of hectares (acres). Owners of large plantations as well as planters on small farms began to grow large amounts of cotton. Cotton was "king."

Cotton growing created a new need for slaves. Before the

Picking cotton in the South

invention of the cotton gin, slavery was beginning to weaken. Planters believed it was getting too expensive to keep slaves. Most farmers in the South did not own slaves. With big profits to be made from cotton, however, planters needed slaves to plant as much cotton as possible. Cotton farming made owning and using slaves more important. Slave owners used their profits from cotton to live comfortable, leisurely lives. And as profits from cotton grew, Southerners supported the system of slavery that made their lifestyle possible.

The West

Cyrus McCormick, a Virginia farmer, changed farming in the West, much as Eli Whitney had done in the South. McCormick spent years working with his father on a mechanical reaper, a machine that would harvest grain. McCormick finished an improved model in 1831, after his father died. He took the reaper out to the wheat fields on his family's farm. As the blades turned, the machine made a clattering noise, but it worked! Then McCormick took his machine to a country fair in Virginia. His neighbors laughed and called it funny-looking.

At first, the noise of the reaper terrified the horses that were pulling it. McCormick was able to calm the horses and continue his demonstration. The farmers were amazed by what they saw. The reaper could do the work of several people at once. Machines like McCormick's reaper made it possible for farmers to harvest more land.

When farmers first settled the land west of the Appalachian Mountains, most of the harvesting and planting was done by hand. Now with the reaper and other machines, farmers could grow far more grain than they could use themselves. They were able to sell this extra supply, or **surplus,** for profit.

By 1850, so much grain was grown in the West that other parts of the country began to buy the western grain. Instead of growing their own grain, they used the western grain to make flour for bread. The fertile land, the new machines, and the hard work of farmers turned the West into the "breadbasket of the nation."

Because the farms of the West were far from the population centers of the East, transportation was very important to the farmers. Riverboats carried crops down the Mississippi to New Orleans. From there, the crops were shipped to eastern ports. After 1825, crops were sent east on the

surplus
an extra supply

Demonstration of McCormick's reaper

Erie Canal. Later, the railroads reached the farming areas of the West. Transportation centers such as Chicago, St. Louis, and Buffalo grew into large cities.

The North, the South, and the West were developing in different ways. It was becoming more difficult for Congress to make laws that pleased all Americans at the same time. The interests of the three sections were not always the same.

Grain elevators at the Grand Central depot in Chicago, Illinois

Section Review

Write your answers on a sheet of paper.
1. What was the Industrial Revolution?
2. Why was New England a good place to build textile factories?
3. Why was factory work dangerous and unhealthy during the middle 1800's?
4. How did Eli Whitney help make cotton "king" in the South?
5. Based on what you have learned about the importance of transportation to farmers, explain how high fuel costs might affect the price of food.

Interpreting a Pie Graph

What were Americans doing for a living in 1850? Were most working on farms or in industry? The pie graph below answers these questions at a glance.

A pie graph is a useful way of showing how the whole of something can be divided into parts. Each part, or segment, of this graph shows the number of Americans employed in each major occupation in 1850.

The largest section of the graph stands for the number of workers involved in agriculture. The smallest segment stands for workers in education. One section stands for workers involved in three industries combined. To find out the total number of workers in 1850, add up the number employed in each industry.

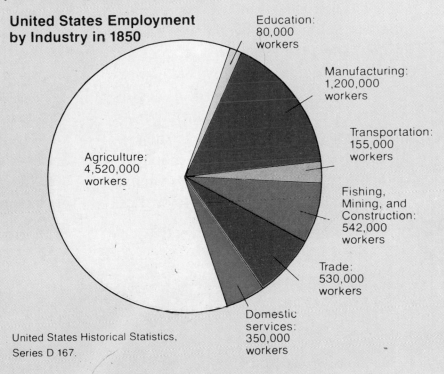

United States Employment by Industry in 1850

Education: 80,000 workers

Manufacturing: 1,200,000 workers

Transportation: 155,000 workers

Fishing, Mining, and Construction: 542,000 workers

Trade: 530,000 workers

Agriculture: 4,520,000 workers

Domestic services: 350,000 workers

United States Historical Statistics, Series D 167.

Practice Your Skills

1. What was the total number of workers employed in the United States in 1850?

2. How many workers were employed in trade? in transportation?

3. Were more people involved in fishing, mining, and construction combined, or in manufacturing?

4. Were there more workers in domestic service or in transportation during the year shown?

American Painting Painters in colonial America imitated the style and subjects of European painting. They painted portraits of important people and events. In the early 1800's, however, a group of painters living in New York State tried something new. They painted scenes of forests, valleys, and low mountains near the Hudson River. Their pictures showed the beauty of the land and the river and the painters' sense of pride in their country. This kind of painting became known as the Hudson River School. This approach encouraged other artists to paint pictures of the unspoiled land. Some of these paintings gave people their first look at the land west of the Appalachian Mountains and the American Indians who lived there.

George Catlin (1792–1872) was the first white person to paint American Indians of the West as they went about their daily activities. He traveled through the Midwest, living among the Plains Indians and painting pictures of their day-to-day life.

Painting by Frederic Remington showing a Pony Express rider who has just changed horses for the next lap of his journey

America

Other painters came from the East—and sometimes from Europe—to paint the West. Karl Bodmer (1809–1893), from France, was a foreign artist who painted American Indians. Alfred Jacob Miller (1810–1874) painted fur-trading scenes. Frederic Remington (1861–1909) painted cowhands and Plains Indians riding on horseback.

Charles Marion Russell (1864–1926) was a real westerner. He worked as a ranch hand himself. His paintings of life on the western range were true to life. Cowhands and other westerners bought his art because it was so real to them.

Albert Bierstadt (**beer**-stat) (1830–1902) painted the Rocky Mountains, and Charles Schreyvogel (**shrie**-voe-gul) (1861–1912) painted the soldiers who protected the western lands taken from the American Indians.

In their paintings, these artists showed the land, the people, and the spirit of the early West.

"Rocky Mountains" by Albert Bierstadt

UNIT REVIEW

Word Work

Write the sentences below on a sheet of paper. Fill in the blanks with the correct words from the list.

frontier   expedition   democracy   missionary   factory

1. For Daniel Boone, the land over the Appalachian Mountains was the new _____.
2. Lewis and Clark's _____ proved that Americans could travel overland to the West.
3. Samuel Slater built the first _____ in the United States.
4. A _____ is a country in which all adult citizens may vote in elections to choose their leaders.
5. Marcus Whitman was a _____.

Knowing the Facts

Write your answers on a sheet of paper.
1. Who were Lewis and Clark? What did they do?
2. Why did California become settled so quickly?
3. What changes in transportation made it easier for people to travel in the United States?

Using What You Know

Choose one of the following activities to do. Follow the instructions given here.
1. Write a report about how goods and people were transported on rivers before the invention of the steamboat. Compare the amount of time needed, the comfort of the passengers, and the distances traveled when people used roads, canals, and railroads. Use your textbook.
2. On an outline map of the United States, draw in the National Road. Use colored pencils to show the different states the road crossed. You may use an historical atlas. Include a map key to help others read your map.

Skills Practice

Use the pie graph shown here to answer the questions below. Write your answers on a sheet of paper.

1. How many years are included in this graph?
2. In that period, how many newcomers arrived in the United States from Great Britain?
3. From what country did the most newcomers come?
4. In total, how many newcomers came to the United States in this period? How did you figure this total?

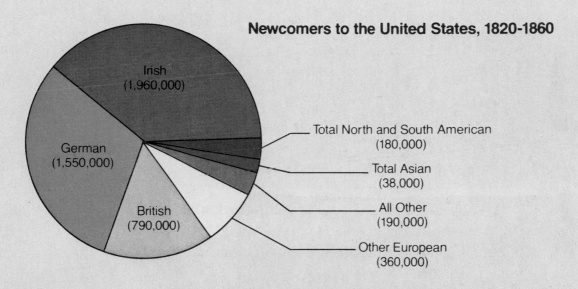

Newcomers to the United States, 1820-1860

Irish (1,960,000)

German (1,550,000)

British (790,000)

Total North and South American (180,000)

Total Asian (38,000)

All Other (190,000)

Other European (360,000)

Your Heritage

Most parts of the United States were very different during the 1800's from what they are today. By studying paintings of American scenes from the nineteenth century, you can observe some of the differences in the land and the way of life. Visit a library or your local historical society to find out what your area looked like during the 1800's. Write a short report about the differences between life then and now.

UNIT 5

The Nation Is Divided

By 1850, the United States had grown until it stretched from the Atlantic to the Pacific. The country's future seemed bright, except for one large problem.

Southerners wanted slavery to be allowed in the new western lands. Northerners were against allowing slavery there. Many people hoped a peaceful solution could be found to the differences between the North and the South. But in the end, the differences led to war.

In this unit, you will read about how Americans first quarreled over the spread of slavery and how the quarrels led to war. You will read about the heroes of these sad years when the people of the United States faced each other on the battlefield.

CHAPTER **11** Slavery Divides the Nation

Cotton was the major cash crop of the South in the middle of the 1800's. And cotton plantations depended on slaves. In the North, many people were not opposed to slavery. But some Northerners spoke out, calling slavery a terrible evil. Soon disagreements grew between the North and the South.

At the end of this chapter, you should be able to:

○ Describe how slaves lived.
○ Explain why some people opposed slavery and identify the leaders of that opposition.
○ Tell how Congress dealt with the issue of slavery.
○ Explain why Abraham Lincoln's debates with Stephen Douglas were important.

1 The Slave System

The democracy that was spreading in the first half of the 1800's was not shared by black Americans. Most blacks were slaves. Under the system of slavery, people were bought and sold as if they were objects instead of human beings.

By the early 1800's, slavery had been outlawed in most Northern states. In the South, however, where "King Cotton" was very important to the economy, the slave system was still strong.

Africa and the Slave Trade

Most of the blacks brought to the United States came from West Africa. Europeans first traveled to Africa around the time of Columbus. By the early 1600's, some Europeans were making a business of bringing Africans to the New World to be sold as slaves.

The voyage from Africa to the New World was a terrible experience for the captured Africans. They were chained together and crowded onto ships. Many died during the

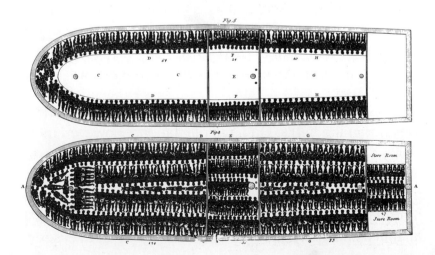

Diagram showing the crowded conditions slaves lived under on board slave ships

ocean crossing. It is estimated that about 10 million Africans were taken to the New World as part of the slave trade.

After they arrived in the United States, slaves were sold at public auctions. Frequently families were divided up to be sold to separate owners. Small children were sometimes taken from their mothers.

Slaves belonged to their owners. They had no rights under the law. Southern states passed laws called slave codes. According to these laws, slaves could not meet together in public. They could not travel without permission. It was also illegal to teach a slave how to read or write. Slaves who disobeyed their owners could be beaten.

In 1808, Congress outlawed the slave trade with Africa. Slaves could no longer be imported to this country. However, the system of slavery continued for nearly 60 years after this.

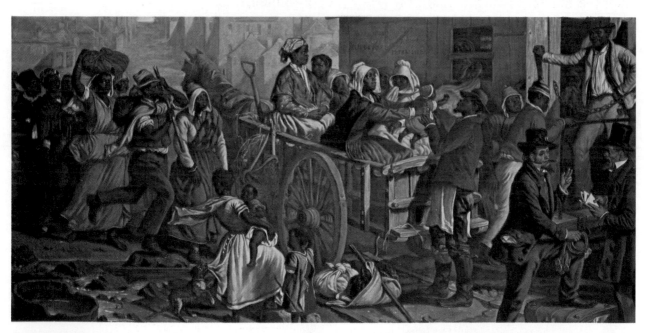

Slave auction

Slave Life

On small farms, slaves and the slave owner often worked together in the fields. On large plantations, however, most slaves rarely saw their owner, or master. Most of the slaves were field slaves. They planted and picked the crops and did other chores on the farm. They worked from early morning until sundown, and sometimes into the night. At all times, they were watched by a boss called an **overseer.**

overseer

a boss who watched over the slaves for a plantation owner

208

House slaves

A small group of slaves, called house slaves, looked after the master's house and family. They prepared meals, cleaned the house, and cared for the owner's children. House slaves were usually better clothed and fed than field slaves.

A slave's life was very hard, but black Americans kept their own faith and dignity alive. Slave marriages were not protected by law. When slave families were separated, family members tried not to lose contact with each other.

The centuries of slavery were hard enough to crush the spirit of a people. Rather than being defeated, however, black Americans survived these years and developed a strong, rich heritage.

Section Review

Write your answers on a sheet of paper.

1. What were the slave codes? Give several examples.

2. Describe what it was like to be a slave on a large plantation in the South.

3. Why do you think the slave codes made it illegal to teach slaves to read and write?

2 Fighting Slavery

By 1830, all Northern states had outlawed slavery. Many Northerners accepted slavery as part of the Southern way of life. However, some people in the North wanted to do away with slavery, or abolish it. These people were called **abolitionists** (ab-uh-**lish**-un-ists). Their cause was known as abolitionism.

Many abolitionists devoted their lives to their cause. They held meetings and gave speeches on the subject.

abolitionist

a person who wanted to do away with slavery

Cover of a pamphlet containing anti-slavery articles

They wrote articles about the evils of slavery. Some helped slaves escape from the South. In the beginning, abolitionists were unpopular. But over the years, more and more people began to support their cause.

The Abolitionists

The first abolitionist leader was William Lloyd Garrison, a Boston newspaper editor. Garrison was a very religious man. For him, slavery was both sinful and against the law. He said slavery went against what was said in the Bible and in the Declaration of Independence.

Garrison thought slaves should be freed, or **liberated.** In 1831, he began writing a newspaper about abolitionism called the *Liberator*. Most Southerners disagreed with Garrison. So did many Northerners.

liberate
to make free

Garrison did not care if his message made people angry. Once, after giving a speech in Boston, Garrison was attacked by a mob that wanted to hang him. The mayor of Boston put Garrison in jail to protect him from the crowd.

Still Garrison continued to give speeches and write about the need to abolish slavery. After a while, people began listening to him. By the 1840's, about 200,000 people had become abolitionists.

Another famous abolitionist was Frederick Douglass. Douglass spent most of his life working to help black people gain their freedom and rights.

Frederick Douglass was born a slave in Maryland. When he was a boy, his master's wife taught him to read and write. This was against the slave code. Douglass was a proud man, and for a slave, pride could mean trouble. So he decided to escape to the North. He had to avoid the slave catchers who captured runaways for a reward. Once in the North, Douglass continued to educate himself.

Douglass traveled all over the North speaking out against slavery. In Rochester, New York, he began a newspaper called the *North Star*. He chose that name because many slaves escaping from the South followed the North Star to freedom. In his newspaper, Douglass reminded his readers that even though blacks had their freedom in the North, they still were not treated fairly.

Frederick Douglass

Harriet Beecher Stowe

Other Voices Against Slavery

Over the years, the abolitionist movement grew stronger. It gained many supporters in 1851, after a New England woman named Harriet Beecher Stowe wrote *Uncle Tom's Cabin,* a story about slavery. In the story, an old slave named Uncle Tom is killed by a cruel overseer named Simon Legree (luh-**gree**). All over the country, people discussed *Uncle Tom's Cabin.* The book convinced many Northerners that slavery was an evil that had to end. Southerners complained that most slave owners were good to their slaves and that the book did not give a true picture of slavery. Years later, when war broke out between the North and the South, Abraham Lincoln called Stowe "the little woman who started this great war."

Poster advertising Uncle Tom's Cabin

Many other women fought against slavery. Elizabeth Cady Stanton and Lucretia Mott worked against slavery as well as fighting for women's rights. At the Seneca Falls Convention, many women spoke out against slavery. Sarah and Angelina Grimké (**grim**-kee), daughters of a rich South Carolina planter, were also active abolitionists. The Grimké sisters traveled around the country, speaking out against slavery and for women's rights.

The Underground Railroad

The Underground Railroad was a secret route to help slaves escape from the South to freedom in the North and Canada. Despite its name, it did not use trains, nor did it follow an underground route.

The Underground Railroad involved blacks and whites. The escape route went beyond the borders of the United States into Canada. People who knew the way guided slaves along a footpath. They traveled at night to avoid being seen. In the daytime, the slaves were hidden in the homes of supporters. These homes were called "stations," and the people who led the slaves out of the South were called "conductors."

The Grimké sisters, Sarah (above) and Angelina (below)

The Underground Railroad

Harriet Tubman

The most famous conductor on the Underground Railroad was an escaped slave herself. Her name was Harriet Tubman. Tubman was born on a Maryland plantation in about 1821.

Tubman escaped in 1849. For 15 years she worked as a conductor, leading over 300 slaves to freedom. She risked her own life many times traveling back into the South to rescue other slaves. Slave owners offered a reward of $40,000 for her capture, dead or alive. But no one could catch her.

Slave Revolts

Blacks sometimes fought back violently against slavery. The most famous revolt was led by a slave preacher named Nat Turner. On August 22, 1831, Turner and his followers began attacking whites. Turner and the other slaves were soon captured and put to death. Many innocent slaves were also killed or sent away to work on distant farms because slave owners were afraid that more revolts might take place. By the end of the rebellion, a few days later, more than 150 people, black and white, had died.

Turner's rebellion greatly frightened white Southerners. Southern state governments passed new laws that made a slave's life even harder.

Section Review

Write your answers on a sheet of paper.
1. Who were the abolitionists?
2. Who was William Lloyd Garrison?
3. How did *Uncle Tom's Cabin* help the abolitionist movement gain more supporters?
4. What was the Underground Railroad?
5. Abolitionists used newspapers and public speeches to win supporters for their cause. What other methods of communication do people use today to win supporters for their causes?

FAMOUS AMERICANS

SOJOURNER TRUTH

"I can't read a book, but I can read the people," Sojourner Truth once said. When Truth said she could "read" people, she meant that she understood how others felt. Truth used this ability to convince people that slavery was wrong and that women should have more rights under the law.

The woman who became known as Sojourner Truth was born a slave in New York in the late 1700's. Her mother named her Isabella and taught her to believe in God, to obey her owner, and to be truthful.

New York State outlawed slavery in 1827, and Isabella became a free woman. But other states still allowed slavery. Isabella decided to help people who were still slaves.

In 1843, Isabella changed her name to Sojourner Truth. She believed she heard a command from God to go out into the world and preach. "Sojourner" means "traveler." So her name meant that she was a traveler who preached the truth.

Although she never went to school, Sojourner Truth was a powerful speaker. Often she sang to her audience as well. Her singing would silence the noisiest crowd.

Sojourner Truth traveled throughout the eastern and midwestern states. Everywhere she went, she spoke out and sang songs for the freedom of black people and the rights of women.

Sojourner Truth feared no opponent. Once a man told her, "I don't care any more for you than I do for the bite of a flea." She replied, "Perhaps not. But . . . I'll keep you scratchin!"

Sojourner Truth died in 1883 in Battle Creek, Michigan. Today, a century after her death, this self-taught former slave is remembered as a woman who lived up to her name. She was a proud but gentle traveler for the truth.

3 Attempts to Avoid War

Many Northerners were not against slavery. They thought there was nothing wrong with Southerners using slaves to grow cotton. But Northerners and Southerners disagreed about permitting slavery in the territories that had not yet become states.

Free States and Slave States

Under the United States Constitution, each state decided for itself whether it would permit slavery. Congress could make no laws about slavery in the states. But Congress could make laws about slavery in the territories.

The problem of slavery in the territories became very serious in 1819. People in the Missouri Territory wrote a constitution that permitted slavery. Then they asked to be admitted to the United States as a state.

At that time, there were an equal number of states that permitted slavery, called slave states, and states that did not permit it, called free states. This balance between free states and slave states meant that each side had the same number of votes in the Senate.

Henry Clay speaking out in Congress

If Missouri became a slave state, there would no longer be a balance. Slave states would have more voting power in Congress than free states. The members of Congress argued about this issue for several months. Finally Henry Clay of Kentucky came up with an idea that was called the Missouri Compromise. The law passed by Congress in 1820 allowed Missouri to join the Union as a slave state. Maine, which had been a part of Massachusetts, was allowed to join as a free state. The Missouri Compromise kept an even balance between free states and slave states.

If these escaping slaves were caught, they had to be returned to their owners under the terms of the Compromise of 1850.

In 1850, Congress faced the problem again. California wanted to join the Union as a free state. But this time there was no other area ready to join as a slave state to keep the balance. Again Henry Clay came up with a compromise. Under the Compromise of 1850, as it was called, California came into the Union as a free state. At the same time, a law was passed saying that slaves who escaped to free states could be captured and sent back to their owners.

The leaders of Congress hoped the Compromise of 1850 would settle the issue of slavery in the territories. But the problem of slavery would not go away. By the 1850's, the North and South were growing into two different nations.

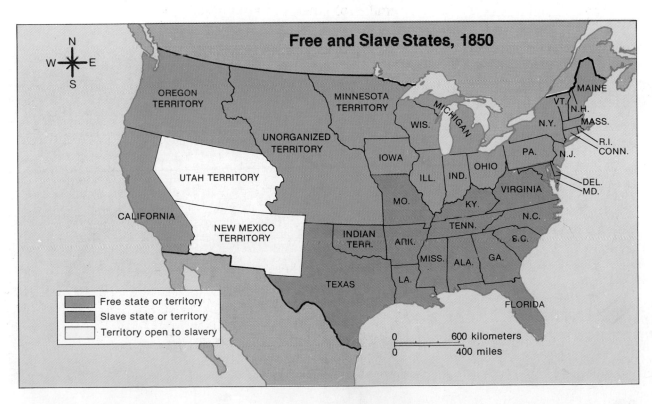

Free and Slave States, 1850

Free state or territory
Slave state or territory
Territory open to slavery

0   600 kilometers
0   400 miles

A New Leader

No election could take place in these years without the issue of slavery coming up. An important election took place in 1858 in Illinois. Senator Stephen Douglas ran for reelection against Abraham Lincoln. The two rivals held a series of talks, or debates, in which they presented different views on the subject of slavery.

Douglas believed that the people living in an area should decide if slavery should be permitted in that area. Lincoln was not an abolitionist. But he was against permitting slavery in the territories. He also did not think the United States could continue to exist as a nation if it was part slave and part free. In one speech, he said: "A house divided against itself cannot stand." Lincoln meant that unless the country decided to be all slave or all free, it would not last. This was an unpopular opinion, but Abraham Lincoln was not afraid to speak his mind. That is one reason people called him Honest Abe. Douglas won the election, but many people were impressed with Lincoln. They would remember him in 1860 when he ran for President.

Abraham Lincoln and Stephen Douglas debating

Abraham Lincoln was born in a log cabin in Kentucky in 1809. He grew up on the frontier, first in Kentucky and then in Indiana. As a boy, young Lincoln loved to read books. After doing the day's chores, he read late into the night by candlelight.

When Lincoln was a young man, he moved with his family to Illinois. He opened a store, but he enjoyed reading and studying more than waiting on his customers. Lincoln studied law and became a lawyer. He was well liked by his neighbors. In 1834, when Lincoln decided to enter politics, they elected him to the Illinois legislature.

Lincoln was a quiet, gentle person who cared deeply about people. In arguing with others about slavery, he never became angry with those who disagreed with him. He simply said slavery was wrong.

Before 1858, few people outside Illinois knew of Lincoln. Because of his debates with Stephen Douglas, Lincoln's fame spread. Even though he was not an abolitionist, people who were against slavery thought of him as a leader for their cause. Most Southerners believed that Lincoln was a threat to the Southern way of life because he was against the extension of slavery. However, Lincoln had enough supporters to win the presidential election in 1860. With his victory, the North and the South moved closer to war.

Abraham Lincoln

Section Review

Write your answers on a sheet of paper.

1. What was the Missouri Compromise?
2. Name two results of the Compromise of 1850.
3. Why was Lincoln opposed to the extension of slavery into the territories?
4. Many Southerners believed slavery was a bad thing, but they believed it was an important part of their way of life. Explain why they might have felt this way.
5. Abraham Lincoln is one of the greatest heroes in American history. Name some ways he is remembered today.

CHAPTER 12 A Nation Divided— The Civil War

The North and South had developed different ways of life. Each region also had different ideas about the rights of the individual states and the powers of the federal government. In 1861, Americans went to war over these differences. Many people believed that the war would decide whether the United States could survive as a nation.

At the end of this chapter, you should be able to:

○ Tell how the election of 1860 led to war.
○ Explain the advantages that each side had during the Civil War.
○ Tell how blacks and women helped in the war.
● Use a resource map to compare the North and the South.
○ Identify two important battles and three generals.

1 The Road to War

The question of states' rights divided the country. Did the states have the right to disobey laws of the federal government? What might happen if the balance of free and slave states in Congress changed? Would the larger group make laws that would anger the smaller group?

There were strong feelings about slavery in both the North and the South. However, the country did not go to war over slavery. It went to war over the issue of keeping the states united in order to preserve the nation.

Election banner for Lincoln in the 1860 Presidential election campaign

The Election of 1860

The election of 1860 showed clearly that the United States was a divided country. Four people ran for President. Each one had different views about slavery. Abraham Lincoln was the candidate of the Republican party. He believed that slavery was wrong. But Lincoln said he would

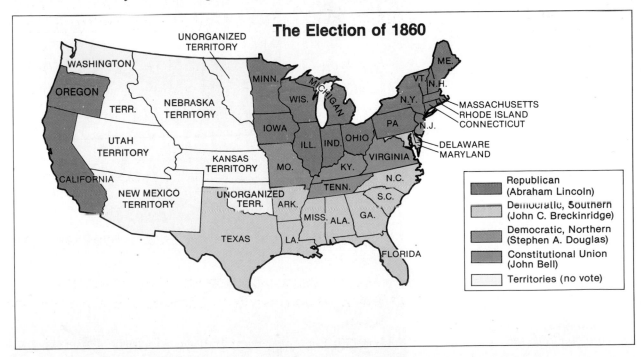

The Election of 1860

WASHINGTON
OREGON
TERR.
UTAH TERRITORY
CALIFORNIA
NEBRASKA TERRITORY
UNORGANIZED TERRITORY
KANSAS TERRITORY
NEW MEXICO TERRITORY
UNORGANIZED TERR.
TEXAS
MINN.
WIS.
MICHIGAN
IOWA
ILL.
IND.
OHIO
MO.
KY.
ARK.
MISS.
ALA.
LA.
TENN.
GA.
S.C.
N.C.
VIRGINIA
PA.
N.Y.
VT.
N.H.
ME.
MASSACHUSETTS
RHODE ISLAND
CONNECTICUT
N.J.
DELAWARE
MARYLAND
FLORIDA

Republican (Abraham Lincoln)
Democratic, Southern (John C. Breckinridge)
Democratic, Northern (Stephen A. Douglas)
Constitutional Union (John Bell)
Territories (no vote)

not end slavery in the South. He did promise to end slavery in the areas that were not yet states. That way, no new slave states would enter the United States. Southerners did not trust Lincoln. Many believed that the Republicans planned to abolish slavery everywhere.

Southerners warned there would be trouble if Lincoln were elected. Lincoln did not win in any of the Southern states. But he did win the national election. Americans waited to see what would happen.

South Carolina was the first to act. On December 20, 1860, South Carolina voted to withdraw, or **secede,** from the United States. By February 1, 1861, Mississippi, Florida, Alabama, Georgia, Louisiana, and Texas had also voted to secede.

secede

to leave or withdraw from

Confederate States of America

The seceding states decided to form their own nation. On February 4, 1861, the Southern states formed the Confederate States of America. Jefferson Davis of Mississippi became President. Davis had been a soldier and a United States senator.

Inauguration of Abraham Lincoln, March 4, 1865

Lincoln Takes Office

Between Lincoln's election and his inauguration in March 1861, the United States had split apart. Some Northerners urged President Lincoln to let the South secede.

At his inauguration, however, Lincoln disagreed. He said that, as President, it was his constitutional duty to keep the nation united.

Lincoln did not want a war. But soon he felt that there was no choice. The Confederacy had taken over several federal forts in Southern states. Fort Sumter, in the harbor of Charleston, South Carolina, was still held by Union, or Northern, troops. Lincoln decided to send badly needed supplies to the fort. He told the South he was sending only food, not soldiers or weapons. He hoped that the South would let the supplies through.

On April 12, 1861, Confederate troops opened fire on Fort Sumter. The next day, Union troops surrendered the fort. It was the beginning of a **civil war**—a war between people of the same nation.

Between April and June, Arkansas, Tennessee, North Carolina, and Virginia joined the Confederacy. This made a total of 11 Confederate states.

Four other states that permitted slavery did not secede. These were Delaware, Maryland, Kentucky, and Missouri. These four states were called border states because they

civil war
a war fought between people of the same nation

The attack on Fort Sumter

were on the border between the North and South. Lincoln's government was able to persuade these states to remain in the Union. However, some people in these states fought for the Confederacy.

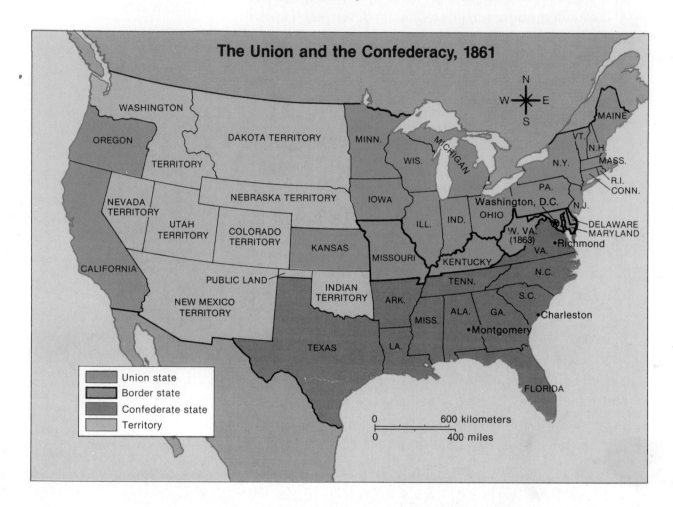

The Union and the Confederacy, 1861

Legend:
- Union state
- Border state
- Confederate state
- Territory

0 — 600 kilometers
0 — 400 miles

Section Review

Write your answers on a sheet of paper.
1. What action did South Carolina take after Lincoln won the election?
2. Who was Jefferson Davis?
3. What is meant by the term "border state"?
4. Who would have been more likely to approve of the South's seceding from the Union: a Northern cotton mill owner or a Northern abolitionist? Explain your answer.

2 Americans at War

After the attack on Fort Sumter, President Lincoln called for 75,000 volunteer soldiers. These soldiers needed time to train. But some congressmen demanded immediate action against the South. So before the Union troops were ready, they were ordered out to fight the Southerners.

Bull Run

The first major battle of the war was on July 12, 1861. It was fought in northern Virginia along a creek called Bull Run. Many people thought it might be the only battle of the war, so they rode out to watch. The road was jammed with carriages full of people. Many of the troops had never been soldiers before. Some of them stopped along the way to pick berries.

When the two armies met at Bull Run, the mood of the day changed quickly. Guns blazed and soldiers died. Southern troops easily defeated the Union army, but it was clear that the North was not going to give up. People on both sides soon realized that this was not going to be a short war full of glory and easy victories. The war was going to demand great courage and sacrifices from Northerners and Southerners alike.

North Against South

Both sides had certain advantages that they felt would help them win the war. The North had more soldiers, more supplies, and better transportation. The South had better generals and was fighting on home ground.

Robert E. Lee, probably the greatest soldier of the Civil War, commanded the Southern armies. Lee was from Virginia. He had spent most of his life in the army. At the outbreak of the Civil War, President Lincoln asked Lee to command the Union troops. Lee loved the United States, and he did not believe in slavery. But he felt he could not fight against his neighbors from Virginia. So he resigned from the United States Army to lead the Confederate troops.

Robert E. Lee

Lee was a great general. He could fight and win when the odds were against him. He organized brilliant surprise attacks on the more powerful Union forces.

Another great Confederate general was Thomas "Stonewall" Jackson. Jackson got his nickname at the battle of Bull Run. Another general saw him rally his men against a Union charge and said, "There is Jackson standing like a stone wall."

Other advantages also helped give the South early victories. White Southerners were fighting to preserve their way of life. For them, the Civil War was a second war for independence. They believed they had a right to secede from the Union, just as the colonists had a right to break away from Great Britain.

Another advantage, at least at the beginning, was that much of the war was fought in the South. Since they were fighting on home ground, the Southern soldiers knew the land better than the Northern troops. Also, Southerners did not have to ship supplies long distances, as did the North.

But soon the North's advantages began to have an effect. Goods and troops could be moved more quickly on the North's better network of railroads. There were nearly 23 million people in the North against about 9 million people in the South. So the North had more people available to fight and help in the war effort. Northern factories could supply uniforms, guns, bullets, and other important items for its army. The South had few factories. And as the war continued, the South had more and more trouble supplying its army.

Resources of the North and South in 1861

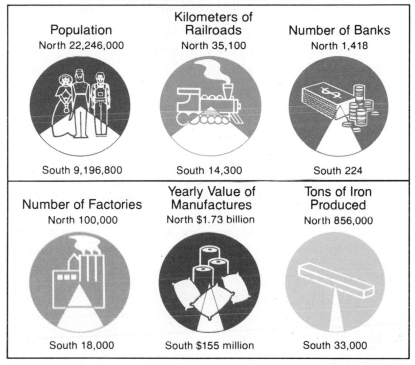

Population	Kilometers of Railroads	Number of Banks
North 22,246,000	North 35,100	North 1,418
South 9,196,800	South 14,300	South 224

Number of Factories	Yearly Value of Manufactures	Tons of Iron Produced
North 100,000	North $1.73 billion	North 856,000
South 18,000	South $155 million	South 33,000

Life on the Home Front

The war involved other people besides soldiers. Thousands of people who were not in the army worked to supply uniforms, guns, bullets, bandages, and food. In both the North and the South, groups of women formed women's aid societies. These groups made uniforms, flags, and bandages. They sent food to the soldiers. They raised money to buy other supplies. While the men were at war, women still had to take care of their families. They also had to run the family farms or businesses.

Some women took on the dangerous work of spying. Harriet Tubman worked as a spy for the Union. She made many trips to the South. Slaves there told her about Confederate troop movements.

Belle Boyd was a famous Southern spy. She was 17 years old when the war began. Union forces occupied the town in Virginia where Boyd lived. She listened carefully to Union soldiers who liked to brag about the military secrets they knew. Soon Boyd found out some very important information. Twice she was caught by Union troops and arrested. Both times, however, the quick-thinking Boyd was able to persuade the soldiers to release her.

Many women took on the difficult work of nursing. The most famous of these was Clara Barton. Barton collected supplies and organized nursing services for the sick and wounded. She used her own home to store the supplies. Then she would deliver them by mule directly to the soldiers on the battlefield.

In 1864, Barton was put in charge of all the nurses for one of the Union armies. She also organized groups of women to bring news of the wounded soldiers to the soldiers' families. After the war, Clara Barton founded the American Red Cross.

(left) Clara Barton
(right) Belle Boyd

Black Soldiers

Blacks also played an important part in the war. At first, they were not allowed to fight in either the Union or the Confederate army. After many white Union soldiers were killed, however, blacks were allowed to become Union soldiers. About 186,000 blacks joined the Union army. One of these soldiers was Major Martin Delany, the first black to become an army officer. Delany served in the army medical corps.

In general, black soldiers were rarely treated as well as white soldiers, but they fought with courage. Twenty black soldiers won the highest award, the Medal of Honor.

Black soldiers fighting for the Union at Fort Wagner, South Carolina

Section Review

Write your answers on a sheet of paper.

1. What was the importance of the battle of Bull Run?
2. What advantages did the South have in the war? What were the North's advantages?
3. How did women and blacks help in the war effort?
4. Wars are difficult times for a nation. People are killed. But people often come together to help during a war. What other national events, besides wars, bring the people of a country together?

The South took an early lead in the Civil War because its army was well organized, it had good generals, and it was fighting on familiar ground. But a war is not won on the battlefields alone. The North had a better network of railroads than the South had. The maps on the next page show other advantages held by the North that greatly influenced the outcome of the war.

The maps show the important agricultural and industrial resources held by both sides at the beginning of the war. The colored areas stand for different kinds of farming, and the picture symbols represent different industries.

Notice that cotton was a major crop in the South, and wheat and corn were major crops in the North. Notice, too, that there was much dairy farming in the North.

Now compare the industrial activities of the two sides. The symbol for mining is a tiny coal car. As you can see, the North had far more mining centers than the South did. It had other industrial strengths as well.

To fight a war, a nation must feed and clothe its army. It must produce guns and ammunition. By comparing these maps, you can see that, from the very beginning, one side was better able to support its army than the other.

Practice Your Skills

1. Which side had more iron works and steel works? more textile mills?
2. In what Southern state were flour and meal milled?
3. Name the types of farming done in the South. How many food products were grown?
4. In what Northern states was mining done? In what Southern states was mining done?

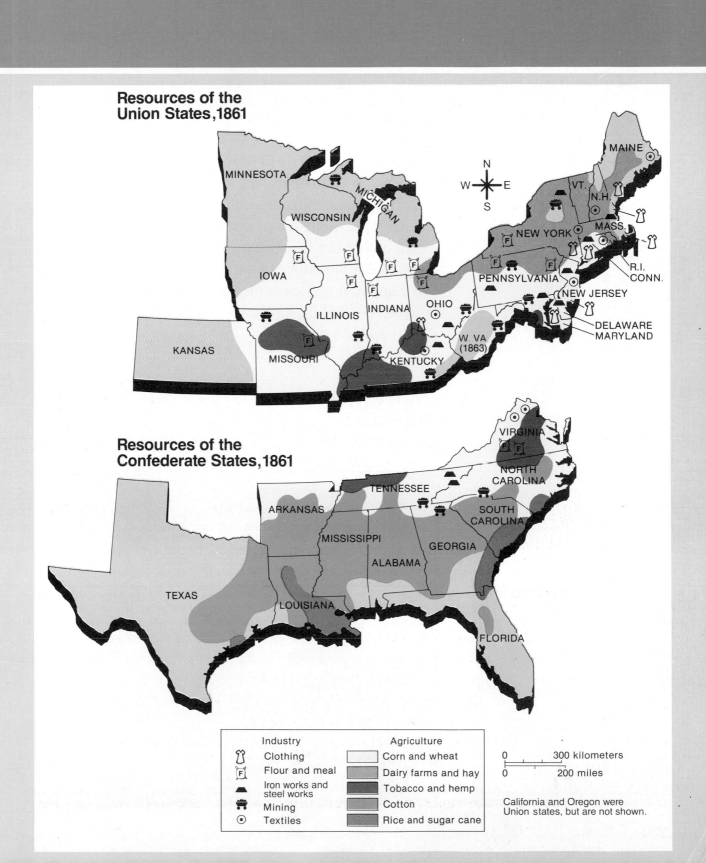

Resources of the Union States, 1861

MAINE

MINNESOTA

MICHIGAN

WISCONSIN

VT.

N.H.

NEW YORK

MASS.

IOWA

PENNSYLVANIA

R.I.
CONN.

ILLINOIS

INDIANA

OHIO

NEW JERSEY

KANSAS

MISSOURI

KENTUCKY

W. VA
(1863)

DELAWARE
MARYLAND

Resources of the Confederate States, 1861

VIRGINIA

NORTH
CAROLINA

TENNESSEE

ARKANSAS

SOUTH
CAROLINA

MISSISSIPPI

GEORGIA

ALABAMA

TEXAS

LOUISIANA

FLORIDA

Industry

🧥 Clothing

Ⓕ Flour and meal

▲ Iron works and steel works

⛏ Mining

⊙ Textiles

Agriculture

Corn and wheat

Dairy farms and hay

Tobacco and hemp

Cotton

Rice and sugar cane

0   300 kilometers

0   200 miles

California and Oregon were
Union states, but are not shown.

3 The War Years

Almost 2.5 million Southerners and Northerners fought in the Civil War. More American soldiers died in this war than in any other.

A Soldier's Life

Many Civil War soldiers were very young. Some were only 16 years old. Few knew what fighting a war was really like. On the battlefields, the cannons and guns made a dreadful noise. Smoke from the cannons made it difficult to see. The wounded and dying were all around.

Still, when the war began, many boys and men were eager to join the army. As the war went on and both sides lost many soldiers, fewer men joined the army. Men had to be drafted—that is, forced by law—to join the army.

A dead Southern sharpshooter lies behind a stone wall he had built for defense at the battle of Gettysburg

Young Confederate soldier, Private Edwin Jennison of Georgia, who was killed in a battle at Malvern Hill, Virginia

Not everyone who was drafted went to war. A man who did not want to fight could pay a substitute to serve in his place. Northerners could also buy their way out of the draft for $300. However, many could not afford to pay.

Both sides had trouble keeping soldiers supplied. For the South, this was more difficult. Many Confederate soldiers fought barefoot. Often they did not have enough food. Medical care was so bad that more soldiers died from disease and infection than from the actual fighting.

The War at Sea

Early in the war, the Union navy began to blockade Southern ports. The Union wanted to prevent Southern ships from trading with European countries for the manufactured goods the South needed.

At first, Southerners did not feel the effects of the blockade. Swift blockade runners moved past the heavier Union gunboats. As the war went on, however, the Union blockade caused great hardship. The South suffered shortages of everything from clothes and food to nails and guns.

Union and Confederate ships fought many battles. The most famous was between a Union ship, the *Monitor,* and a Confederate ship, the *Merrimac.* Unlike the earlier ships that were built entirely of wood, the *Monitor* and the *Merrimac* were covered with iron. Cannonballs could not damage them.

Iron-covered ships fighting during the Civil War

On March 9, 1862, the two ships met on the James River near Hampton, Virginia. They battled for nearly four hours without either side winning. Later both ships were sunk. But the value of iron-covered ships was proven. The *Monitor* and the *Merrimac* became the models for later United States warships.

Freedom for Slaves

In September 1862, President Lincoln issued an important order called the **Emancipation Proclamation** (ih-man-suh-**pay**-shun prock-luh-**may**-shun). Emancipation means freedom.

The Emancipation Proclamation said that, beginning on January 1, 1863, all slaves in the Confederacy would be free. Lincoln had no way of enforcing his proclamation. But as the Union army began to win battles, slaves in conquered areas of the South were freed.

The Emancipation Proclamation did not free slaves in the border states that fought with the Union. It only freed slaves in the Confederacy. Still, slaves and abolitionists throughout the country were grateful for the proclamation.

Emancipation Proclamation
President Lincoln's order that granted freedom to slaves in the Confederate states

Painting celebrating the Emancipation Proclamation

Gettysburg

In 1863, Confederate leaders thought that Union forces might surrender if the South could win a battle in the North. They knew that Lincoln was having difficulty finding a general who could defeat Robert E. Lee. The South believed this was its chance for victory.

In June 1863, Lee marched into Pennsylvania. The Union army met Lee's forces at Gettysburg on July 1. For two days, the armies battled. Then, on July 3, Lee sent a large unit under General George Pickett to attack the main Union position. This was on a hill called Cemetery Ridge.

The Confederates bravely fought their way to the top of the ridge. But the Union forces held their ground. After a few minutes, the Confederates were forced to retreat.

Pickett's Charge, as the attack was called, was the turning point of the war. If the Confederates had been able to take Cemetery Ridge, they would have won the battle. They would have gained a stronghold in the North. From there they might have tried to invade all the Union states. Instead it was the beginning of the end for the Southern cause.

On November 19, 1863, President Lincoln went to Gettysburg to dedicate a cemetery for the fallen soldiers. He spoke only a short time. But the simple words of his Gettysyburg Address are still remembered. Lincoln said "that this nation, under God, shall have a new birth of freedom—and that government of the people, by the people, for the people, shall not perish [disappear] from the earth."

Battle of Gettysburg

The South Is Defeated

In 1864, Lincoln finally found a general to lead the Union armies to victory. He was Ulysses (yoo-**liss**-eez) S. Grant. Grant had won an important battle at Vicksburg, Mississippi, in 1863. With that victory, the entire Mississippi Valley came under Union control.

For one year, Grant and Lee fought a series of battles. Even though neither side won a great victory, Grant had the advantage. Lee was running out of troops and supplies.

In the summer of 1864, a Union general, William T. Sherman, captured Atlanta, Georgia. In November 1864, Sherman began a march through Georgia, from Atlanta to Savannah on the eastern coast. As Sherman's troops marched, they destroyed plantations, towns, and farms. Sherman wanted to destroy anything that could help the South. For years afterward, Southerners spoke bitterly about Sherman's march to the sea. In January 1865, Sherman began a drive through South and North Carolina. He destroyed farms and towns in those states as well.

Meanwhile, in Virginia, Grant finally closed in on Lee. On April 5, 1865, Grant captured Richmond. By April 7, the Confederate forces that had tried to retreat farther south were surrounded. At last, on April 9, Lee surrendered in a farmhouse near Appomattox (ap-uh-**mat**-iks) Court House. With Lee's surrender, the war was over.

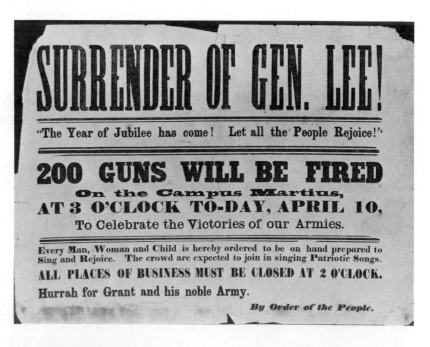

Newspaper headline announcing the surrender of General Robert E. Lee to the Union army

The Final Shot

On the evening of April 14, 1865, President Lincoln and his wife went to see a play at Ford's Theater, in Washington, D.C. During the play, John Wilkes Booth, an actor and a Southerner, shot the President. Lincoln died the next morning.

Picture showing what the assassination of President Lincoln might have looked like

Section Review

Write your answers on a sheet of paper.
1. Name three things that made life hard for soldiers on both sides during the Civil War.
2. How were the *Monitor* and the *Merrimac* different from earlier ships?
3. What was the Emancipation Proclamation?
4. Lincoln's Emancipation Proclamation freed slaves in the Confederacy but not in the border states. Why do you think Lincoln limited emancipation in this way?

CHAPTER 13 Reconstruction

Freed blacks in the South after the Civil War

President Lincoln had planned for a period of rebuilding after the war. New leaders for the South had to be chosen. Good relations between the North and the South had to be restored. Lincoln had hoped the rebuilding, or Reconstruction, would go quickly. But after Lincoln's death, Americans quarreled over how to proceed with Reconstruction.

At the end of this chapter, you should be able to:
- ○ Compare the Reconstruction plans made by President Andrew Johnson and by Congress.
- ○ Explain why Congress and President Johnson disagreed about Reconstruction.
- ○ Identify the constitutional amendments passed during the Reconstruction period.
- ○ Explain how sharecropping worked.
- ○ Describe how the South changed after Reconstruction.

1 The South After War

After the war, much of the South was in ruins. Fields that had been planted in cotton were overgrown with weeds and brush. The economy was destroyed. The Confederacy had printed its own money. Now the money was worthless.

More than 250,000 Southerners had died in the fighting. Many people were homeless. Freed slaves had no place to live and no way to make a living. Confederate soldiers were allowed to go home. But often their homes had been destroyed. Returning soldiers found few jobs in the ruined economy.

The political leaders of the South had suffered a painful defeat. Reconstruction would be a long and difficult process.

Governing the South

Before the end of the war, President Lincoln had begun work on plans for Reconstruction. He told the nation that he would act "with malice [ill will] toward none; [and] charity for all."

The ruins of Richmond, Virginia, after the Civil War

Lincoln's plan for the reconstruction of the South was simple. First, he said he would give **amnesty,** or a pardon, to all Southerners who would take an oath of loyalty to the United States. Important leaders of the Confederacy, however, would be denied amnesty. They would be held responsible for having broken the law. Second, states would be allowed to rejoin the United States when one tenth of the voters had taken the oath of loyalty.

President Andrew Johnson

When Lincoln died, Vice-President Andrew Johnson became President. During the first year of Johnson's presidency, the Thirteenth Amendment to the Constitution was passed. This amendment outlawed slavery in all parts of the United States.

Johnson had a plan for Reconstruction that was similar to Lincoln's. Under Johnson's plan, Southern states had to take back their original vote to secede from the United States. They also had to accept the Thirteenth Amendment. Johnson said he would grant amnesty to most Confederates who would swear an oath of loyalty to the United States.

Under President Johnson's plan, Southern states were free to elect representatives to their state legislatures. The Southern state governments acted quickly to restrict the freedom of blacks. They passed laws called "black codes." These laws prevented blacks from voting, living in certain places, and working at certain jobs. News of the black codes made Northerners very angry. Slavery had been abolished, but life for blacks in the South seemed the same.

Johnson's plan also allowed Southern states to elect representatives to Congress. Many of the people elected to Congress from the South had been leaders of the Confederacy. The new congressmen from the South faced a very unfriendly welcome when they came to Washington. Northern and Western members of Congress refused to let the Southerners take their seats. Many people in the North felt that President Johnson's Reconstruction plan was not harsh enough. In 1867, President Johnson and Congress began a struggle over who would control Reconstruction.

Andrew Johnson

Congress and Reconstruction

Andrew Johnson had not been elected by the voters. He became President because of the death of President Lincoln. As a former slave owner, Johnson was not trusted by many Northerners. One Northerner who was very outspoken against Johnson's Reconstruction plan was Thaddeus Stevens.

Stevens was a congressman from Pennsylvania. He had been an abolitionist before the war. Stevens believed that very extreme, or **radical,** policies were the only way to change conditions in the South. Stevens and other members of the Republican party who agreed with him were called Radical Republicans.

The Radical Republicans had enough supporters in Congress to pass their own program of Reconstruction. They did away with the Southern state governments set up under Johnson's plan. They declared that only Congress could decide who would control Reconstruction and govern the South. They divided the South into five military sections, or districts. A United States army general was appointed governor of each district.

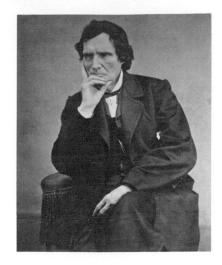

Thaddeus Stevens

radical
extreme

Robert B. Eliot of South Carolina, was one of several blacks elected to Congress during Reconstruction.

Southern states had to start all over in forming new governments. People who had been leaders of the Confederacy were not allowed to vote or hold office. Each state had to write a new state constitution. In addition to adopting the Thirteenth Amendment, the states also had to accept two more new amendments to the United States Constitution. The Fourteenth Amendment said people of every race must be treated equally under the law. The Fifteenth Amendment gave black men the right to vote.

President Johnson and Congress

President Johnson and Congress continued to disagree about Reconstruction. Congress passed laws limiting the powers of the President. Johnson refused to accept these laws. In 1868, the House of Representatives voted to accuse Johnson of not enforcing the Reconstruction acts and of treating Congress with disrespect. They voted to put him on trial for not carrying out his constitutional duties. This process of bringing charges against a government official is known as **impeachment.**

Under the Constitution, members of the House may vote to accuse a government official of high crimes and of fail-

impeachment
the process of bringing charges against a government official

President Andrew Johnson being served papers ordering him to appear in Congress for his impeachment trial

242

ing to uphold the Constitution. Then the government official is tried in the Senate. If two thirds of the senators believe the government official is guilty, he or she is removed from office.

Johnson's trial in the Senate went on for one and a half months. Finally, on May 16, 1868, the Senate called for a vote. The vote in the Senate was very close. Thirty-five senators said Johnson was guilty of high crimes. Nineteen supported the President. Andrew Johnson missed being removed from office by just one vote.

FAC-SIMILE OF TICKET OF ADMISSION TO THE IMPEACHMENT TRIAL.

Tickets like this one admitted people to the impeachment trial of President Andrew Johnson.

Section Review

Write your answers on a sheet of paper.

1. What were conditions in the South like after the Civil War ended?
2. Who were the Radical Republicans? How did their plan for Reconstruction differ from Johnson's?
3. What do the Thirteenth, Fourteenth, and Fifteenth amendments say?
4. During the Reconstruction period, President Johnson and Congress had strong disagreements. Name an issue on which the President and the Congress disagree today.

2 A New Way of Life

For both blacks and whites, life in the South was very different after the Civil War. The old plantations that had depended on slavery could no longer operate. Farming and business had suffered terribly during the war. Many people had lost their homes and all their money.

Sharecropping

After the Civil War, plantation owners found that their Confederate money was worthless. They had no money to hire people to work on their land.

Southern landowners came up with a different way of making money from their land. The landowners allowed farmers to live and work on their plantations. The landowner also supplied seeds, work animals, and farm tools. In exchange, the farmers gave the landowners a large share of the crops raised on the land. This arrangement was called **sharecropping.**

During the growing season, sharecroppers would buy food and supplies on credit. Then when the harvest was in, they would pay their bills using their share of the crops.

sharecropping

a system of farming in which farmers rent land from landowners and pay their rent with a share of the crops they grow

Black sharecroppers picking cotton in the South after the Civil War

Often their share of the crops was not enough to pay all their debts. So from one year to the next, sharecroppers were almost always in debt. Sometimes they could not afford to buy enough food and clothing for their families.

Many of the newly freed blacks became sharecroppers. For them, the Civil War had brought freedom from slavery. But their lives were still filled with days of hard work and hunger.

The Freedmen's Bureau

In 1865, Congress set up an organization called the Freedmen's Bureau to help the freed slaves. The bureau provided food, schooling, and hospital care to blacks in the South. By 1870, there were several hundred thousand blacks in school. The Freedmen's Bureau also gave support to black colleges, such as Howard University, in Washington, D.C.

Freedmen's Bureau school in Vicksburg, Mississippi

Blacks Vote and Hold Office

The Fifteenth Amendment, which gave black men the right to vote, meant that blacks could run for government office. The first black candidates were elected to important offices across the South. Hiram Revels was appointed to

Hiram Revels

carpetbagger
name used to describe a Northerner who moved to the South to take part in Reconstruction governments

scalawag
name given to a white Southerner who took part in Reconstruction governments

finish the United States Senate term in place of a famous Confederate leader, Jefferson Davis. In 1875, Blanche K. Bruce became the first black man elected to the United States Senate.

Carpetbaggers and Scalawags

Under the Radical Republicans' Reconstruction plan, most of the old Confederate leaders could not take part in government. The new leaders of the South came from both the North and the South. They were disliked by people who had been loyal to the South during the war.

The Northerners who moved to the South to take part in the new state governments were called **carpetbaggers.** They got their name from the suitcases they carried, which were made from pieces of carpet. Some were not concerned with being good public officials. Their goal was to get rich. Others, however, did work hard to improve conditions in the South.

The white Southerners who were allowed to take part in government under the Reconstruction plan were called **scalawags** (**scal**-uh-wagz). Many Southerners were angry that the carpetbaggers and scalawags were running the state governments. Reconstruction was supposed to bring the North and the South together again. Instead the new Reconstruction leaders of the South added to the angry feelings between the two sections of the nation.

In this cartoon of a carpetbagger, the bag in front represents the faults of others which he always sees. The bag in back represents his own faults which he never sees.

246

The Ku Klux Klan

Some white Southerners were totally opposed to Reconstruction. They formed a secret organization called the Ku Klux Klan. The Klan believed that black people were not entitled to the same rights as white people. Klan members rode around in white, ghostlike costumes with hoods that kept their faces hidden. They frightened blacks and sometimes harmed them to stop them from voting. They wanted to keep blacks from using their rights as citizens. The Klan did not have many members. But few people tried to stop the Klan. Bitterness and hatred continued to spread across the South.

Two members of the Ku Klux Klan in their disguises

Section Review

Write your answers on a sheet of paper.
1. What was sharecropping? How did it work?
2. What did the Freedmen's Bureau do to help blacks?
3. Explain what carpetbaggers and scalawags were.
4. What was the Ku Klux Klan?
5. Today there are many black government officials. Name two blacks who have served in local, state, or national government.

3 The New South

Reconstruction lasted from 1865 until 1877. During the Reconstruction years, the South began to rebuild, despite great bitterness and hardship. Soon people talked about a "new" South. But the problem of poor relations between blacks and whites remained for years, not only in the South but in Northern communities as well.

The End of Reconstruction

Reconstruction began to lose support in the 1870's. Many Northerners became disappointed in the Reconstruction governments in the South. Some of these governments were run by people who were corrupt. Some carpetbaggers and scalawags were stealing money from the people of the South.

Blacks were not able to show their support for Reconstruction. Organizations like the Ku Klux Klan frightened many blacks and prevented them from voting. Reconstruction governments gradually lost power. By 1876, Southern whites who were against Reconstruction had gained control in 8 of the 11 states of the old Confederacy.

There was great confusion in the 1876 election for President. It appeared that Samuel J. Tilden, the Democratic candidate, got more votes than Rutherford B. Hayes, the Republican candidate. But there were disagreements about the exact number of votes each man received. Congress appointed an electoral commission to decide the outcome of the election. The commission, which had more Republican members than Democratic members, announced that Hayes was the winner.

All over the nation, Democrats protested. Most Southerners were Democrats, and some of them even talked of war. Finally an agreement was made. Hayes would be President, but he would end Reconstruction by removing United States troops from the South. Under the Radical Reconstruction plan, United States troops had occupied the South to support Reconstruction governments. When

Campaign poster for Samuel Tilden in the 1876 Presidential election campaign

Hayes removed the United States troops, the last Reconstruction governments ended.

Jim Crow Laws

In the years after Reconstruction ended, the governments in the South passed laws that discriminated against blacks. These laws were passed to keep blacks from taking part in Southern society. Some Southern whites had used the name "Jim Crow" as an insulting way of referring to black people. These new laws were called Jim Crow laws. The purpose of the Jim Crow laws was to separate blacks from whites. This separation of people on the basis of race is called **segregation.**

Under Jim Crow laws, blacks had to ride in separate railroad cars, go to different schools, and even drink at separate water fountains. In 1896, the United States Supreme Court ruled that Jim Crow laws were legal if what the blacks had was equal to what the whites had.

At the same time, Southern governments passed laws that made it difficult for black men to vote. There were taxes that only blacks had to pay and tests that only blacks had to take before they could vote. Most blacks were poor and had never been allowed to learn to read and write. These laws kept most blacks from voting.

segregation

separation of people of different races

Jim Crow laws remained in effect in many Southern states until the middle of this century. This photograph shows that separate entrances were required for blacks and whites at this movie theater.

New Black Leaders

Life under the Jim Crow laws was very hard for Southern blacks. During this time, two new black leaders, each with different ideas, spoke out on the segregation issue.

Booker T. Washington was a teacher and a writer who had been born a slave. In 1881, he started a school for blacks in Tuskegee (tuss-**kee**-gee), Alabama. At his school, Tuskegee Institute, students studied farming, shoemaking, or carpentry. These were skills the students could use to earn a living.

Washington believed that if blacks educated themselves and learned skills, whites would eventually view blacks as equals. In this way, Washington believed segregation would gradually end.

W.E.B. Du Bois (doo **boyss**), a black author and editor, had very different views on how to end segregation. Du Bois believed segregation laws should be changed immediately. In 1909, Du Bois helped start the National Association for the Advancement of Colored People, called the NAACP for short. The NAACP, which still exists, worked to promote legal and political rights for blacks. With the help of the NAACP, some Jim Crow laws were declared illegal.

The New South

During the 1870's, cotton planting increased in the South. Sharecroppers began to grow cotton on the plantation lands. In new areas, including parts of Texas, cotton was planted for the first time. Old crops, such as tobacco, rice, and corn, were also being planted once again.

The South had always been a farming area. After the war, industry started to develop there too. In 1870, Birmingham, Alabama, was surrounded by cotton fields. By 1910, Birmingham was one of the country's leading iron and steel centers.

There were other changes as well. When textile mills began to be built in the early 1900's, small Southern farming towns became busy mill centers. Railroads damaged during the war were repaired, and new railroad lines were built. Improvements in transportation helped bring new industry to the South.

Booker T. Washington

W.E.B. Du Bois

By the early 1900's, the South was still mostly a farming area. But the industry of the new South was changing the way many Southerners worked and lived.

Sugar refinery in Louisiana after the Civil War

Section Review

Write your answers on a sheet of paper.

1. How was the dispute over the 1876 presidential election resolved?
2. What were Jim Crow laws?
3. Reconstruction was supposed to solve many problems in the South. Which of these problems continued to exist after 1877?
4. How was the new South different from the South before the Civil War?
5. Booker T. Washington and W.E.B. Du Bois had very different ideas on how to end segregation. What are some advantages to each man's approach?

Picturing the Civil War At the beginning of the Civil War, there were two ways to make pictures of events, places, and people. People could make a copy of a scene by drawing or painting it. Or they could use a new method of making pictures called photography. Mathew Brady and Winslow Homer were two Americans who used these arts to record scenes of the Civil War.

Mathew Brady was the most famous photographer of the Civil War period. Photography was still very new then. Brady was one of the pioneers of this new art.

Winslow Homer was one of the coun-

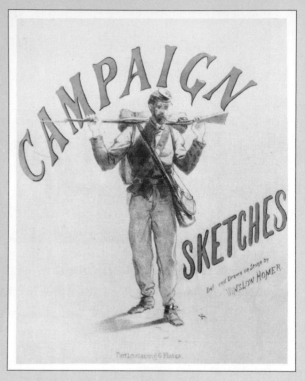

Title page of a book of Civil War sketches by Winslow Homer

Photograph by Mathew Brady showing Union army camp life in 1862

try's leading artists. Born in Massachusetts in 1836, Homer became famous as a magazine illustrator. He later became known for his paintings of the sea and ships.

When the Civil War broke out, both Brady and Homer went to the battlefront. Each re-created the events in his own way.

Brady formed a team with three other photographers—M. Alexander Gardner, Timothy O'Sullivan, and George N. Bernard. These men brought the heavy camera equipment to war areas. Sometimes they risked their lives to take pictures of the war. Brady and his team photographed towns that had been destroyed, soldiers, and battlefields.

There had been many paintings of battles before. But Brady and his team were the first to photograph actual battles and war conditions.

Winslow Homer had seen some of the war photographs. He was struck by how real they looked. Homer began to draw and paint his pictures to look like photographs. His pictures did not usually show particular battles. Instead Homer painted general scenes of army life. He showed what it was like to be a soldier.

One of his paintings, "A Sharp-shooter on Picket Duty," shows a single soldier sitting high up in a tree. The soldier is taking careful aim, his long rifle held steady against a branch.

Homer's most famous Civil War painting is "Prisoners from the Front." In the painting, a young Union officer faces a group of battered-looking Confederate soldiers.

Winslow Homer's paintings and the photographs by Brady's team gave many people in the United States firsthand views of war.

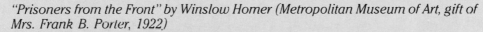

"Prisoners from the Front" by Winslow Homer (Metropolitan Museum of Art, gift of Mrs. Frank B. Porter, 1922)

UNIT REVIEW

Word Work

Write the sentences below on a sheet of paper. Fill in the blanks with the correct words from the list.

secede   abolitionist   overseer
       sharecropping   impeachment

1. A person who wanted to put an end to slavery was called an _____ .
2. Field slaves were watched by a boss called an _____ .
3. After the election of Abraham Lincoln in 1860, Southern states voted to _____ from the United States.
4. President Johnson was put through the process of _____ by Congress.
5. _____ was a system of farming that developed in the South after the Civil War.

Knowing the Facts

Write your answers on a sheet of paper.

1. What was the Underground Railroad? How did it work?
2. How did Congress try to balance the interests of free and slave states?
3. Why did Southern states secede from the United States?
4. What advantages did the South have during the Civil War? What were the advantages of the North?
5. How was the Radical Republicans' plan for Reconstruction different from the plans of Lincoln and Johnson?

Using What You Know

Choose one of the following activities to do. Follow the instructions given here.

1. Make a time line of the important developments in the United States from 1850 to 1877. Include at least seven events. Explain the importance of the events you chose.

2. Choose one person you have read about and write a two-page story of her or his life. Select a Civil War officer, black leader, or other individual who interests you. Use this textbook and an encyclopedia.

Skills Practice

Use these maps to answer the questions below. Write your answers on a sheet of paper.

1. At the beginning of the war, did the North or the South have more cities with a population of over 100,000?

2. Which side had the most railroads?

3. Which side had more advantages at the beginning of the war? Explain your answer.

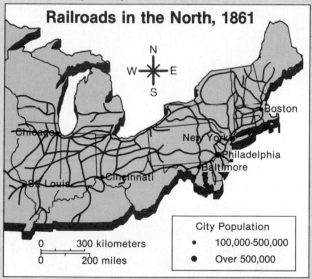

Railroads in the North, 1861

N
W E
S

Boston
Chicago
New York
Philadelphia
Baltimore
St. Louis
Cincinnati

0   300 kilometers
0   200 miles

City Population
• 100,000-500,000
● Over 500,000

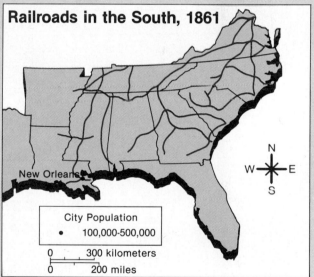

Railroads in the South, 1861

New Orleans

N
W E
S

City Population
• 100,000-500,000

0   300 kilometers
0   200 miles

Your Heritage

Thousands of soldiers have died for their country in wars. Often war memorials are built to honor them.

Find out from your local library if there are any war memorials in your community. Find out which wars are represented by these memorials. Write a short report about the memorials in your area.

UNIT

6

Growth
and Change

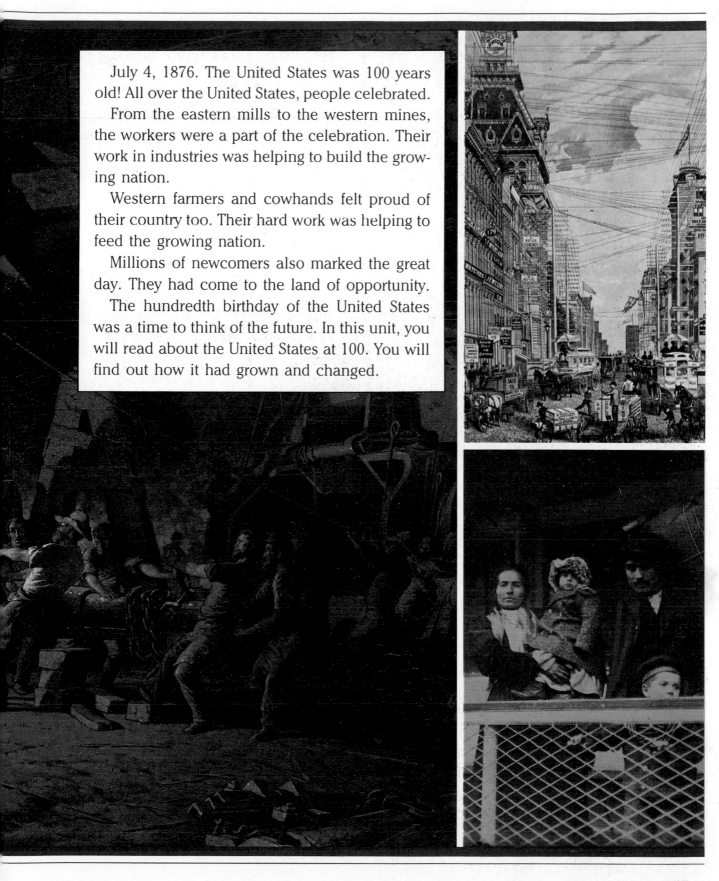

July 4, 1876. The United States was 100 years old! All over the United States, people celebrated.

From the eastern mills to the western mines, the workers were a part of the celebration. Their work in industries was helping to build the growing nation.

Western farmers and cowhands felt proud of their country too. Their hard work was helping to feed the growing nation.

Millions of newcomers also marked the great day. They had come to the land of opportunity.

The hundredth birthday of the United States was a time to think of the future. In this unit, you will read about the United States at 100. You will find out how it had grown and changed.

14 Changes on the Frontier

For many years, the Plains Indians had called the grasslands of the West their home. Powerful and free, they roamed over this vast region.

After the Civil War, many people from the East headed for the frontier to settle on the lands of the Plains Indians. They changed the West and the way the Indians lived. In this chapter, you will read about these changes on the western frontier.

At the end of this chapter, you should be able to:

○ Tell who the homesteaders were and how they lived.

● Interpret a cross-sectional diagram.

○ Describe mining and ranching in the West.

○ Explain why the American Indians and new settlers clashed on the western frontier.

1 Settling the West

In 1803, the Louisiana Purchase added the Great Plains and other areas to the United States. But for decades, few easterners settled there. To them, the plains sounded like a dangerous and difficult place to live. American Indians and buffalo herds roamed across the land. There were few trees for building houses, barns, and fences. The summers were very hot and the winters were very cold. Then, in 1862, Congress decided to give away some land in the plains. Congress passed a law called the Homestead Act.

The Homestead Act

Under the Homestead Act, any citizen 21 years or older could become the owner of 64 hectares (160 acres) of government land by living on it and farming it for five years. The people who went west to claim this free land were called **homesteaders.**

When the Civil War ended, thousands of homesteaders headed for Kansas, Nebraska, Colorado, and the Dakotas. They were soldiers, former slaves, and newcomers to the United States, all eager for their own land. Some traveled on horseback, others by wagon. But most of them headed for their new homes by railroad.

homesteader
a person who settled on government land and owned it after five years

Fast Travel and Good Land

In the mid-1860's, railroad companies added thousands of kilometers (miles) of track to their lines. The railroads reached farther and farther west. Still, most people thought it would be impossible to build a railroad all the way across the continent. In 1862, Congress decided to let two companies begin building a **transcontinental** railroad, or a railroad across the continent. It was completed in 1869.

The transcontinental railroad companies did more than

transcontinental
going from one side of the continent to the other

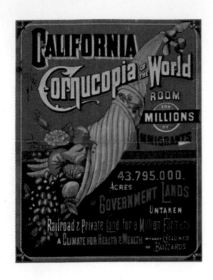

Railroad poster advertising the agricultural riches to be found in California

Newcomers on the railroad that will take them to their new homes in the West

build and run the railroads. The government had given them millions of hectares (acres) of land along their railroad tracks. The companies decided to sell this land to settlers.

Railroad land was near markets and transportation. It was often better than homestead land. In addition, the railroads lent money to settlers for farm equipment, seeds, and livestock. Railroad advertisements convinced many Americans to move to the West.

Agents from the railroads went to Europe to find customers for the land. Many people in Scandinavia, Germany, and Great Britain bought the cheap railroad land. Soon people from these countries arrived in the West. They went to Minnesota, Wisconsin, and the Dakotas. By 1880, 70 percent of the people living in these areas were newcomers to the United States or the children of newcomers.

Houses on the Prairie

The settlers who went to the Great Plains had to build houses. But there were few trees on the plains. Without trees, there could be no wooden houses. So many homesteaders built their first homes from grass and earth.

The grass, or sod, was a mass of tightly packed roots.

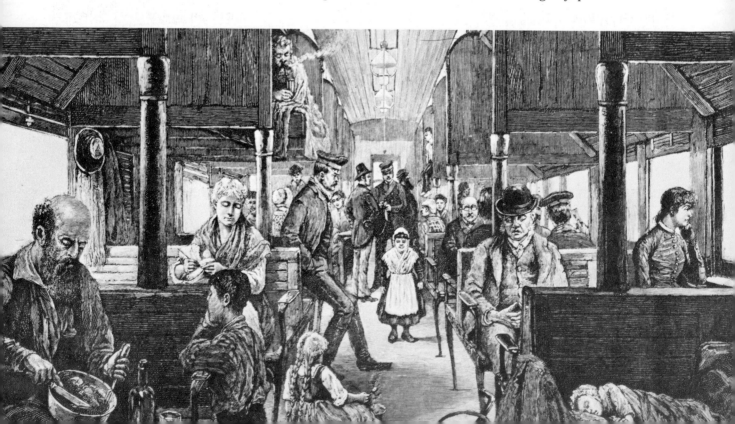

Large blocks of it were cut and used like bricks to build walls. Later on, the railroads brought wood, and the settlers were able to replace their sod homes with wooden ones.

Once their houses were built, the homesteaders planted crops. This meant plowing through the tough sod. Homesteaders spent so much time plowing that they were called sodbusters.

The homesteaders' main crops were wheat and corn. When it rained, the crops did well. But on the western part of the Great Plains, there was often not enough rain. Years of dry weather destroyed many crops. So did grasshoppers. In 1874, millions of these insects ate everything in sight.

The hard life drove many homesteaders back east. But others came to take their places. With irrigation and better equipment, the Great Plains eventually became the best farming area in the nation.

The Spees family, homesteaders on the Great Plains

Section Review

Write your answers on a sheet of paper.
1. What were the terms of the Homestead Act?
2. In what ways did the railroads help settle the West?
3. Why do you think people were willing to give up the things they were used to and become homesteaders?

Interpreting a Cross-sectional Diagram

The soil that lies beneath the thick grasses of the Great Plains is the richest soil anywhere on the earth. The cross-sectional diagram below shows what this prairie soil would look like if you could cut out a block of it and look at it from the side. As you can see, soil is composed of several layers.

The topsoil is the surface layer of the soil. Composed of much decayed plant material, it is the most fertile, or the richest, layer. From this layer, plant roots take in nutrients, or food. The roots of grasses or other forms of plant life combined with the topsoil form sod.

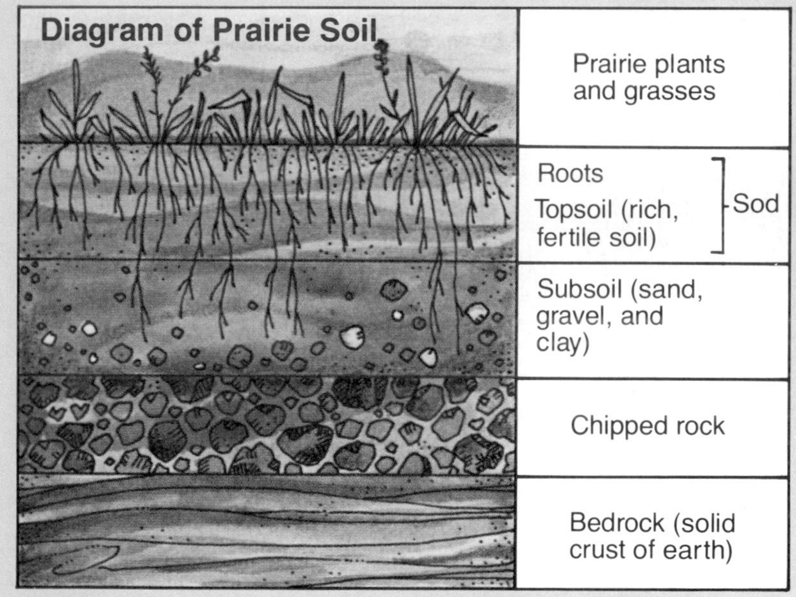

The subsoil is the next layer. It is a mixture of sand, gravel, and clay. Chipped rock and bedrock form the two bottom layers of soil. These layers hold no nutrients for plants. By studying the diagram, you can see why it was difficult for homesteaders to plow the land.

Diagram of Prairie Soil

Prairie plants and grasses
Roots / Topsoil (rich, fertile soil) — Sod
Subsoil (sand, gravel, and clay)
Chipped rock
Bedrock (solid crust of earth)

Practice Your Skills

1. In which layer of soil would you plant seeds? Why?
2. Why would deep sod be hard to plow?
3. What lies just below the topsoil? Would crops grow well in that layer? Why or why not?
4. Which do you think is the hardest layer?

2 Ranching and Mining

The land of the West was used for more than farms. The wide-open plains provided plenty of grass for large herds of cattle. And with every new discovery of gold and silver, more people rushed west, hoping to make their fortunes from this new rich land.

Cowhand in the snow

Home on the Range

Many ranchers made their way to Texas. The cattle there were a hardy breed with giant horns. The spread between the horns sometimes reached 2.7 meters (9 feet)! The Texans called the cattle longhorns.

At first, herds of longhorns could roam freely and still stay separate from other herds. The Texas grazing land, or **range,** was wide open. As the country became more settled, cattle from many different ranches roamed together. Ranchers placed a mark, or brand, on each animal's hide. The brand stood for a particular owner.

range

a large area of land where cattle graze

In the spring and fall, cowhands from each ranch rode out to round up their cattle. Life was hard for these cowhands. They lived out in the open for months at a time. They slept on the ground and ate poor food, working in rain and shine.

One of the cowhand's toughest jobs was the cattle drive—getting the cattle to market. To get the cattle to markets in Chicago, the cattle had to be driven from Texas to Abilene, Kansas. From there they were shipped by train to Chicago. In order to reach the railroad in Abilene, cowhands drove the cattle north. They could usually expect some kind of trouble during these long cattle drives. Often cattle thieves, called rustlers, would try to steal the cattle. Sometimes the cattle would get frightened and stampede, running wildly for kilometers (miles). Also, cattle could easily drown while crossing rivers. Crossing the homesteaders' land caused problems too.

Cowhands driving a herd of longhorn cattle

Range Wars

Conflicts developed between the homesteaders and ranchers. The ranchers felt that the open range belonged to them. Farms got in their way. The cowhands often allowed their herds to trample a farmer's fields and crops. At first, there was not much that farmers could do because they did not have fences that could stop the cattle.

Then, in 1873, a new type of wire fence was invented that solved the homesteaders' problem. Strands of steel wire were twisted together. Sharp points, or barbs, were spaced along the wires to make barbed wire.

The farmers used barbed-wire fences to keep cattle off

Advertisement for barbed wire

their fields. Then the ranchers began putting up barbed-wire fences too. They fenced in their herds on government land that they did not own. Sometimes they fenced in water holes so that farm animals could not get to them.

Angry farmers fought back. They cut the ranchers' wires. Soon both sides were cutting wires. Shooting wars, called range wars, began. They went on throughout the 1880's. Eventually the ranchers were forced to give up the public land or buy it for their herds. And later farmers began to raise cattle themselves. The days of the open range and the long cattle drives drew to a close.

Silver Dollars

While cowhands roamed the ranges for less than one dollar per day, miners rushed west to strike it rich. In 1849, the gold rush began in California. In 1859, a silver rush started in Nevada. Further discoveries of gold, silver, and copper continued to attract people to the West throughout the rest of the century.

Nevada, Colorado, and Montana were silver country. With a little luck, a miner could find $25 worth of silver in a stream each day. With a lot of luck, a miner could become a millionaire.

The silver in the streams was easily found. Miners scooped up gravel from the streambed and picked out the pieces of silver. More silver lay far below the ground. Deep mines had to be dug to get it. Large mills and refineries were built to process the silver. The silver mines and mills provided jobs for western workers. Later, when the silver became more difficult to find, copper was discovered. This mineral became as important as silver. The copper was used to make electrical wire.

Western miners built many cities and towns. Some, such as Denver, Colorado, and Boise, Idaho, became important industrial and population centers. Others were deserted as soon as the silver and copper ran out. Today these deserted towns, called ghost towns, can still be found in the valleys of the West.

Helena, Montana, in 1866

Section Review

Write your answers on a sheet of paper.
1. What were the cattle drives?
2. What led to range wars between the farmers and the ranchers?
3. Name some things that we use today that are made out of silver and copper.

3 A Way of Life Ends

In the first half of the nineteenth century, the United States government decided that the Mississippi River would be a dividing line. The land west of the river would be Indian Territory. No settlers could live there. This land was the homeland of hundreds of thousands of American Indians. The Plains Indians lived there. So did tribes from the southern and eastern United States. These tribes had been forced to move west when settlers took their lands.

The American Indians thought the western lands would be theirs forever. The United States government made this promise to them in 1830. Then white settlers started to arrive. At first, miners and traders simply passed across the Indian lands on their way to California. But by 1860, homesteaders and ranchers were settling on the plains. Railroad crews arrived too, and they began killing the Indians' most important resource—the buffalo.

Piles of buffalo skins

In 1860, there were about 300,000 American Indians on the Great Plains. Some 175,000 white Americans were living there too. But more white people were coming from the East and from California. Caught in the middle, the Indians tried to defend their land.

Trains and the Buffalo

The companies that built railroads across the plains opened the way west. The railroads carried people and supplies to farms and ranches. They brought mining equipment and weapons west. They shipped western grain and cattle east. Yet in opening the way west, the railroads also disrupted the Plains Indians' way of life.

The end to the Plains Indians' way of life started with the killing of the buffalo. Railroad crews, laying track, shot buffalo for food. Famous hunters such as "Buffalo Bill" Cody killed enough buffalo to feed 1,000 workers for more than a year. Even after the railroads were built, the hunting continued. Railroad workers feared that a racing herd of buffalo might overturn a train. They hired hunters to kill the buffalo.

At the same time, buffalo shooting became a sport. Rich easterners rode out to join in the hunt. Next came the hide hunters. Travelers bought buffalo coats and buffalo robes for warmth. In three years, hide hunters killed 9 million buffalo. Their hunting was wasteful because they used only the animals' hides.

Chief Red Cloud

In the 1860's, there had been about 12 million buffalo on the plains. By 1877, about 1,000 were left. The Plains Indians depended on the buffalo for food, clothing, and shelter. Without the buffalo, the Indians' way of life would end.

Fighting Back

Most American Indians decided to fight instead of accepting the loss of their lands and way of life. One tribe that fought back was the Sioux. The Sioux were a powerful tribe of the northern plains. They had modern guns, well-trained horses, and many fighters.

In 1862, a small group of Sioux in Minnesota attacked settlers who had taken their land. Soldiers caught 38 Sioux and hanged them. After that, other tribes also fought to protect their homelands.

The United States government sent thousands of soldiers to the West. These soldiers, trained to fight on horseback, were called cavalry. They built forts and patrolled American Indian territory. This action brought on more and more fighting.

The American Indians fought bravely. They won many battles and made many peace treaties. None of these treaties was honored by the United States government, however. The Indians could do little to stop the ever-spreading flow of soldiers and settlers. In the end, the Indians were forced to live on lands, called **reservations,** set aside for them by the government.

The Black Hills of South Dakota were part of the Sioux reservation. To the Sioux, these mountains were a holy place—the home of their god, or great spirit. In a treaty signed in 1868, the United States government promised that this land would be theirs forever.

In 1874, gold was discovered in the Black Hills. Gold-hungry miners invaded the Sioux holy land. The government tried to buy the land from the Sioux. The Sioux refused, and in 1876, United States soldiers marched into the area.

reservation
an area of land set aside by the government as a home for American Indians

"Buffalo Bill" Cody, at the left, with other buffalo hunters

Battle of the Little Bighorn

Colonel George Custer led some of the soldiers. Two chiefs leading the Sioux were Sitting Bull and Crazy Horse. Custer attacked the Sioux and their Cheyenne allies at the Little Bighorn River. It was one of the few battles in which the Indians were not outnumbered. Custer and all his men were killed.

It was a great victory for the American Indians. Yet it led to more suffering and loss of freedom. Outraged by Custer's defeat, the government took the Black Hills away from the Indians and sent more soldiers into the area. All winter, they hunted down and killed the Sioux. Crazy Horse was captured and killed. Sitting Bull escaped to Canada. The Sioux had most of their reservation taken from them. But they went back to live on the land that was still theirs.

Chief Joseph of the Nez Percés

Chief Joseph

The Nez Percé (**nezz** per-**say**) Indians lived west of the Rocky Mountains. This peaceful tribe had always gotten along well with whites. Then, in 1855, the United States took most of their territory in Idaho, Washington, and Oregon. Settlers and miners tried to take the rest in the 1870's.

In 1877, rather than lose the rest of their land, the Nez Percés fought back. United States soldiers were sent to force them off the land. The Nez Percé leader, Chief Joseph, resisted. After winning a few small battles, he and his followers decided it was best to leave the United States and escape to Canada. There they hoped to live in freedom. Soldiers chased them more than 2,720 kilometers (1,700 miles) and finally surrounded them, just 64 kilometers (40 miles) from the Canadian border. Over one half of Joseph's people were dead.

Chief Joseph surrendered when the government promised that the Nez Percés could return to their homeland. But the promise was broken. "I am tired of talk that comes to nothing," Chief Joseph wrote in 1879. "It makes my heart sick when I remember all the good words and all the broken promises." Most Nez Percés were sent to live on a reservation in Oklahoma. Unable to adjust to the change in climate, many died.

Closing the Frontier

By 1880, almost all the American Indians in the United States had been pushed onto reservations. The last to surrender was Geronimo. He was a leader of the Apaches, the fierce fighters of the Southwest.

Geronimo was greatly feared in Mexico and Arizona. His raids against miners, settlers, and soldiers came fast and often. Again and again, troops chased him through the mountains. He finally surrendered in 1886.

Geronimo's capture marked the end of the warfare between the American Indians and whites. After years of broken treaties and defeats in battle, the Indians' traditional way of life came to an end.

Geronimo

Section Review

Write your answers on a sheet of paper.
1. Why did the buffalo disappear from the Great Plains?
2. Why did Colonel Custer march against the Sioux?
3. Explain how the railroads both helped and hurt people living on the Great Plains.

15 Industrial Growth

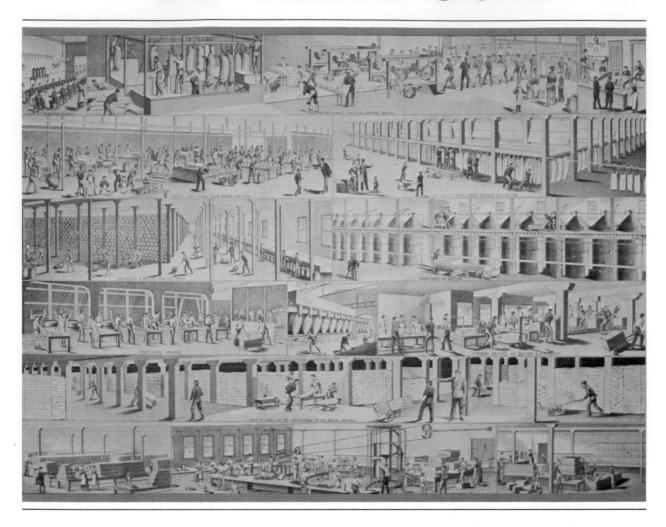

Interior of a pork packing plant

During the second half of the 1800's, the United States entered the industrial age. Mines, mills, factories, and railroads were expanding and improving. American inventors contributed to this industrial growth. In this chapter, you will read about the growth of industry in the United States.

At the end of this chapter, you should be able to:

○ Explain how the growth of railroads helped American industries to grow.

○ Trace the growth of big business in the United States.

● Use an index to locate cities on a map.

○ Tell how inventions changed life and business.

● Use a pictograph to measure increases in production.

1 The Railroad Boom

By 1893, there were almost 320,000 kilometers (200,000 miles) of railroad track in our country. That is enough to circle the world eight times! More people worked for the railroads than for any other industry.

It took huge amounts of steel, iron, and wood to build the railroads. Railroad companies bought as much steel as Americans could make. Whole forests were cut down to make railroad ties.

Many industries began to move their goods by rail. Railroads made it possible for many Americans to buy things not made or grown near their homes. For example, a woman or man in Vermont could make bread with Minnesota flour and bake it in an Ohio-made stove.

The Transcontinental Railroad

Many Americans hoped a transcontinental railroad would be built to link the eastern and western halves of the continent. Such a railroad would make it easier for farmers and factory owners to move food and goods. The railroad would also help passengers who wanted to travel across the country. By 1864, two companies had started to build a railroad across the United States.

Starting in Sacramento, California, the Central Pacific Company worked eastward. The company had to cut through the Sierra Nevada (see-**err**-uh nuh-**vad**-uh) Mountains. The workers drilled and blasted through the mountains. They bridged deep valleys and wide canyons.

More than 10,000 of the workers who built the railroad were newcomers from China. After working on the railroad, many of the Chinese stayed in this country.

Meanwhile, the Union Pacific Company was building westward. Since railroads already linked the east with the midwest, the company started in Omaha, Nebraska, and worked across the flat plains of the midwest. Most of the Union Pacific workers were Irish newcomers.

Finally the two tracks were joined at Promontory (**prom**-un-tor-ee), Utah. On May 10, 1869, Irish and Chinese workers put the last two rails in place. The last spike—a golden one—was pounded into the rail with a silver hammer. The east and west were linked.

People all across the nation cheered the news of the completion of the transcontinental railroad. Fire station bells rang out in Philadelphia, Pennsylvania, and people waved American flags when they heard the news. In Omaha, Nebraska, 100 guns were fired, and fireworks lit up the sky as part of the celebration. In Chicago, Illinois, thousands of people marched through the streets in a parade.

The Railroads Combine

By 1875, dozens of railroads crisscrossed every eastern state. Each railroad company had its own route and set its own prices, or rates.

There were so many railroad companies in the United States that passengers could often choose from among several. The railroad companies competed with each other for customers. This kept rates low. However, it was not convenient to use many small lines. Someone traveling a long distance usually had to change railroad lines several times along the way.

Union Pacific railroad workers excavating a canyon to lay tracks for the transcontinental railroad

By 1880, the railroad companies began to combine, or **consolidate.** Bigger railroad companies bought smaller ones. This meant people and freight could travel farther on the same line.

As the railroad companies became bigger, their owners became more powerful. The small group of railroad owners often discussed what prices to charge. They set rates that were similar and high.

consolidate
to combine or unite

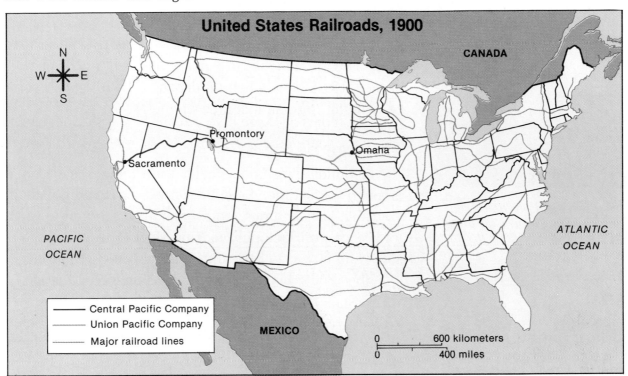

United States Railroads, 1900

Central Pacific Company
Union Pacific Company
Major railroad lines

PACIFIC OCEAN

ATLANTIC OCEAN

CANADA

MEXICO

Promontory

Omaha

Sacramento

0   600 kilometers
0   400 miles

Section Review

Write your answers on a sheet of paper.
1. In what ways did the railroad help other American industries to grow?
2. What two groups of newcomers were most responsible for building the transcontinental railroad?
3. In what ways did railroad consolidation help people who used the railroads? How did it hurt them?
4. Rail travel had a tremendous effect on American life. Name some changes brought about by the development of rail travel.

2 Steel and Oil

In 1844, some surveyors in Minnesota noticed something unusual. The magnetic needle of their compass swung crazily from side to side. They soon learned the reason. Beneath their feet lay the world's greatest deposit of iron ore, the basic element used in making steel.

A few years later, a Pennsylvania man also came upon something unusual. Near his house, a greasy, black ooze seeped up through the ground. He tried lighting the ooze. It burned! He had found an oil deposit. The oil would soon become an important source of energy.

The Age of Steel

As a building material, steel has advantages over iron. It is tough yet flexible. It can be shaped, or **forged,** without cracking. For centuries, ironworkers had labored in small forges, or iron factories, making steel. The process was slow, and only small amounts of steel could be produced.

In the 1850's, two men, working separately, developed a way to speed up the steel-making process. One of the men, William Kelly, was a Kentucky kettle maker. The other, Henry Bessemer (**bess**-uh-mer), was an English factory owner.

The new process they both developed meant that steel could be made on a large scale. The process became known as the Kelly-Bessemer method. What was needed next was someone who understood the importance of the new process. Using the Kelly-Bessemer method, the right person could develop a huge, money-making industry out of the production of steel.

Andrew Carnegie, Man of Steel

In his youth, telegraph messenger Andrew Carnegie (**kahr**-nuh-gee) earned $2.50 per week. By the time he retired, his fortune was worth $250 million. In making his fortune, Carnegie helped shape the steel industry in the United States.

At the age of 18, Carnegie went to work for the Pennsyl-

The first oil well in the United States, and the man who drilled it, E.L. Drake, who is at the right

forge

to work into shape by heating or hammering

vania Railroad. Carnegie learned that iron was a poor construction material for the railroad. Iron rails often cracked and had to be replaced. Iron bridges weakened under a train's weight. Carnegie knew that steel would be a stronger building material. He began working on ways to increase steel production.

Carnegie saved some money and used it to buy part of a small iron company. Eventually he became the owner of several companies. After he learned about the Kelly-Bessemer method of making steel, Carnegie decided to build a huge steel mill. He bought iron and coal mines in Minnesota. He bought ships and trains to transport the iron and coal. Never in the history of the United States had there been such a powerful businessman. By 1900, Carnegie's steel mill was producing 2.7 million tonnes (3 million tons) of steel per year.

In 1901, when his business was at its peak, Carnegie sold it. He retired and spent much of his time and money on projects to help others. Carnegie especially loved libraries. He started more than 2,800 of them in the United States and around the world.

Steel plant in Bethlehem, Pennsylvania

The Oil Business

The first oil drilling in the United States was done by Edwin Drake in Titusville (**tite**-us-vill), Pennsylvania, in 1859. In the same year, John D. Rockefeller left his home in Cleveland, Ohio. He went to Pennsylvania hoping to make his fortune in the oil business. Drilling wells seemed too risky to him. But he knew he could make money **refining** crude oil, or changing it into usable products such as kerosene, a liquid fuel.

Back in Cleveland, Rockefeller opened a refinery. He had a good mind for business. Soon he was able to buy up many small refineries in the Cleveland area.

Rockefeller's company, Standard Oil, was able to use railroad rates to drive other oil refineries out of business. Since he shipped so much oil by rail, Rockefeller could demand cheaper shipping rates from the railroad companies. Smaller refineries had to pay the full rates. Because their transportation costs were higher, small refineries could not sell oil as cheaply as Rockefeller could. Many small oil companies failed, and Rockefeller bought them.

refining

making finer or purer

Cartoon illustrating the powerful hold Standard Oil had on government and industry

The many different companies that made up Standard Oil were run by Rockefeller and those in business with him. In 1882, this group of companies, or **trust,** produced about 90 percent of the country's oil.

Many people complained that Standard Oil had grown too big. The company had complete control over the oil-refining industry. It was a **monopoly.** People demanded that Standard Oil be broken up into smaller, competing companies. In 1892, the company was divided up.

Rockefeller reorganized Standard Oil. He wanted to continue to direct the business of the smaller oil companies. But in 1911, the United States Supreme Court ruled that Standard Oil had too much control over the industry. It was divided once again into separate, competing companies.

Trusts and Big Business

Standard Oil set a pattern for big business in the United States. Other business people tried to gain control in their industries. Trusts soon controlled the production of sugar, tobacco, cattle, salt, leather, and even bicycles.

The big companies forced many small companies to close or sell out to them. As a result, there was less variety in many American products. But in some cases, big companies could make and sell goods more cheaply. From 1865 to 1897, prices fell steadily in the United States.

trust
a group of businesses that unite in order to control the production and price of certain goods

monopoly
a company that completely controls an industry

Section Review

Write your answers on a sheet of paper.
1. Why did the railroads prefer to use steel rather than iron for rails?
2. How did Andrew Carnegie make his fortune? How did he use his fortune to help others?
3. How did Standard Oil use the railroads to establish a monopoly?
4. Why would products lose variety if a few big companies controlled an industry?

Using Atlas Coordinates

OHIO
(Map on page 41)

Cincinnati A4
Circleville B3
Cleveland C1
Columbus B3
Coshocton C2
Dayton A3
Defiance A1
Delaware B2
Elyria C1
Euclid C1
Findlay B2

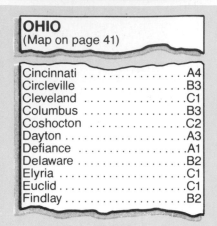

Ten different Presidents served the United States in the years between the Civil War and 1900. Five of them, including Rutherford B. Hayes, were born in Ohio. If Hayes had been born in a large city, such as Cleveland, it would be easy to find his birthplace on a map. But Hayes was born in the small town of Delaware, Ohio. To locate that town on a map, you would use an atlas index.

Notice that in an atlas index, two map coordinates are listed for each city and town. To find the town of Delaware, Ohio, in this atlas, you would look up the coordinates for Delaware in the index and turn to the map of Ohio on page 41. Then you would look for the coordinates for Delaware—B2—on that map. The letter coordinates appear along the top of the map. The number coordinates appear along the side of the map. Delaware is located in the box where row B meets row 2.

Practice Your Skills

1. What are the coordinates for Cleveland? for Circleville?
   Which city is closer to Delaware?
2. What are the coordinates for Columbus? for Dayton?
   Which city is closer to Cleveland? to Cincinnati?
3. What three cities are found in C1?

3 The Age of Invention

In 1790, the founders of the United States passed the first **patent** laws. A patent (**pat**-unt) is a government document that protects an inventor. For a certain number of years, only the inventor can make or sell a patented invention. No one can copy it.

The period following the Civil War brought a rush for patents by American inventors. But even before then, inventors had started to change the way Americans worked and lived.

Inventions on the Farm

The farmers on the plains had big problems. One problem was their plows. Instead of the plows breaking the sod, the sod often broke their wooden plows. Iron plows were not much better. When the sod was wet, it stuck to the iron plow.

A blacksmith named John Deere solved the farmers' problem. Deere tried making his steel saw into a plow. It cut through sod cleanly. Deere's steel plow made it easier to plow the sod plains.

patent

a government document that gives an inventor the right to make and sell a new invention for a certain number of years

Threshing machine on a farm in Oregon

In 1847, Cyrus McCormick opened a factory in Chicago to manufacture the reaper. Within a few years, he was selling thousands of his machines. McCormick's success encouraged others to invent new machines for agriculture. Machines soon plowed, planted, hoed, and harvested. With machinery to help, fewer people were needed to work on the farms. Americans became the most productive farmers on earth.

Bell's Telephone

Sound and speech were what mattered most to Alexander Graham Bell. Like his father, the Scottish-born inventor was an authority on sound. He spent hours studying how the human ear worked. During the day, he taught deaf people to speak. At night, he worked on his inventions.

Bell and his assistant, Thomas Watson, discovered how to send sound waves over wire. In 1876, Bell patented the telephone. It was probably the most important patent ever given.

By 1900, there were about one million telephones in the United States. The use of the telephone improved communications in business and family life. Business people could talk to buyers and sellers who worked far from them. Big companies with many offices could keep in constant touch by telephone. People could "visit" with relatives and friends who lived in far away places by means of the telephone. Thanks to the telephone, news could travel faster.

Alexander Graham Bell at the opening of the long distance telephone line from New York to Chicago in 1892

People could tell others of important events as soon as they happened. Bell's invention changed the lives of people around the world.

Henry Ford's Automobiles

Henry Ford was not the first person to think of a self-powered automobile. A steam bus had chugged through London five years before Ford was born. By 1904, Henry Ford was one of 178 American automobile makers.

Most people made cars for the rich. Ford wanted to make an automobile that anyone could afford. To keep prices low, he looked for ways to build cars quickly. Ford decided to build cars using an **assembly line.** Workers stood in a line alongside a moving belt. Cars were built, or assembled, on the belt. The belt moved the cars from one worker to the next. Each worker put a different piece of the car into place. At the end of the assembly line, a finished car rolled off the belt. By 1915, Ford's Detroit, Michigan, factory could produce a car from start to finish in just 93 minutes.

As time went by, the assembly line reduced costs. The early Ford car, called the Model T, cost $950 in 1909. In 1917 it cost only $345. In that year, Ford sold 730,000 of his Model T's.

assembly line
a method of producing goods in which workers put together a product as it moves past them on a moving belt

The final stage of the Ford Motor Company's assembly line in 1913

The Wrights in Flight

At about the same time that Ford was building his first cars in Detroit, Wilbur and Orville Wright were building a gasoline-powered airplane in Dayton, Ohio. They tried it out on a windy beach at Kitty Hawk, North Carolina, on December 17, 1903. The brothers made four successful flights that day. The longest flight lasted almost a minute and covered about 260 meters (852 feet).

The Wright Brothers' first flight at Kitty Hawk, North Carolina

The Wrights kept working to improve their airplanes. Their planes took them higher and farther. Their aircraft was patented in 1906. By 1909, they began manufacturing and selling them.

The first airplane flights did little to change people's daily lives. Then, in 1914, a plane was used to carry passengers from one part of Florida to another. Four years later, the post office began offering airmail service from

New York City to Washington, D.C. The age of air transportation had begun.

Changes at Work and at Home

Inventions changed office and factory life. At one time, all business letters and reports had to be written by hand. People spent hours copying words and numbers. Then, in 1867, C.L. Sholes, a Wisconsin printer, developed the typewriting machine. Within 15 years, almost every office had at least one typewriter. By the early 1900's, another new invention was being tried out in some factories. Air conditioners were used to make the air cooler and cleaner.

Another invention led to changes in the size and shape of new buildings. The invention of the electric elevator in 1889 led to the construction of tall buildings, called skyscrapers. City centers became more crowded as more people and businesses moved into the skyscrapers.

Inventions were beginning to make changes in people's home life too. Many helpful inventions followed the development of electricity by several scientists in the 1870's. The electric vacuum cleaner, invented in 1899, helped homemakers do their work faster and more effectively. So did the invention of the electric washing machine in 1907.

An early model of the washing machine

Section Review

Write your answers on a sheet of paper.

1. In what way did John Deere's invention make farms more productive?
2. How did Henry Ford change production methods in his factory? What effect did this have?
3. Choose three inventions described in this section and explain how they saved time for the people who used them.
4. Name a recent invention and explain how it is changing people's lives.

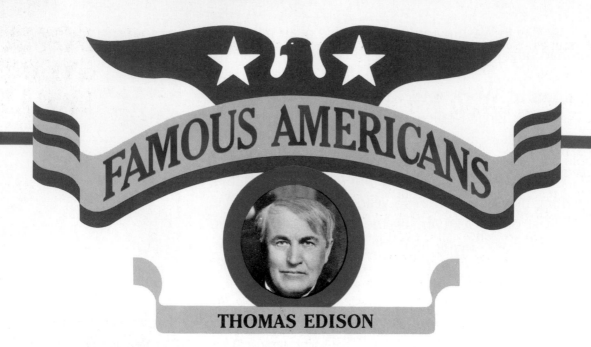

FAMOUS AMERICANS

THOMAS EDISON

Thomas Alva Edison was an American hero in his own time. Edison was a self-made man. He taught himself most of what he knew. And his inventions made life easier for people everywhere.

Thomas Edison may have been the world's greatest inventor. He was granted more than 1,000 patents. His inventions, and improvements on other people's inventions, made possible many of the things we take for granted in modern life.

Edison invented a light bulb for home and office use. The light bulb was much easier to use than gas lights or kerosene lamps.

Edison improved early models of the telegraph, telephone, and motion-picture camera and projector. His most unusual invention, however, was the phonograph. The first words Edison recorded to be played back on his machine were "Mary had a little lamb." Many people who heard it for the first time in 1877 were amazed. They could not believe a machine could "speak."

The man who became known as a wizard was full of curiosity as a boy. He never stopped asking questions about how different things were made or how they worked. For every question, he performed experiments to find the answer. By the time he was 12, he was an expert in chemistry and physics.

Edison was interested in many subjects. Throughout his life, he studied literature, medicine, and music as well as science.

People asked him how it felt to be a genius. He replied, "Genius is one percent inspiration and 99 percent perspiration." Today people's lives are full of light and sound that Edison's hard work helped to make possible.

Interpreting a Pictograph

Before 1908, when Henry Ford built his first Model T, automobiles were rare in the United States. At that time, only the rich could afford automobiles. The pictograph below shows how automobile production increased after Ford began assembly-line production of the Model T.

A pictograph presents information by means of symbols. A pictograph symbol stands for a number of objects or an amount. Part of a symbol represents a fraction of the number or of the amount.

In this pictograph, each Model T symbol stands for 100,000 automobiles, so a half symbol stands for 50,000 cars and a quarter symbol stands for 25,000 cars. Smaller fractions of the symbol, such as the one next to the year 1900 on this pictograph, are hard to read precisely. Here the wheel represents 8,000 cars, or less than one tenth of a whole symbol. To figure the number of cars produced each year, add all the symbols and symbol fractions.

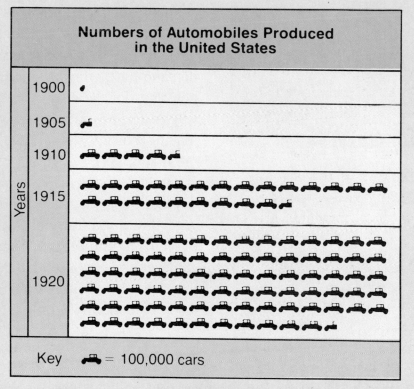

Numbers of Automobiles Produced in the United States

Key 🚗 = 100,000 cars

Practice Your Skills

1. What does the key on this graph tell you?
2. About how many cars were produced in 1910?
3. How many more cars were produced in 1915 than in 1910? in 1920 than in 1910?

4 People with New Ideas

In the late 1800's, the United States was changing more rapidly than ever. Along with new industries and inventions, Americans began to look at their surroundings in new ways.

New Plants and Food Products

George Washington Carver was a former slave. He used his knowledge of science and his imagination to help southern agriculture. By 1880, cotton had worn out much southern soil. Carver urged southerners to plant soybeans, peanuts, and sweet potatoes. These crops restored important minerals to the soil. But when farmers followed Carver's advice, they had trouble selling the new crops. The demand for them was small. So Carver worked on finding new uses for the crops. Over the years, he found 300 new ways to use peanuts and sweet potatoes. People were soon making plastics, dyes, flour, medicines, and fertilizer from the plants.

Luther Burbank also put plants to work for people. In his huge gardens, he produced over 800 new varieties of fruits, vegetables, and flowers. Once he tested 30,000 new kinds of plums to find the one that tasted best. His most famous achievement was the Idaho potato. It is said that this potato added a billion dollars' worth of business to the world's economy in only 50 years.

Modern Architecture

Louis Sullivan was a leader in developing a new type of architecture. At the turn of the century, most buildings were still being modeled after styles that had been popular for centuries. Many banks, for example, were designed to look like Greek temples. Sullivan felt that buildings should have no unnecessary lines or parts. Sullivan designed buildings whose style reflected their use. The Wainwright Building in St. Louis, Missouri, was a skyscraper he designed.

George Washington Carver

The Wainwright Building in St. Louis, Missouri designed by Louis Sullivan

An American Writer

Samuel Clemens, known as Mark Twain, wrote the way many frontier Americans really spoke. He proved that American writers could gain an audience without using the formal style of writing that was popular in Great Britain.

Twain was an adventurer. He grew up in a Missouri town, but his travels took him all over the United States. In novels such as *Huckleberry Finn* and *Tom Sawyer,* he captured the American spirit of adventure.

Samuel Clemens, known as Mark Twain

Section Review

Write your answers on a sheet of paper.

1. What important problem did George Washington Carver solve?

2. What was new about Mark Twain's style of writing?

3. George Washington Carver found new uses for crops. Name some things you use today in school that are made out of plants.

CHAPTER 16 Cities, People, and Industry

Hester Street in New York City as painted by George Luks

By 1890, many cities in the United States had grown. They were lively places, with wonderful sights to see and things to do. Many of them, however, were overcrowded. Many city people worked in dangerous factories and lived in poor housing. How did the cities get that way? In this chapter, you will find out. You will also learn about the people who lived and worked in the cities of the United States. And you will read about some Americans who tried to improve the conditions in the cities.

At the end of this chapter, you should be able to:

○ Describe how and why cities in the United States grew.
○ Name some problems that factory workers faced.
○ Explain why newcomers came to the United States.
● Read a time zone map.
○ Explain the Progressive Movement.

1 American Cities Grow

As industry grew in the United States, so did the nation's cities. Many businesses built their factories in or near cities. Cities provided factory owners with local markets for their goods and with transportation to distant markets. Cities attracted **immigrants,** or newcomers, to the United States, providing factory owners with the workers they needed. Young Americans who had been born on farms or in small towns also came to cities to find new kinds of work to do and new, exciting places to live.

By 1900, there were 38 cities in the United States that had more than 100,000 people. The United States was becoming an **urban** nation—a nation of cities.

Problems of City Life

Many cities grew quickly. There was no time to prepare for their growth. Immigrants needed places to live right away. Some city homes were turned into rooming houses to ease the housing shortage. Many small buildings were torn down. In their place, builders put up **tenements,** or crowded apartment houses.

immigrant
a foreign-born settler

urban
having to do with a city or cities

tenement
apartment house, especially one that is run-down, very crowded, or poorly built

Interior of a tenement in New York City around 1889

The early tenements were poorly built. Many rooms had no windows. Whole blocks of buildings had no pipes to supply fresh water. There was no good way to get rid of waste water, or sewage, either. And when winter came, many tenements had no heat.

Most of the people who lived in the tenements were new to the cities. They were poor and had nowhere else to live. A crowded area of a city with poor housing is called a **slum.** As cities grew, so did the slums.

Diseases spread rapidly in many slums, partly because drinking water was often unclean and partly because of overcrowding. Outbreaks of disease made officials in some cities realize that slums were dangerous. Some cities passed laws to have water lines built that would carry water to all parts of the city. They had sewage lines built to carry away waste. People were hired to collect and remove trash.

City officials also had to fight another problem—fires. Fires spread quickly in the crowded cities. In 1871, a huge fire destroyed most of Chicago. The next year, Boston had a major fire. To prevent fires, some cities and states outlawed the construction of wooden buildings. They also ruled that new buildings had to be spaced farther apart to keep fires from spreading so quickly.

Busy Streets

As the cities grew, more and more people crowded the streets. Many immigrants sold goods from wagons or pushcarts. Others did business from stands and tables on city sidewalks. To get around the city, most people had to

Rear of a tenement building in New York City

walk. Some cities had streetcars that were pulled by horses. But the streetcars were slow.

By the end of the 1800's, electric streetcars called trolley cars had been installed in some cities. The trolley cars enabled people to travel more quickly within the cities. By using the trolleys, people could get to work faster or look for work in other neighborhoods. They could also visit neighborhoods outside their own.

There was much noise and activity in the streets of many cities. Workers were digging trenches to hold water and sewer pipes. They also put down gas lines. In addition, the first telephone and electric wires were being strung overhead. In some cities, the wires seemed to fill the sky.

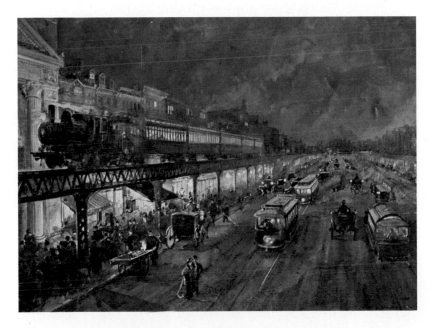

The busy streets of New York City as painted by Louis Sonntag in 1895

Section Review

Write your answers on a sheet of paper.
1. What groups of people were moving to the cities in the early 1900's?
2. What types of transportation did people in cities use?
3. Do cities still have problems with poor housing and frequent fires? List some other problems people are trying to solve in today's cities.

2 Workers and Factories

Many of the people who worked in factories in the United States during the late 1800's were unhappy with conditions. They believed that factory owners were getting rich, while they worked long hours for low pay.

Eventually the workers decided to act. They joined together to ask for shorter workdays. They asked for better pay and safer workplaces too.

Mass Production

Large factories were able to produce goods quickly and cheaply by using machines to do the easier tasks. Making many goods quickly by machine is called **mass production.** Prices fell because goods could be produced so quickly. Many Americans could suddenly afford things they could never before buy.

Mass production also changed the lives of most workers. Most factory jobs were not very satisfying. Working on an assembly line in a factory meant that a worker had to do the same task over and over, day after day. Instead of taking pride in their work, many workers became bored and unhappy.

mass production

the use of machines to manufacture goods cheaply and quickly

Women packing chipped meat in cans on an assembly line in Chicago, Illinois

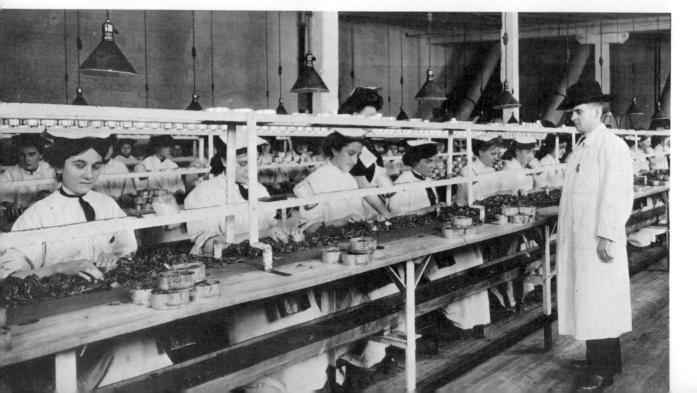

Children working in a vegetable cannery in Baltimore, Maryland

Poor Working Conditions

Some workers were also unhappy about their working conditions. In 1900, the average worker earned less than $10 per week. This was considered very low pay. Many workers made much less. Some did not earn enough to feed their families.

In some industries, people were paid for each piece of work they finished. A clothing worker might be paid a penny for every shirt he or she sewed together. People had to work very quickly to make enough money to support themselves.

What made things worse was that many factories were unhealthy and unsafe. Workers did not wear masks to protect their lungs from dangerous gases. Workers handled harsh chemicals without wearing gloves to protect their hands. Some people, trying to work 12-hour days, actually fell asleep at their jobs. Some were injured or killed by machinery. Those who were injured received no help or money from their employers.

In many of these dangerous workplaces, a large number of the workers were children. In 1890, more than one million girls and boys under age 16 were working. They spent 12-hour days in mills, mines, and factories.

Labor Unions

Slowly workers in the United States realized that they would have to group together to improve their working conditions. The groups they formed to fight for their rights were called **labor unions.**

The first unions were made up of people who worked at the same craft. Printers were in one union, and carpenters, in another. Later, unions were formed that tried to bring together all the workers in an industry. For example, the American Railway Union was open to almost all railway workers, no matter what their job.

In 1886, several different unions decided to work together. These unions formed the American Federation of Labor, or the AFL. The AFL only permitted skilled workers to join the union. But, by 1900, the AFL had about half a million members. The AFL's first president was Samuel Gompers, an immigrant from Great Britain.

Each union in the AFL helped the others fight for better pay, shorter hours, and safer workplaces. Gompers encouraged union leaders to bargain with factory owners and employers for better wages and shorter working hours. When bargaining failed, union members sometimes went on **strike.** When workers strike, they refuse to return to their jobs until an agreement is reached with their employers. With the AFL's support, striking workers were able to win some improvements. By 1918, the unions had become a strong political force in the United States.

labor union
organization of workers which tries to improve its members' wages and working conditions

strike
a refusal to work until workers can reach an agreement with their employer

Section Review

Write your answers on a sheet of paper.
1. How did mass production change workers' lives?
2. What are labor unions? What working conditions did they want to change in the late 1800's?
3. How might your life be different if you lived in the early 1900's and worked in a factory?

3 Nation of Immigrants

Between 1865 and 1915, about 26 million immigrants came to the United States. They came from different lands and for different reasons. But the immigrants all had one thing in common. They all saw the United States as a land of hope and opportunity.

Immigration Before 1890

Until the 1890's, most immigrants came from northern and western Europe. They came from Ireland, Germany, Scotland, England, Norway, and Sweden. In Europe, most of them had been farmers who worked on someone else's land.

The promise of owning large farms drew most of these immigrants to the United States. Land was much cheaper in the United States. After 1862, the Homestead Act offered free land in the western United States to those who promised to settle there. Thousands of immigrants took advantage of this act.

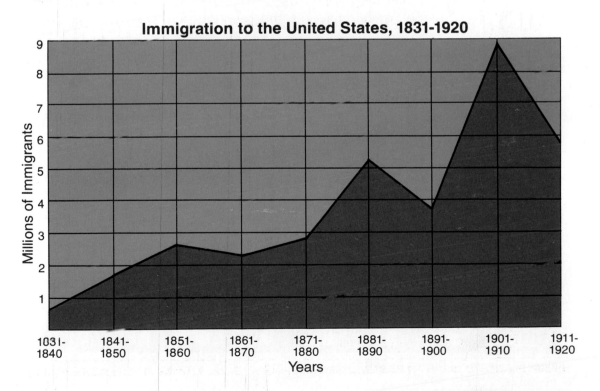

Immigration to the United States, 1831-1920

Years

Millions of Immigrants

Immigrants came from northern and western Europe for other reasons too. Many Germans came to escape being treated unfairly for their religious and political beliefs. Many Irish came to escape hunger. The potato was a major source of food in Ireland. When potato crops began to fail in 1845, thousands of Irish people left for the United States.

Immigration After 1890

As the years passed, the pattern of immigration changed. By the 1890's, about 52 of every 100 American immigrants were from southern and eastern Europe. The new immigrants came from Italy, Greece, Poland, and Russia.

Many of these immigrants came to escape poverty. In Italy, much of the land was no longer fertile. Old-fashioned farming methods could not produce enough food. In Greece, too, agriculture had failed. Greek workers faced low wages and high prices. Conditions were so bad there that one out of every four male workers in Greece moved to the United States.

Other immigrants came to escape unfair laws. For a long time, different peoples under Russian rule, including Poles, Finns, and Lithuanians, had been allowed to speak their own languages and keep their customs. Suddenly the Russian government demanded that these groups become

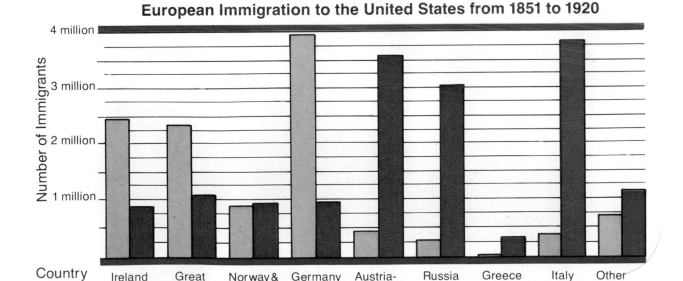

European Immigration to the United States from 1851 to 1920

Number of Immigrants

Country of Origin: Ireland, Great Britain, Norway & Sweden, Germany, Austria-Hungary, Russia, Greece, Italy, Other European

■ 1851-1890   ■ 1891-1920

more like Russians. Rather than do this, many of these people moved to the United States.

Almost 40 percent of the people who came from Russia and nearby Poland were Jewish. Jews had long been the victims of unfair laws in eastern Europe. They were forced to live in separate areas and were not allowed to hold certain jobs. To escape these conditions, they settled in the United States.

By the time these newer immigrants arrived in the United States, much of the good farmland had been claimed. So these immigrants settled in or near cities. They worked in factories, mines, and mills.

Immigrants from Asia

Another important attraction for immigrants was gold. News of the California gold rush of 1849 spread around the world. Some Chinese were drawn to the United States when they heard that gold had been discovered. By 1852, about 25,000 Chinese had reached California. By 1880, the number of Chinese immigrants had risen to 100,000.

Most of the first Chinese immigrants were young men. They thought of the United States as a place to make money quickly. Some returned to China with their gold. But many others stayed and opened their own businesses. Thousands worked on the transcontinental railroad. By 1884, half of California's agricultural workers were Chinese.

Chinese immigrants in San Francisco, California

Immigrants waiting to enter the United States around 1900

Hawaii was a stepping-stone to the United States for many Japanese. Japanese workers began arriving in Hawaii in 1885. They were invited there by American sugar and pineapple planters. Farm labor in Hawaii was always in short supply.

Beginning in the 1890's, many Japanese began moving to the United States. By 1910, more than 70,000 Japanese had moved on to California. Like the Chinese, the Japanese often worked in agriculture. Many of the Japanese immigrants bought or rented land in California. Often, they took the land no one else wanted. Through hard work and scientific methods, Japanese farmers turned the land into rich farms.

Agriculture helped the Japanese succeed in the United States. By 1920, Japanese immigrants owned or rented almost 200,000 hectares (500,000 acres) of farmland. In addition to farms, the Japanese started fishing and canning businesses too.

Problems of Immigrants

Once they got to the United States, immigrants faced many problems. One of their most immediate problems was language. Most immigrants came from countries where English was not spoken. When they arrived in the United States, they did not understand the street signs or newspapers. It was difficult to find a job. They could not communicate with most Americans. To solve this problem, many immigrants took special classes to learn English.

Immigrant children attending school

The immigrants who settled in the cities had another problem. Most of them had lived on farms in their native lands. Suddenly the immigrants found themselves in crowded cities. Their way of life changed completely. It was a difficult change to get used to.

Some immigrants were made to feel unwelcome by people in the United States. This usually happened when jobs were scarce. Immigrants in need of jobs were usually willing to work for low pay. American workers feared that immigrants might take their jobs.

Chinese and Japanese immigrants were made to feel especially unwelcome because they dressed and looked so different from other Americans. Immigrants from Europe could become American citizens. But those from China and Japan could not. In 1882, a law was passed that said no more immigrants from China could come to the United States. Later laws made it difficult for Japanese immigrants to buy farmland. These unfair laws were in effect for many years.

Whether working on a farm or in a factory, the immigrants worked hard. They hoped that eventually they would improve their lives. Some gave up and returned to the countries they had left behind. But many stayed to start new lives for themselves and their children.

A butcher shop in San Francisco, California, run by Chinese immigrants

Slowing Down Immigration

By 1900, many Americans were talking about limiting immigration. They claimed there was not enough room or work for so many newcomers.

In 1921, Congress passed a law that said only 350,000 immigrants could enter the United States each year. The law also let more people come from some countries than from others. The law slowed down the pace of immigration to the United States.

Immigrant Contributions

The United States today is a rich and varied place because of the customs, styles, and traditions brought here from other countries. Dances such as the polka and the jig were first danced in other countries. Many holiday traditions, such as the way we celebrate the beginning of a new year, were brought to the United States by newcomers. The immigrants' influence is especially easy to see in the foods we eat. Hamburgers, pizza, egg rolls, chili, and sauerkraut were all first brought to the United States by people from other nations.

As immigrants settled in the United States, they began to learn to live as Americans. Most learned English and adopted many "American" customs, even though they also held on to some of their native traditions. Little by little, some of these traditions and customs became part of American culture too.

Some immigrants did not give up their native ways. They continued to live according to their native customs. They still spoke their native languages. They lived in **ethnic** neighborhoods—places where people with the same customs and backgrounds lived.

Many immigrants to the United States in the late 1800's and early 1900's made important contributions to our society. Hungarian-born Joseph Pulitzer was a famous journalist and publisher. Mary Anderson, a Swedish immigrant, became a labor union organizer and an official in the United States Department of Labor. Claude McKay, of Jamaica in the Caribbean, was a respected novelist and poet. Charles Steinmetz, a German immigrant, helped

ethnic

having to do with a group of people who share the same customs, language, and culture

Thomas Edison develop uses for electricity in the United States. Irving Berlin, a Russian immigrant, wrote "God Bless America." Simon Rodia was an Italian immigrant sculptor who built a group of unusual, attention-getting towers in Watts, California.

Irving Berlin

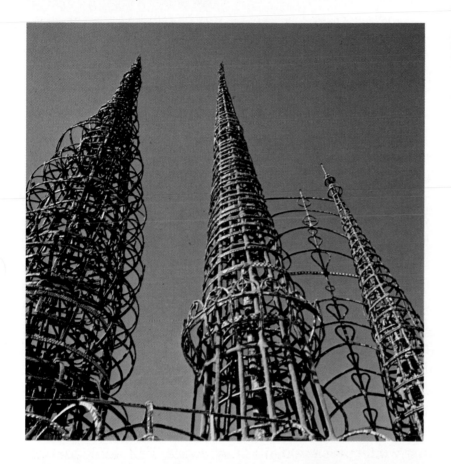

The Rodia Towers in Watts, California, designed by Simon Rodia

Section Review

Write your answers on a sheet of paper.

1. How did most of the western European immigrants earn their livings? What kinds of jobs did the eastern European and Asian immigrants get?
2. Why did the first Chinese immigrants come to the United States?
3. Name one important problem most immigrants faced.
4. Do immigrants still come to the United States? Give two examples.

Understanding International Time Zones

Many immigrants traveled to this country from distant lands at the end of the nineteenth century. These travelers may have found it difficult to keep track of time. That is because they passed through many different time zones as they crossed continents and oceans.

Because the earth is a round body that rotates on its axis, morning arrives in different parts of the world at different times. To help us keep track of the passage of time on the earth, we divide the world into 24 time zones. Each time zone covers 15° of longitude. The time change from one zone to the next is one hour.

Look at the map of international time zones on the next page. After an international conference in 1884, the Prime Meridian, located at 0° longitude, was chosen as the starting point for figuring time. Moving toward the west, the time in each zone is one hour earlier than in the zone before it. Moving toward the east, the time in each zone is one hour later.

If you moved to a point 180° west of the Prime Meridian, you would pass through 12 time zones. That would make it 12 hours earlier than at 0°. But 180° east of the Prime Meridian is 12 hours later. Therefore, as you cross the 180th meridian, the difference in time is a full 24 hours, or one day. An imaginary line is located at the 180th meridian. This line, called the international date line, marks the starting point of each new day. If you traveled west across this line, you would add a day to your calendar. If you traveled east across it, you would subtract a day. At any time of the day or night, there are always two different calendar days on the earth. If you flew west from Honolulu, Hawaii, to Tokyo, Japan, early one Sunday morning, you would arrive in Tokyo a few hours later. However, you would have "lost" a day by crossing the international date line. In Tokyo, it would already be Monday morning! If you then left Tokyo on Monday morning and flew east back to Honolulu, you would again cross the international date line. But this time, you would "gain" a day and arrive in Honolulu on Sunday morning.

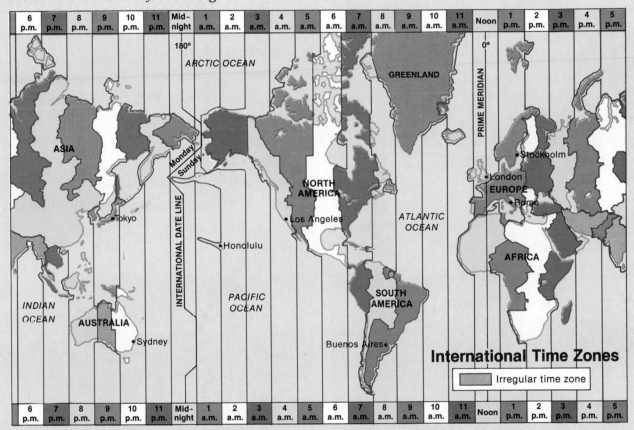

| 6 p.m. | 7 p.m. | 8 p.m. | 9 p.m. | 10 p.m. | 11 p.m. | Mid-night | 1 a.m. | 2 a.m. | 3 a.m. | 4 a.m. | 5 a.m. | 6 a.m. | 7 a.m. | 8 a.m. | 9 a.m. | 10 a.m. | 11 a.m. | Noon | 1 p.m. | 2 p.m. | 3 p.m. | 4 p.m. | 5 p.m. |

International Time Zones

Irregular time zone

═══ Practice Your Skills ═══

1. When it is noon in Buenos Aires, what time is it in London? in Honolulu? in Stockholm?

2. How many time zones divide Africa? South America?

3. If you left Sydney, Australia, early Friday morning and flew east, on what day would you arrive in Los Angeles, California? Why?

4 Progressive Movement

In 1900, some Americans were very rich. Many were very poor. A lot of Americans, however, were somewhere in the middle, in a middle class.

At that time, members of this middle class began to talk about the problems of government and business in the United States. Many wanted to change, or **reform,** society for the better. Their efforts to improve life in the United States were called the Progressive Movement.

Leaving It Up to the People

In 1900, business leaders would not take responsibility for their workers' health and safety. They refused to spend money to make their factories safe. Factory owners also refused to check the quality of the goods being produced.

Government leaders did not think the government should be responsible for people's well-being, or **welfare,** either. For example, the government did not help people who were too old or too sick to work.

The government did help big business, however. Many

reform

to improve living conditions, government, health care, and working conditions

welfare

condition of being well and having enough money

These two pictures show the contrasts that existed in American life in the early 1900's. Some people were very wealthy, while many were poor.

government workers took illegal payments, or **bribes,** from business leaders. In return, the government workers did favors for businesses. For example, a government leader who took a bribe might see to it that a business did not have to pay high taxes.

The Muckrakers

In a way, the United States in 1900 was like a lake. On the surface, things looked bright and clear. The nation's problems were below the surface, like the mud, or muck, in a lake.

It is not hard to see how this happened. Slums were set apart from nicer neighborhoods. Most well-to-do people avoided the slums. Factories were closed to the public. Only the workers knew what went on inside. Most people went about their daily lives and did not look closely at problems. The government did not take responsibility for solving any of society's problems either.

Cover of a magazine that contained a story investigating Rockefeller's Standard Oil Company

But a concerned group of writers in the United States began "stirring up the muck." They wanted Americans to know the truth. They investigated dishonest politicians and businesses. Using facts and figures, they pointed out the problems. These writers were called **muckrakers.**

Muckraker stories appeared in popular magazines. Millions of people read them. One famous muckraker, Ida Tarbell, wrote a series of magazine articles exposing the unfair business practices of Rockefeller's Standard Oil Company. Another muckraker, Lincoln Steffens, wrote about government corruption in cities like St. Louis, Minneapolis, and Milwaukee. The articles by the muckrakers shocked and angered middle-class Americans. Many Americans decided to vote for leaders who promised to fight these wrongdoings.

The Reformers

The movement for reform began to make progress in 1901. President Theodore Roosevelt became the leading speaker and worker for reform.

Roosevelt began by breaking up some of the big business trusts. For this, he was nicknamed the "trust buster." Under Roosevelt, a Department of Commerce and Labor was set up. Roosevelt also gained greater government control over railroads. For the first time, government was taking an interest in making businesses act fairly.

In 1906, Roosevelt supported the Pure Food and Drug Act. This reform called for government inspections of food-processing plants and better labeling of drug products. Because of this act, fewer useless drugs and unclean foods reached the public.

Other reformers worked with people, especially those in city slums. In 1889, Jane Addams founded Hull House in Chicago. It was a community center for immigrants and the poor, or a **settlement house.** In New York, Lillian Wald organized nursing services for slum dwellers. She also established the Henry Street Settlement, another community center.

settlement house

a center that offers community members social, educational, and recreational activities

NO MOLLY-CODDLING HERE

(This is the prevailing Wall Street notion of President Roosevelt's attitude toward corporate interests.)

From the *Globe* (New York)

Cartoon showing President Theodore Roosevelt as a trust buster

Hull House in Chicago, Illinois

Thanks to the efforts of reformers such as Addams and Wald, many states passed laws that limited child labor. Other laws set standards to make factories safer places to work. Laws also set minimum pay and maximum hours for female workers.

In 1912, Americans elected another reformer to the White House. President Woodrow Wilson continued the fight against the trusts. He also helped establish the eight-hour workday in some industries.

Section Review

Write your answers on a sheet of paper.

1. Who were the muckrakers? What did they achieve?
2. Describe the reforms that President Theodore Roosevelt worked for.
3. Who were Jane Addams and Lillian Wald? How did they contribute to the Progressive Movement?
4. Based on your readings, what groups do you think might have been opposed to reform in 1900? Why?

State Fairs Every year, hundreds of thousands of people gather to enjoy the carnival rides, agricultural competitions, and sights and sounds that can be found at a state fair.

State fairs began as farming fairs about 180 years ago. In 1810, the Berkshire Agricultural Society held a fair that set the pattern for many fairs. That fair, called the Berkshire Cattle Show, was held in Pittsfield, Massachusetts. Cattle farmers showed off their prize animals. Judges picked the best examples of each breed. Farm women exhibited their jellies, pickles, and preserves.

Thirty-one years later, New Yorkers held a state fair. And in 1854, California and Iowa had state fairs of their own.

The fairs were a way for country families to celebrate the harvest. Fairs gave farmers a chance to show off their best crops and animals. Farmers with prize-winning cattle could expect to get a good price for their calves.

As fairs grew in size, they became centers for exchanging information about farming. Farmers could learn about new methods of planting or about fighting crop diseases. New products, such as time-saving machinery, were displayed.

Western fairs often included rodeos, where cowhands could show off their roping and riding skills. In sheep-raising country, there were contests to see who could cut the wool off, or shear, a sheep the fastest. Hay baling, corn husking, and plowing contests were other popular fair activities.

By the end of the 1800's, many state and county fairs also included carnivals, with rides, fireworks, and sideshows. Often families would travel hundreds of miles to spend a few days at the fair. For many, it was the highlight of the year.

UNIT REVIEW

Word Work

Write the sentences below on a sheet of paper. Fill in the blanks with the correct words from the list.

tenements   strike   transcontinental
              bribes   consolidate

1. Many immigrants lived in poorly built _____ .
2. In order to provide better service, many small American railroads began to _____ .
3. When workers' demands for better wages and conditions are not met, they may go on _____ .
4. Muckrakers wrote about senators who accepted _____ .
5. On the _____ railroad, one could travel from New York to California.

Knowing the Facts

Write your answers on a sheet of paper.
1. How did the Homestead Act help to settle the West?
2. What part did the railroads play in developing industry?
3. Which inventions changed American home life?
4. What problems did immigrants face when they arrived in the United States?
5. What was the Progressive Movement?

Using What You Know

Choose one of the following activities. Follow the instructions given here.
1. Prepare a history of your family. Interview older relatives to find out how your family came to this country.
2. Write a two-page report about any American invention. Explain who invented it and why. Also describe the effects of the invention on American life.

Skills Practice

Use this map to answer the questions below. Write your answers on a sheet of paper.

1. How many time zones separate the Prime Meridian and the international date line?
2. When it is noon in London, what time is it in Chicago?
3. When it is noon in Honolulu, Hawaii, what time is it in Anchorage, Alaska?
4. If you flew west from Los Angeles on Monday, on what day would you arrive in Tokyo?

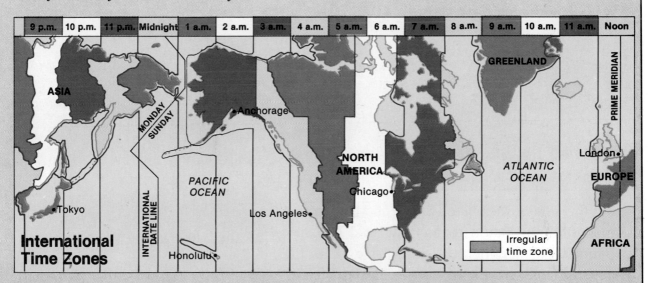

Your Heritage

Find out what your state was like in 1900. List the names of its railroads and the industries that were developing in your area. Find out about any factories, mills, and mines that were important at the turn of the century. Also find out about any immigrant groups that lived in your area. You should be able to find most of this information in your local library.

UNIT 7

The United States Gains Power in the World

In the 1800's, the United States changed from a small farming nation to an industrial one that spanned the continent. During these years the United States was not very involved in the affairs of other countries. Toward the end of the 1800's, however, this situation was changing.

Between 1900 and 1945, the United States faced many challenges at home and overseas. The country went through a period of economic growth. Then it suffered through hard times. The nation took part in two world wars. By 1945, the United States had become the strongest and richest nation on the earth. In this unit, you will learn how and why the United States became a major power in the world.

Teaching old Dogs new tricks

CHAPTER 17 The United States in World Affairs

American forces at San Juan Hill, Cuba, during the Spanish-American War

As the United States grew, its interest in the affairs of other nations increased. By the end of the nineteenth century, the country needed markets in other nations to sell all the goods it could produce. It needed raw materials from other nations to use in its factories. Because of its new interests in foreign countries, the United States was drawn into world affairs and the troubles between nations. This led the United States into two wars: first in 1898 and again in 1917.

At the end of this chapter, you should be able to:
○ Explain the changes that took place in the United States between 1800 and 1900.
○ Describe the causes of the Spanish-American War.
○ Explain why the United States entered World War I.
● Compare and contrast population maps.

1 Our Changing Role

By the 1890's, the United States had grown into a mighty nation. The United States had business interests in other countries. Business leaders thought the United States should be more involved in the affairs of these nations. Many Americans also thought that their country should help spread democracy to other nations. They wanted other peoples to become free and independent and to be able to choose their own governments.

A Century of Growth

In 1800, the United States was a small country of 16 states and less than 6 million people. Most people lived on

Poster for the 1893 World's Fair

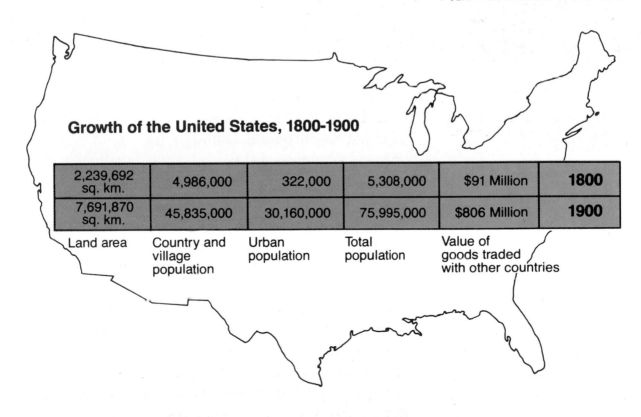

Growth of the United States, 1800-1900

Land area	Country and village population	Urban population	Total population	Value of goods traded with other countries	
2,239,692 sq. km.	4,986,000	322,000	5,308,000	$91 Million	**1800**
7,691,870 sq. km.	45,835,000	30,160,000	75,995,000	$806 Million	**1900**

William Randolph Hearst

Drawing of a Spanish officer by Frederic Remington

farms or in small villages. The frontier of the United States was slowly moving west.

By 1900, the United States stretched more than 4,500 kilometers (2,800 miles) from the Atlantic Ocean to the Pacific Ocean. About 76 million people lived in its 45 states. Almost half of these people lived in cities. Many worked in factories and offices. The United States had become an industrial nation.

In 1800, it took months to travel by ship across the Atlantic Ocean to Europe. By 1900, steamships made the crossing in a week. Telegraph messages sent by underwater cable could reach Europe the same day they were sent.

Trouble in Cuba

In the 1890's, news stories from Cuba caught the interest of Americans. Cuba was a Spanish colony that was fighting for its independence. Many Americans sympathized with the Cuban patriots. They were upset by news that the Spanish were mistreating the Cubans. In addition, some Americans had invested $100 million in the Cuban sugar industry. They wanted to support Cuba in order to protect their investment.

During this time, two leading newspapers in New York City were competing to sell the most papers. The two papers, the *Journal* and the *World,* often printed news stories that were exaggerated or based on rumor. These stories got attention and helped to sell more papers.

The owner of the *Journal* was William Randolph Hearst. He was eager to outsell the *World,* owned by Joseph Pulitzer (**poohl**-it-ser). Hearst sent Frederic Remington, one of the best-known artists in the United States, to Cuba. Hearst wanted the artist to draw pictures of the fighting. Remington sent Hearst a message saying that everything seemed peaceful in Cuba. Hearst sent back this famous reply: "You furnish the pictures, and I'll furnish the war."

Hearst and Pulitzer each printed stories about Spanish cruelty to the Cubans and to Americans living in Cuba. The stories upset many Americans. People began to talk of going to war against Spain.

President William McKinley wanted to avoid war. He

sent the battleship *Maine* to the Cuban capital of Havana to protect Americans and their property. McKinley hoped that this would ease the problems. The Spanish rulers of Cuba welcomed the Americans. But on the night of February 15, 1898, the *Maine* suddenly exploded. Some 260 American sailors were killed.

Americans were furious. The Spanish denied they were responsible for blowing up the *Maine.* Even today no one knows what caused the explosion. Still, newspapers in the United States blamed the Spanish. Most Americans believed what they read in the papers. In April 1898, Spain and the United States went to war.

The Spanish-American War

Americans were willing to fight. First, however, new army units had to be formed. Some Americans felt so strongly that they volunteered to form their own units. Theodore Roosevelt formed one new army unit, called the Rough Riders. In Cuba, the Rough Riders helped win the battle of San Juan (san **wahn**) Hill.

The Spanish-American War was fought in other Spanish colonies too. In the Philippine Islands, Commodore George Dewey of the United States won a great naval victory at Manila Bay. American soldiers also defeated the Spanish on the Caribbean island of Puerto Rico. In 10 weeks, the war was over.

Theodore Roosevelt and the Rough Riders

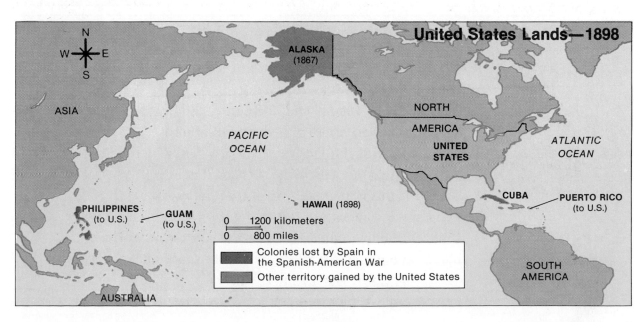

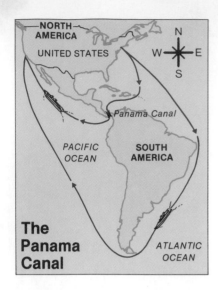

The Panama Canal

The United States Expands

The United States and Spain signed a peace treaty. Spain agreed to let Cuba become an independent nation. And Spain gave the United States control of Puerto Rico, the Philippine Islands, and the island of Guam in the Pacific Ocean.

The former Spanish colonies were not the first new lands to come under American control. In 1867, the United States had bought Alaska from Russia. And in 1898, the United States took control of Hawaii.

Now the United States held territory in both the Atlantic and Pacific oceans. American leaders knew that it was more important than ever that warships be able to get from one ocean to the other quickly. President Theodore Roosevelt decided that the United States should build a canal across Panama, the narrowest area of land between the Atlantic and Pacific oceans. Panama agreed to let the United States build a canal. In 1903, Roosevelt gave the order to "make the dirt fly!"

And the dirt really did fly! An army of men had to cut through jungles, hills, and swamps to build the canal. Still, it was not until 1914 that the first ship made its way through the Panama Canal.

Section Review

Write your answers on a sheet of paper.
1. What changes took place in the United States between 1800 and 1900?
2. How did the *World* and the *Journal* encourage the United States to enter into war with Spain?
3. What territories did the United States gain as a result of the Spanish-American War?
4. Why was the Panama Canal important?
5. The United States went through great changes between 1800 and 1900. What changes do you think will take place by the year 2000? Explain your answers.

2 World War I

The United States was becoming one of the most powerful nations in the world. Americans soon found that being a world power meant getting involved in world problems. In the summer of 1914, war broke out in Europe. The war expanded to Europe's colonies in Africa and Asia. Americans wondered if the war overseas would spread to the United States too.

The First Shots

Europe had been at peace for many years, but it was not an easy peace. Nations quarreled with each other over colonies and trade. For several years, the countries of Europe had been divided into two **alliances.** An alliance is a group of nations that agrees to help each other, especially in times of trouble. On one side were Great Britain, France,

alliance

a group of nations that agrees to help each other

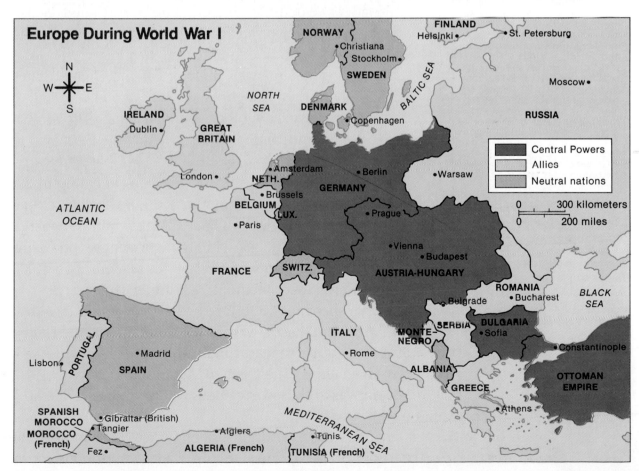

Europe During World War I

Legend:
- Central Powers
- Allies
- Neutral nations

0 300 kilometers
0 200 miles

OCEAN STEAMSHIPS.

CUNARD

EUROPE VIA LIVERPOOL
LUSITANIA

Fastest and Largest Steamer
now in Atlantic Service Sails
SATURDAY, MAY 1, 10 A. M.
Transylvania, Fri., May 7, 5 P.M.
Orduna, - - Tues., May 18, 10 A.M.
Tuscania, - - Fri., May 21, 5 P.M._
LUSITANIA, Sat., May 29, 10 A.M.
Transylvania, Fri., June 4, 5 P.M.

Gibraltar—Genoa—Naples—Piraeus
S.S. Carpathia, Thur., May 13, Noon

ROUND THE WORLD TOURS
Through bookings to all principal Ports
of the World.
Company's Office. 21-24 State St., N. Y.

NOTICE!

TRAVELLERS intending to embark on the Atlantic voyage are reminded that a state of war exists between Germany and her allies and Great Britain and her allies; that the zone of war includes the waters adjacent to the British Isles; that, in accordance with formal notice given by the Imperial German Government, vessels flying the flag of Great Britain, or of any of her allies, are liable to destruction in those waters and that travellers sailing in the war-zone on ships of Great Britain or her allies do so at their own risk.

IMPERIAL GERMAN EMBASSY

WASHINGTON, D. C., APRIL 22, 1915.

Advertisement that appeared in American newspapers for the Lusitania, *with a warning from the Germans of the possible dangers of sailing on a British ship*

Russia, and other smaller countries. This group of countries was called the Allies. The Allies were opposed by the Central Powers. Germany and Austria-Hungary were the most powerful members of the Central Powers. The countries in each alliance promised to help each other in case of attack.

By 1914, both sides were heavily armed. It seemed as if anything could set off a war. One of the major trouble spots was Serbia, a small nation in southeastern Europe. In June 1914, Archduke Francis Ferdinand of Austria-Hungary was shot and killed while visiting Serbia. Austria-Hungary responded to the killing by invading Serbia. The Serbs asked Russia for help and got it. Because of the alliance system, almost all of Europe was at war within a week. Since the fighting involved so many nations, people called it a world war.

Staying Out of War

President Woodrow Wilson said the United States should not get involved in the war. Wilson hoped the United States would be able to stay neutral.

Remaining neutral was difficult for the United States because the war was fought on the seas as well as on land. The British navy had blockaded Germany. The British hoped to prevent supplies from reaching the Germans. In return, the German navy sank British ships that were carrying supplies. American ships were soon caught up in the fighting on the high seas. In May 1915, a German submarine sank the British luxury liner *Lusitania* off the coast of Ireland. The liner was carrying both passengers and arms from the United States to Great Britain. More than 1,000 people were killed, including 128 Americans.

Many Americans were angry at Germany and talked of war. President Wilson warned the Germans that the United States would go to war if the Germans continued to sink passenger ships. The Germans promised to stop. In 1916, Wilson was reelected President with the slogan: "He kept us out of war."

In 1917, however, the Germans broke their promise to President Wilson. The Germans wanted to stop American ships from bringing needed goods to Britain. So German submarines sank some American ships. Wilson believed that these sinkings were open acts of war against the American people. In April 1917, Congress declared war on the Central Powers.

The War at Home

Once war was declared, the United States moved into action. First an army had to be organized and trained. Congress passed a law that required all men between the ages of 18 and 45 to register for the army. By November 1918, almost 3 million men had been drafted into the armed forces.

Weapons and uniforms were needed to supply the American soldiers. President Wilson appointed Bernard Baruch (buh-**rook**) to lead an organization called the War Industries Board. Baruch was a successful businessman. He was famous for getting things done. The War Industries Board directed the production of supplies needed for the war. Automobile factories began to make jeeps and tanks. Clothing factories switched over to making army uniforms.

United States Army recruitment poster

Photograph showing conditions in the trenches during World War I

The war involved people on the home front as well as soldiers on the battlefields. The need for war goods created many jobs in factories. Most factories were in the Northeast and Midwest. Many people from the South moved north to cities such as New York, Detroit, and Chicago to work in the factories.

Soldiers at War

At the time the United States entered the war, neither the Allies nor the Central Powers were winning. Neither side was able to break through the opponent's lines. Soldiers on both sides dug long ditches, or trenches, across the battlefield. In the middle was "no man's land." Sometimes one side would try to advance. The soldiers would go over the top of the trenches into "no man's land." There they were forced back by two of the new weapons of this war: the machine gun and barbed wire. Soldiers tried to cut their way through the thick barbed wire. But many were shot down by machine guns. This kind of fighting was called trench warfare.

Over 2 million American soldiers were sent to Europe, mainly to France. The Americans were welcomed by the Allies who had lost many soldiers in three years of war.

In July 1918, the Allies stopped a major German advance into France. The Allies were aided by American troops led by General John J. Pershing. This was the turning point of the war. From then on, the German army retreated.

The Peace That Failed

Austria-Hungary finally surrendered on November 3, 1918. On November 11, Germany surrendered. The war was over.

After the war, President Wilson traveled to France to help write the peace treaty. Wilson hoped to make a peace that would prevent war forever. His idea was a "peace without victory." This meant that no country would be a winner. No country would be a loser. Wilson believed that "only a peace between equals" could last.

Wilson's peace plan was called the Fourteen Points. The fourteenth point was the main part of his plan. It called for the establishment of an organization called the League of Nations. Wilson wanted all countries to belong to the League. Member countries could bring their complaints to the League and settle them without going to war, he hoped.

Many Americans did not like Wilson's plan for the League of Nations. They said the United States should no longer be involved in the affairs of other countries. They wanted to go back to being neutral.

The other Allies did not agree with Wilson's idea of peace without victory. They wanted to see Germany's army destroyed. They wanted Germany to pay for the damages of the war. In the end, there was a compromise. Wilson agreed that Germany should pay for the damages of the war. The Allies agreed to accept his plan for the League of Nations.

Wilson traveled across the United States trying to gain support for the peace treaty and the League of Nations. But in the end, the Senate rejected it. The League was established without the United States. When war broke out again in Europe in 1939, the League was unable to stop it.

Woodrow Wilson

Section Review

Write your answers on a sheet of paper.
1. Explain how the system of alliances caused World War I. Who were the Allies? the Central Powers?
2. What was trench warfare?
3. Describe Wilson's plan for peace.
4. By 1900, the United States had become a world power. Name some nations that are world powers today.

Comparing and Contrasting Population Maps

The population maps on the next page give several kinds of information about the growth of the United States. The top map shows how much of our country was settled in 1800. At that time, the population numbered 5,308,483. The bottom map shows the settled areas of our country a century later, when the population had increased to 75,994,575 people. The colors on the maps show how densely, or thickly, populated each settled area was. Study the color key for each map. You will be able to tell how densely settled each part of our country was in 1800 and 1900.

A star symbol on each map marks the population center for each time period. It shows that half the population lived to the east of the symbol. The other half of the population lived to the west of the symbol.

Compare one map with the other. You can see how our country grew from 1800 to 1900. The settled areas increased in population. The population center of our country shifted farther west. And new communities and states were founded.

Practice Your Skills

1. What body of water marked the western boundary of the country in 1800? Where was the population center then?
2. Where was the population center in 1900? What was the country's western boundary at that time? How many people lived in each square kilometer in the Boston area in 1800? in 1900?
3. In 1900, were there more areas of densest population to the east or to the west of the Mississippi River?
4. In 1800, around what cities was the population densest?

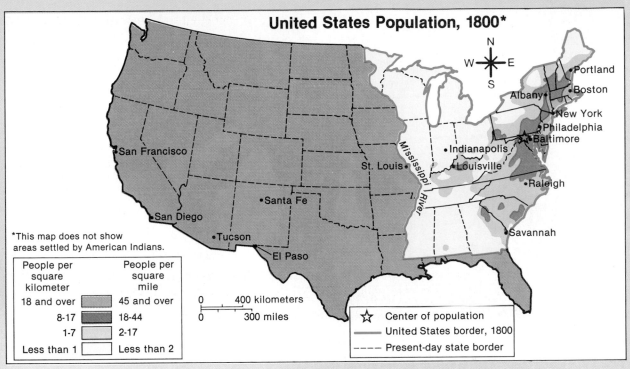

United States Population, 1800*

*This map does not show areas settled by American Indians.

People per square kilometer		People per square mile
18 and over		45 and over
8-17		18-44
1-7		2-17
Less than 1		Less than 2

0   400 kilometers
0   300 miles

☆ Center of population
━━ United States border, 1800
- - - Present-day state border

Portland
Boston
Albany
New York
Philadelphia
Baltimore
Indianapolis
St. Louis
Louisville
Raleigh
Savannah
San Francisco
San Diego
Tucson
Santa Fe
El Paso
Mississippi River

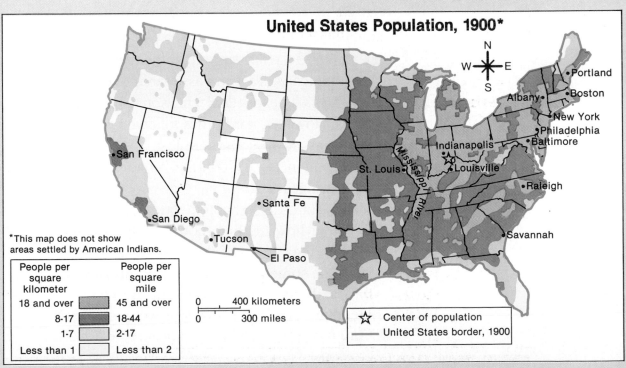

United States Population, 1900*

*This map does not show areas settled by American Indians.

People per square kilometer		People per square mile
18 and over		45 and over
8-17		18-44
1-7		2-17
Less than 1		Less than 2

0   400 kilometers
0   300 miles

☆ Center of population
━━ United States border, 1900

Portland
Boston
Albany
New York
Philadelphia
Baltimore
Indianapolis
St. Louis
Louisville
Raleigh
Savannah
San Francisco
San Diego
Tucson
Santa Fe
El Paso
Mississippi River

CHAPTER 18 The 1920's and the Great Depression

August   25 Cents

World War I had been a time of sacrifice for many Americans, both at home and abroad. When the war was over, they wanted to relax and enjoy themselves. For a while, many Americans did lead easy, carefree lives. Times were good. Business expanded, and some people even made fortunes. However, hard times followed good times. Business slowed down, jobs were lost, and the Great Depression began. In the 1930's, the American people had to make sacrifices again.

At the end of this chapter, you should be able to:
○ Describe how the automobile changed American life.
○ Explain the causes of the Great Depression.
○ Describe some of the problems Americans faced during the 1930's.
○ Identify Franklin Delano Roosevelt and the New Deal.
● Compare maps showing moisture regions and wind erosion.

1 After World War I

World War I brought changes for women and blacks in the United States. Women won the right to vote. Many blacks moved from farms in the South to factory jobs in northern cities. Within a few decades, the black population in major cities grew very quickly. But blacks found that discrimination was as common in the North as it had been in the South.

Women Get the Vote

Throughout the 1800's, there had been slow progress in the area of women's rights. By 1860, a New York law permitted married women to buy and sell property and spend the wages they earned.

After the Civil War, women hoped to be given equality with men. They were disappointed, however. The Fifteenth Amendment gave the vote to black men but not to women. In 1869, Elizabeth Cady Stanton and Susan B. Anthony started a movement to gain the right to vote, or **suffrage,** for women. Women who joined the movement were called suffragists.

suffrage
the right to vote

Women's suffrage parade in New York City in 1912

Group of San Francisco suffragists celebrating California's ratification of the Nineteenth Amendment in November 1919.

Stanton and Anthony traveled around the country trying to win supporters for the cause. In 1869, Wyoming Territory became the first place in the United States to allow suffrage for women. Other western territories followed Wyoming's example. Then, in 1890, Wyoming became the first state in the Union to allow women to vote.

Even with this progress, the leaders of the women's suffrage movement realized that some states would not willingly grant women the right to vote. So women began working to have a women's suffrage amendment added to the Constitution.

Suffragists worked hard for many years to bring attention to their cause. They held meetings and marches. They protested in front of the White House. Some suffragists were arrested. In jail, they went on hunger strikes, refusing to eat. Their protests succeeded in bringing national attention to the cause of women's suffrage.

World War I helped change people's thinking about women's suffrage. Many men saw the contributions made by women to the war effort. Others recognized that in a war fought for democracy, democracy should begin at home. President Wilson finally supported a women's suffrage amendment to the Constitution.

By 1920, 36 of the 48 states voted to accept the Nineteenth Amendment to the Constitution, giving women the right to vote. It became law. That year, women across the nation voted for the first time in a presidential election.

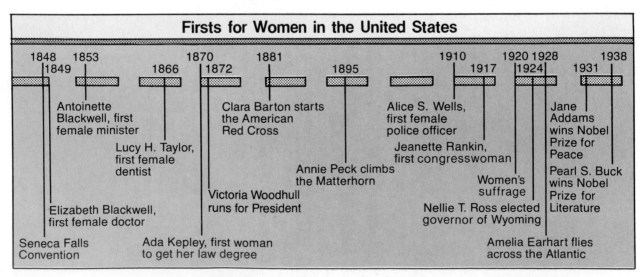

Firsts for Women in the United States

1848 1853 · 1870 1881 · · 1910 1920 1928 · 1938
1849 · 1866 1872 · 1895 · 1917 1924 · 1931

Antoinette Blackwell, first female minister

Lucy H. Taylor, first female dentist

Clara Barton starts the American Red Cross

Annie Peck climbs the Matterhorn

Victoria Woodhull runs for President

Elizabeth Blackwell, first female doctor

Alice S. Wells, first female police officer

Jeanette Rankin, first congresswoman

Women's suffrage

Nellie T. Ross elected governor of Wyoming

Jane Addams wins Nobel Prize for Peace

Pearl S. Buck wins Nobel Prize for Literature

Seneca Falls Convention

Ada Kepley, first woman to get her law degree

Amelia Earhart flies across the Atlantic

Blacks After the War

Black soldiers returned from Europe with high hopes. They had fought bravely in the trenches and won many honors. They, too, had heard President Wilson speak of the war as one to make the world safe for democracy. Blacks hoped they would be treated more fairly after the war than they had been in the past.

Instead, when they returned home, most blacks found that conditions had not improved. Many blacks who had moved to northern cities found that they were treated no better there than they had been in the South. In addition, some white workers were angry that they had to compete for jobs with black soldiers returning from the war. Almost everywhere they went, blacks faced discrimination. Blacks were often denied jobs because of their color. Some whites refused to sell homes or rent apartments to blacks.

In the summer of 1919, riots broke out in many American cities. White crowds attacked blacks, and blacks fought back. A riot in Chicago left more than 30 people dead and hundreds injured. There was rioting in Washington, D.C. Officials there had to call in soldiers to try to put an end to the violence.

The situation was made worse by the Ku Klux Klan. The Klan had died out after Reconstruction. A new Ku Klux Klan was organized in 1915. It attracted people who did not like blacks, Catholics, Jews, and foreigners. At its peak in the mid-1920's, the Klan had between 4 and 5 million members. The Klan preached hatred of, and the use of violence toward, blacks.

Southern Blacks Move North, 1900-1930

(bar graph, vertical axis labeled "Thousands" with values 100, 200, 300, 400, 500, 600, 700; horizontal axis labeled 1900-1910, 1910-1920, 1920-1930)

Ku Klux Klan march in Washington, D.C. during the 1920's

President Warren G. Harding, at left, and Vice-President Calvin Coolidge

A Return to Normalcy

In 1920, Warren G. Harding was the Republican candidate for President. Harding said he would help the nation "return to normalcy." By normalcy, Harding meant that Americans would no longer be asked to make sacrifices for others. They would return to life the way it had been before the war. Many Americans did not want to get involved in the affairs of other nations. They wanted to forget about problems and responsibilities. Many found Harding's promise of a return to normalcy appealing. Warren G. Harding was elected President of the United States in 1920.

Section Review

Write your answers on a sheet of paper.

1. Why were leaders of the women's rights movement disappointed after the Civil War?
2. How did World War I raise the hopes of blacks?
3. Explain what Warren Harding meant by his promise of a "return to normalcy."
4. In the past, women fought to get the right to vote. What rights are some women fighting for today?

2 The Roaring Twenties

The decade called the Roaring Twenties got its name because of the tremendous excitement, "roaring" good times, and change that filled those years. Some people called it the time of the wonderful nonsense. Years later, the 1920's were remembered most of all as the time when many Americans had fun.

A Nation on Wheels

The automobile first became popular in the United States during the 1920's. The car had been invented nearly 30 years earlier. But the first cars were expensive and not very reliable. Then, in 1908, Henry Ford produced a practical car called the Model T. Other people called Ford's car the Tin Lizzie. It shook, rattled, and sputtered, but it worked.

Some people said the Tin Lizzie looked like a black box on wheels. Yet people bought the cars. Between 1908 and 1927, more than 15 million Model T's were sold.

Model T's seemed to last forever. They were easy to fix. Spare parts were ready-made and simple to install. The cars were lightweight. This was important because many roads in the United States were not paved. The roads usu-

A traffic jam in the early 1900's

Ford Motor Company assembly line

ally turned to mud in the rain. A Model T that was stuck in the mud could easily be pulled out.

Henry Ford's great achievement was making a car that many people could afford. In 1908, the Model T cost more than $800. In those days, that was not cheap. But Ford used the assembly line to cut costs. He put an assembly line in his factory in 1913. By 1916, the price of a Model T was below $400. It was the cheapest car on the road. By 1925, one Model T rolled off the assembly line every 10 seconds. The price was only $260.

Henry Ford had a lot of new ideas. In 1914, he announced that he would pay all his workers at least $5 per day. Until then, some of his workers earned $1 and some earned $2.50 per day. If workers had more money, Ford argued, they would spend that money on cars and other goods. Then business would grow and everyone would benefit.

Ford's new wages angered many other business owners. They kept their workers' wages low in order to make the largest possible profits. Ford also angered people who had invested money in his company. Instead of dividing up all the profits among the investors, Ford wanted to use the extra money to build bigger and better automobile factories. In the long run, however, Ford's ideas were followed by other businesses.

The automobile changed the way Americans worked, traveled, and relaxed. People no longer had to live close to the places where they worked. Those people who lived in rural areas could drive into town to visit friends or shop. And people who lived in cities could get away for an afternoon in the country.

Cars had a big effect on business as well. Gasoline and tires were needed to keep the cars running. Steel was used in making cars, so the steel industry grew. Because people traveled more, more restaurants and hotels were needed.

Good Times

The 1920's were considered a great time to be alive. People went out, had fun, and did not worry about the future. They invented new ways to dress, new words to use, and new ways to have fun.

Many women cut their hair and wore their skirts short. These women were called flappers. Young men began to wear raccoon coats and straw hats called boaters. People loved a new dance known as the Charleston, where they kicked their legs and waved their arms wildly. No longer did they have to face their partners, hold hands, and dance calmly to the music.

Along with new ways of dressing and new ways of dancing came a new way of speaking. A boring person was said to be "a flat tire." An interesting person was "the bee's knees," and an important person, "a big cheese."

People also invented new kinds of games or fads. They held contests to see who could keep dancing the longest. A man named Shipwreck Kelley set a record for sitting at the top of a flagpole—23 days and seven hours. People also had fun driving cars.

Magazine cover showing the "roaring" good times of the 1920's

Family in Hood River County, Oregon, listening to the radio in 1925

Helen Wills Moody

The entire family could enjoy another twenties craze—radio. Radio station KDKA went on the air in Pittsburgh in 1920. It was the first station to go into business. On election night that year, about 500 people heard on KDKA that Warren G. Harding had been elected President. Soon almost everyone wanted a radio.

Radio stations were set up all across the country. They broadcast concerts by jazz bands and symphony orchestras. There were also comedy and mystery shows. Listening to the radio became a favorite family entertainment.

Another family entertainment was the movies. Movies in the 1920's had no sound. Usually a piano was played along with the movie. The actors' words were printed on the screen. People enjoyed watching such stars as Charlie Chaplin, Rudolph Valentino, and Gloria Swanson. By the end of the 1920's, the first sound movies, or talkies, were made. They were a great hit.

An Age of Heroes

The 1920's was a time for heroes, especially in sports. Babe Ruth, the first great home-run hitter in baseball, was loved by baseball fans across the nation. Red Grange was a great football player. Bill Tilden and Helen Wills Moody were tennis champions for many years. Gertrude Ederle became the first woman to swim from Great Britain to France across the English Channel.

One of the greatest heroes of the age was an airplane pilot named Charles A. Lindbergh. In 1927, Lindbergh flew his small plane from New York to Paris. He was the first person in history to fly across the Atlantic Ocean alone.

It was a long, dangerous trip for Lindbergh. But he made it. About 33 hours after taking off, he landed in Paris. A huge crowd was waiting for him. Cheering, they surrounded his plane when he landed. When he returned to New York, Lindbergh was welcomed with the biggest parade ever held in that city.

Getting Rich

During the 1920's, many people made money by buying shares, or **stocks,** in different companies. The place where shares are bought and sold is called the **stock market.** The price of a company's stock depends on business conditions, profits, and whether people think the company will be successful. If many buyers want to buy stock in a company, the price of the stock will rise. If many stock owners want to sell their stock, the price will go down. In the 1920's, stock prices seemed to go in only one direction: up. There were stories of shoeshine boys and office workers making fortunes overnight in the stock market.

Charles Lindbergh

stock
a share in a business or company

stock market
a place where shares in companies are bought and sold

The New York Stock Exchange in the 1920's

installment buying
paying part of the purchase price of an item and making regular payments plus interest for the rest of the amount

interest
a charge for borrowing money

Twice the cleaning...
twice the leisure!

Premier Duplex

Advertisement for one of the new appliances of the 1920's, the vacuum cleaner

People were making more money than ever before. Companies used advertising to encourage people to buy their products. Advertising became important to business during the 1920's.

Another way of encouraging people to buy more goods was called **installment buying.** When people bought an item on the installment plan, they had to pay only a small part of the total price for the item. Each month they paid another small amount, or an installment. The installment included an extra charge for the unpaid amount called **interest.** People paid installments until the item they purchased had been paid for in full. Installment buying led to more sales of all kinds of goods in the 1920's.

As long as people were earning a lot of money, installment buying seemed like a good idea. But some experts warned that too many Americans owed too much money. If people suddenly lost their jobs, they would not be able to pay their debts. Then business would suffer. Few people listened to these warnings, however. Business was expanding. People kept buying on the installment plan.

Stores were offering a wide range of new products for Americans to spend their money on. New appliances, such as washing machines, refrigerators, and vacuum cleaners, made housework much easier.

Section Review

Write your answers on a sheet of paper.
1. What other industries expanded because of the popularity of the automobile?
2. What were some of the new ways to dress, to talk, and to have fun that people invented in the 1920's?
3. How did businesses encourage people to buy more goods?
4. You have read what families did to have fun in the 1920's. What kinds of things do families do to have fun in the 1980's? Are any of these things the same?

3 Depression Years

The fun-filled, trouble-free days of the 1920's came to a sudden end. In the 1930's, the United States and the world faced one of the worst times in history. Thirteen to 15 million people were out of work in the United States alone. Great industries stopped producing. Businesses closed. Hard times replaced the get-rich years.

The Crash

Not everyone was getting rich during the Roaring Twenties. Those years were difficult ones for farmers. New farming methods had improved harvests. But the huge harvests meant lower prices because people did not need, and could not use, all the food that was for sale. Many farmers lost money on their crops. In addition, many Americans spent more money than they really had. They had bought many things, including stocks, on the installment plan.

In October 1929, the big trouble began. Stock market prices had been at a record high. Thousands of shares were for sale at a high price. Because the prices were so high, there were no buyers. So the prices fell. When the shares finally sold at low prices, people began to worry. Low prices meant trouble for those who had paid high prices for their stocks. They were afraid they would lose

After the stock market crashed, many people feared that banks would fail too. They rushed to their banks to withdraw all of their money.

their money. Now everyone wanted to sell before prices went even lower. But there were no buyers.

Tuesday, October 29, 1929, was called Black Tuesday. Stock prices dropped further, and billions of dollars were lost on that one day. Many people had all their money invested in stocks that were now worthless. Some people lost all their money overnight. The stock market had crashed.

The stock market crash was terrible for business. People had less money to spend on goods. This meant businesses were selling less. Many companies were left with goods they could not sell. So there was no demand to make new goods. Therefore, factories were closed down. This meant that people lost their jobs. As unemployment spread, there were even fewer customers for goods. So even more factories closed down, and more workers lost their jobs.

The Depression

depression
a time when the economy fails to grow and many people are out of work

The United States was in a **depression,** a time when the economy fails to grow and many people are out of work. By 1932, one-quarter of all the workers in the country could not find jobs. Many people had to work part-time or take jobs that did not use their special skills. They worried about keeping even those jobs. Others lined up for free bowls of soup or tramped about the country looking for a job.

Unemployed men lining up for free bowls of soup during the depression

Life was not much better for farmers during the 1930's. Farm prices had been very low in the 1920's. Many farmers had been forced to borrow money from banks to meet their expenses and stay in business. By the 1930's, many farmers owed money to the banks. When they could not pay, the banks took over their farms. Farmers protested when banks tried to sell the land. They had no place to go and no work to do.

The weather also created great hardships. For several years in the Midwest, there was a terrible drought. A drought is a period of little or no rainfall. The rich topsoil of the Great Plains turned to dust and was blown away. Huge dust storms moved across the prairies blotting out the sun and blowing through cracks in houses. People began to call the Great Plains area the Dust Bowl. Many farmers just gave up. They packed their belongings onto the tops of their Model T's and set out for California. There many farmers found work picking fruit and vegetables. Whole families lived in shacks or camped out in their cars in the California countryside. They did not earn enough money to pay for decent housing.

Drought and strong winds turned the Great Plains into a Dust Bowl during the 1930's. This is a photograph of a farm in Dallam County, Texas, in 1937.

Many farm families, like this one, gave up during the Dust Bowl years and headed for California.

Franklin D. Roosevelt

The New Deal

In 1932, Franklin Delano Roosevelt was elected President. Roosevelt had promised the American people a "new deal." Under the New Deal, Roosevelt said, government would be responsible for helping people during the hard times. Right after he was elected, Roosevelt began working on the problems of the depression.

Roosevelt brought new people into the government. College professors, business people, economists, and labor experts—he went after the best minds available. Soon newspapers were calling Roosevelt's people the Brain Trust.

Roosevelt told the Brain Trust that fast action was needed. If one plan did not work, the government should admit it and try something else. The important thing was to try something.

As soon as Roosevelt was inaugurated, the Brain Trust was ready. In the first 100 days of Roosevelt's term of office, many new laws were passed. New Deal laws had two goals. The first was to give some relief for the suffering brought on by the depression. The second was to help farmers and businesses hurt by the depression.

The New Deal helped people by putting them to work. Americans built new roads, schools, hospitals, bridges, tunnels, and dams. Under the New Deal, some young men were sent to camps in rural areas. There they worked at conserving the nation's land, forests, and water. Actors and musicians were paid to put on shows. Artists and writers were paid to paint and write. The government also set up a system of payments to help people too old to work and for

Artists working on a government sponsored project during the depression

people who were out of work. The system was part of the Social Security Act.

The New Deal helped business people and farmers. The government asked businesses to draw up agreements setting fair prices for goods and fair production levels. This way companies would not produce more goods than could be sold.

Under the New Deal, the government paid farmers to plant less so food prices could rise. The government helped farmers keep their lands by giving them more time to pay off their loans or by lending them money. For farmers in the Tennessee River Valley, the government constructed dams in a project called the Tennessee Valley Authority. Farmers in the valley gained protection from floods, richer soil for farming, and cheap electricity.

Not everyone was in favor of the New Deal. Some thought it was wrong for the government to take such a large role in helping people, business, and agriculture. Later some people complained that the New Deal was not helping to end the depression. The economy improved at first, but toward the end of 1937, business began to fail once again.

Still, the New Deal helped millions of Americans. It gave people hope when they needed it. And it changed the way Americans thought of their government. For the first time, the government took responsibility for helping people in need.

One way to earn money during the depression was to enter a dance contest.

Life in the Thirties

Life was hard in the 1930's, but Americans helped each other when they could. They thought up new ways to keep their spirits high and help each other at the same time. People would hold rent parties at which each guest pitched in a little money. The money would be used to pay the rent. And everyone would have a good time too.

With hard times, families became closer. Since they had less money, people spent more time at home. Instead of buying such things as clothes or toys, people made them themselves at home. Listening to radio shows was also a popular family activity.

To get away from their troubles, people went to the movies. For only a quarter, people could see two movies and a film about current events, called a newsreel. People flocked to see their favorite movie stars. Fred Astaire and Ginger Rogers were two of their favorites. Gangster films, Westerns, and musicals were the most popular films during the thirties.

Two popular film stars of the 1930's were Ginger Rogers and Fred Astaire.

Section Review

Write your answers on a sheet of paper.
1. What effect did the stock market crash of 1929 have on business?
2. What happened to many farmers during the depression?
3. What were two goals of the New Deal?
4. How did programs of the New Deal help people?
5. What are two New Deal programs that have lasted into the 1980's?

FAMOUS AMERICANS

ELEANOR ROOSEVELT

All over the world, Eleanor Roosevelt was known as a dedicated worker for human rights. As a public figure and as a speaker and writer, she worked for social causes all her life.

Anna Eleanor Roosevelt was born in 1884. Her parents died when she was young and she was raised by her grandmother. Eleanor felt herself to be shy and very unattractive. She tried to overcome these problems most of her life. As a young girl, she became interested in helping others. She worked in a settlement house aiding immigrants. When she was 21, she married Franklin D. Roosevelt, who later became President of the United States.

After her marriage, Eleanor Roosevelt raised a family and supported the career of her husband. He was elected to the New York state senate in 1910.

In 1921, Franklin Roosevelt was paralyzed by polio. Eleanor Roosevelt helped to keep him interested in politics by at-tending meetings and telling him what she heard and saw. By the time her husband became governor of New York in 1928, Eleanor Roosevelt had become a public figure herself. She was known as a leader in the field of rights for working women and in the field of education.

During the 12 years of her husband's presidency (1933–1945), Eleanor Roosevelt traveled widely, finding out for the President how people lived and what they needed. She supported full equality for minorities. She fought against poor housing by helping to set up a model community. She wrote books and articles on her life in the White House.

After her husband's death, Eleanor Roosevelt worked for international human rights. Until her death in 1962, Eleanor Roosevelt continued to work for the causes she believed in. Her tireless fight for human rights won the respect of people around the world.

Comparing a Moisture Region Map and a Wind Erosion Map

The map at the top of the next page is a type of climate map. It divides the lower Great Plains states into four moisture regions. The map on the bottom of the page shows what areas of those states had the worst wind erosion during the 1930 drought years. By comparing one map to the other, you can discover why this five-state area became known as the Dust Bowl.

As you can see, much of the lower Great Plains is normally semiarid, or partly desertlike. During the 1930's, rainfall in the area was lower than usual. Much cropland became scorched and withered, leaving the dry soil unprotected. The drought was followed by unusually strong winds. Midwestern farmers watched helplessly as their valuable soil blew away.

Study the key on the moisture regions map. As you can see, the color yellow shows semiarid areas while the color green shows semihumid areas. Now study the wind erosion map. You can see that severe wind erosion occurred mainly in the semiarid area where the five states meet.

Practice Your Skills

1. In what parts of the five states was wind erosion severe in 1935 and 1936? Is this area mainly semiarid or semihumid?
2. Was the area of severe wind erosion larger in 1938 than in 1940?
3. Describe the area of severest wind erosion. Over what years did this erosion occur?
4. Was the area of severest wind erosion semiarid or semihumid?

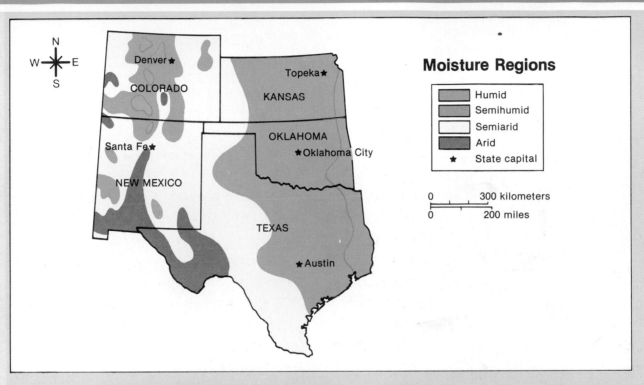

Moisture Regions

Legend:
- Humid
- Semihumid
- Semiarid
- Arid
- ★ State capital

0 ——— 300 kilometers
0 ——— 200 miles

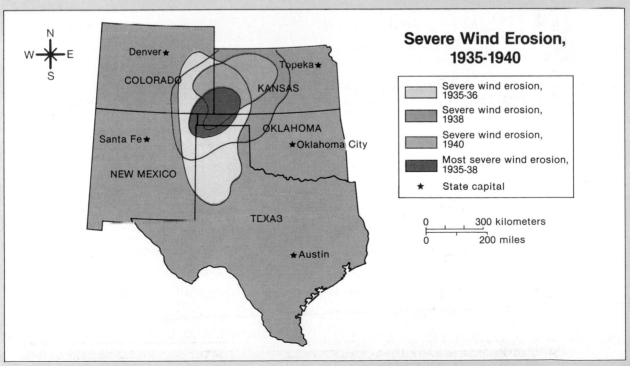

Severe Wind Erosion, 1935-1940

Legend:
- Severe wind erosion, 1935-36
- Severe wind erosion, 1938
- Severe wind erosion, 1940
- Most severe wind erosion, 1935-38
- ★ State capital

0 ——— 300 kilometers
0 ——— 200 miles

CHAPTER 19 World War II

There was bad news from Europe and Asia in the late 1930's. The governments of Germany, Italy, and Japan were trying to gain control of other lands. Their actions brought the threat of another war.

At first, Americans tried to ignore that threat. But by 1939, war had come. It was the beginning of World War II. About two years later, the United States entered the war.

At the end of this chapter, you should be able to:

○ Explain the causes of World War II.
○ Describe how the United States got involved in the war.
○ Explain how the war with Japan came to an end.
○ Describe how Americans at home supported the war effort.

1 The Seeds of War

The depression brought hard times all over the world. In Germany, the people supported a leader who they thought would help their nation. He brought hatred instead. He blamed Germany's problems on the harsh terms of the treaty that ended World War I. He also blamed certain groups of people—especially Jews. Many people believed him. His name was Adolf Hitler. At the end of the 1930's, he set out to make Germany a world power again.

Adolf Hitler and the Nazis

Adolf Hitler had been a German soldier in World War I. Like many Germans, he was disappointed by Germany's defeat in the war. But unlike many of his fellow Germans, Hitler believed that Germany had lost the war because it had been betrayed by the Jews. There was absolutely no truth to this idea. Hitler also believed that the treaty, signed at the end of World War I, was unfair to Germany. The treaty took away land Germany had once held. It forbade Germany to have powerful armed forces. Hitler wanted Germany to be a great nation once again. Hitler founded the Nazi Party. Together with his followers, he began to spread his beliefs. Hitler called the German people a superior race, or "master race." He said they deserved to rule the world.

German soldiers parading in front of Adolf Hitler

In Germany, Jews were forced to identify themselves by wearing a yellow star.

concentration camp
a prison for those the government says are its enemies

Children in a German concentration camp

Some Germans did not take Hitler seriously at first. They did not think he really meant all that he said. But Hitler's speeches and his political methods were clever. People began to believe he would be able to solve Germany's economic problems and make the nation a world power again. In 1933, Hitler and the Nazis were elected to lead Germany.

Hitler soon made himself dictator of Germany. Dictators rule countries by force. Hitler began preparing for war by building up the German army. The Nazis also began to punish anyone whose race, religion, or politics they did not like. Jews in particular suffered. Synagogues were burned. Jews were forbidden to work at certain jobs or live in certain areas. When out on the street, Jews had to wear a yellow star so that they could be easily identified. Often Jews were beaten by Nazis.

The Nazis built huge prisons called **concentration camps.** Jews, Catholics, Slavs, Poles, and others whom Hitler considered enemies were rounded up and sent to these camps. People who were strong enough were forced to work as slaves. Those too weak to work, children, and old people were killed soon after they arrived at the camps.

About 6 million Jews died in Hitler's concentration camps. This is known as the Holocaust. A holocaust is a very terrible event. It was the first time in history that a plan was organized and carried out to kill so many people of one race or religion.

The Axis

Germany was not the only country in Europe ruled by a dictator. A few years after World War I, a man named Benito Mussolini (buh-**nee**-toe moo-suh-**lee**-nee) talked about the glory of the Roman Empire. At that time, Rome had ruled most of Europe and parts of Africa and Asia. Mussolini wanted to make Italy, like Rome, a ruling nation.

In Asia, a military group came to power in Japan. They too believed in the "glory" of ruling over other nations. Japan lacked many raw materials that it depended on for its manufacturing. The new Japanese rulers talked of conquering areas of the world that had these raw materials. They hoped to take control of areas in Asia and islands in the Pacific Ocean.

In the 1930's, Germany, Italy, and Japan formed an alliance called the Axis. They promised to help each other in the event of a war. The Allies, led by Great Britain and France, opposed the Axis.

Japan was the first nation to use military might. In 1931, the Japanese army invaded a part of China called Manchuria. In 1935, Italy invaded parts of Africa. Germany took over Austria and part of Czechoslovakia (check-uh-sloe-**vah**-kee-uh). European leaders, eager to avoid war, kept allowing Hitler to take what he wanted. But there was no satisfying the desire for power of these rulers. On September 1, 1939, the German army invaded Poland. Great Britain and France had agreed to come to Poland's aid if Germany attacked. On September 3, 1939, they declared war on Germany.

Adolf Hitler, at left, and Benito Mussolini

General Hideki Tojo, Prime Minister of Japan

The First Years of War

The Poles fought bravely, but the German army conquered Poland in less than three weeks. The Germans used a new tactic called a **blitzkrieg** (**blits**-kreeg), or lightning war. Fast-moving tanks and aircraft focused their attacks on one area. They soon stopped all resistance. The attack was so swift that Poland's allies, Great Britain and France, had no time to come to Poland's aid.

In the spring of 1940, Germany turned its attention to western Europe. The Germans invaded and took control of

blitzkrieg
lightning war; a fast-moving attack of tanks and aircraft focused on one area

German bombing raids destroyed many buildings in Great Britain during the battle of Britain.

Denmark, Norway, Luxembourg, The Netherlands, and Belgium. The French army was thought to be very strong. But Germany, with help from Italy, defeated the French in a few weeks.

By June 1940, Great Britain stood alone against the Nazis. German planes made terrifying bombing raids against British cities, railroads, and factories. All night long, the bombs dropped. Pilots of the British air force tried to fight off the German planes.

Hitler's plan was to break the spirit of the British and destroy Great Britain's ability to defend itself. Then the Germans would cross the English Channel, from France. They would invade and take control of Great Britain. But the British Royal Air Force shot down many German planes. Hitler decided it was too costly to invade Great Britain. The battle of Britain was the Allies' first victory.

Several months later, German armies marched east toward the Soviet Union. Germany and the Soviet Union had signed an agreement in 1939, saying that the two countries would not fight with each other. However, Germany wanted to gain control of the Soviet Union's oil fields and raw materials. In June 1941, Germany invaded the Soviet Union. But the Germans were not able to conquer the huge Soviet nation. Because of the invasion, the Soviet Union joined forces with the Allies. In November 1942, the Soviet troops halted the German advance and began pushing the Germans back toward Germany.

Section Review

Write your answers on a sheet of paper.

1. How did Hitler come to power in Germany?
2. Which countries joined the Axis? the Allies?
3. How did Hitler plan to conquer Great Britain? Why did his plan fail?
4. How does the geography of Great Britain make it easier to defend than Poland or France?

2 Americans at War

Americans read about what was happening in Europe and Asia in their newspapers. At first, many Americans thought the United States should not get involved in the struggles of other countries. But by the time the United States finally did go to war, Americans realized that the survival of freedom in Europe was at stake. And if the Axis got control of Europe, Americans and their way of life would be in danger.

Americans Argue About the War

During the 1930's, Americans had been divided about what the United States should do. Some people were sure that the Axis powers were preparing for war. Sooner or later, these people said, there will be a war. They wanted the United States to be ready. It was certainly clear that the Axis countries did not respect the rights of any of the democratic nations.

But most Americans did not want to think about another war. Many people said that the United States would have been better off staying out of World War I. It had cost the lives of more than 100,000 Americans. And nothing seemed to have been solved by going to war.

A rally of Americans who were opposed to American involvement in World War II

At first, President Roosevelt was against the United States getting involved. But as Hitler grew bolder, Roosevelt realized that one day the United States might have to fight. Americans were afraid that Hitler was gaining so much power he might become a threat to the United States.

In 1940, President Roosevelt and Congress took action to get the country ready. The army began drafting soldiers. The navy was strengthened. More planes were built. Roosevelt met Winston Churchill, the leader of Great Britain. The United States agreed to help Great Britain by lending arms, ships, and supplies. The United States stayed out of the fighting, but it was giving more and more support to the Allied side.

Pearl Harbor

The warships of the United States Pacific Fleet were the pride of the United States Navy. They were based at Pearl Harbor in Hawaii. On Sunday morning, December 7, 1941, Japanese warplanes suddenly appeared in the sky over Hawaii. The planes dove out of the sky, toward the warships. Hundreds of bombs fell on the ships. In a matter of hours, many American fighting ships had been damaged or sunk. More than 2,000 people had been killed.

Japan wanted to control Southeast Asia. The Japanese knew that the United States naval forces could interfere in Southeast Asia. By attacking Pearl Harbor, Japan hoped to prevent United States interference.

The Japanese attack on Pearl Harbor stunned Americans. President Roosevelt and the Congress acted quickly. On December 8, 1941, the United States declared war on Japan. A few days later, the United States entered the war against both Germany and Italy.

The Japanese attack on Pearl Harbor

The United States Fights Back

The Japanese thought their attack would weaken the United States for a long time. But they did not count on how quickly the United States would be able to rebuild its fleet.

In June 1942, the Japanese and the American navies fought a huge battle off Midway Island in the Pacific. For the first time, naval battles were fought in the air as well as on the sea. Aircraft carriers acted like floating airports for the many fighter planes and bombers. At Midway, American planes sank four Japanese aircraft carriers.

The battle of Midway ended any threat of a Japanese attack on the mainland of the United States. But Japan was far from being beaten. Japan had invaded and held many Pacific islands and countries.

At the beginning of the war, Japan had invaded the Philippine Islands. There they defeated a large American force of more than 75,000 soldiers. The American commander, General Douglas MacArthur, was ordered by Roosevelt to flee to Australia. There he organized the Allied land forces that would push the Japanese, island by island, back to Japan. One of the most costly battles was the fight for the island of Iwo Jima (**ee**-woe **jee**-muh). Almost 4,200 Americans and more than 20,000 enemy troops died there before the Americans won. It took three years for the United States to push the Japanese back to Japan.

Battle of Midway

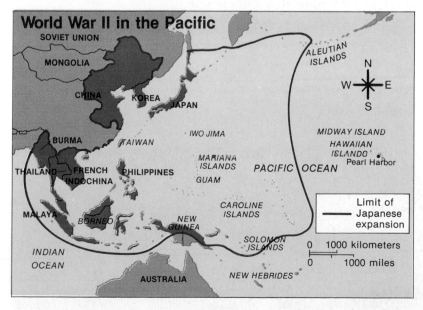

D Day

By 1942, Germany and Italy controlled most of the European continent. In 1943, the Allies invaded Italy. The Italian government surrendered within two months, but the German army in Italy continued to fight. Slowly the Allies began to drive the Germans back.

Meanwhile the Allies planned a huge invasion of France. An American general, Dwight D. Eisenhower, was named commander of all the Allied armies. It took many months for Eisenhower and other generals to plan the invasion. A large army was gathered in southern Great Britain. Thousands of ships and boats were brought there to help ferry the army across the rough seas of the English Channel.

The day for the invasion was called D Day. The success of the invasion depended on good weather for a smooth channel crossing. Twice the invasion had to be put off because of storms.

Finally on the night of June 5, 1944, the Allied army boarded ships in Great Britain. A giant fleet of 600 warships and 4,000 smaller landing boats carried 176,000 Allied soldiers toward France. The soldiers were from the United States, Great Britain, Canada, France, Poland and many other nations. Overhead, 11,000 Allied aircraft bombed the German positions in France. In the early dawn hours of June 6, the Allies fought their way onto the beaches. By nightfall, the Allies were in France.

Allied troops storm the beaches of France during the D Day invasion

Section Review

Write your answers on a sheet of paper.
1. Why were many Americans unwilling to become involved in the troubles in Europe and Asia in the 1930's?
2. How did the United States prepare for war?
3. Why was the battle of Midway Island important?
4. What is meant by D Day? What did the Allies hope to do?
5. Many nations worked together to fight against the Axis during World War II. In what ways do nations cooperate during peacetime?

3 The Last Act

The D Day invasion marked the beginning of the end for Germany. Four months after D Day, France and Belgium were freed of German control. Then the battle for Germany began. By May 1945, Germany surrendered. Meanwhile, United States forces in the Pacific were getting closer to Japan.

Death of a President

Americans received a shock in April 1945. President Roosevelt died. He was 63 years old. Roosevelt had not been in very good health. Still, in November 1944, he had been elected to a fourth term as President. Roosevelt served as President longer than anyone else in United States history.

Harry Truman's Tough Choice

When Roosevelt died, Vice-President Harry S Truman became President. He was soon faced with a very tough decision. American scientists had developed a new weapon, the atomic bomb, or A-bomb. Scientists were amazed by the power of a single A-bomb. One A-bomb had the force of thousands of tonnes (tons) of explosives.

An atomic bomb explosion

Nagasaki, Japan, after the atomic bomb had been dropped on the city

Some advisers urged President Truman to drop an A-bomb on a Japanese city. They said that when the Japanese saw how destructive an A-bomb could be, they would surely surrender. Otherwise the United States would have to invade Japan. An invasion of Japan would cost many American lives. Some advisers claimed that as many as one million American soldiers would die if the United States attempted such an invasion.

Some scientists were against using the A-bomb. They argued that the bomb's power was not still fully known. It was not only the bomb's explosion that killed. The bomb also gave off a deadly poison called radiation. The radiation lasted in the air for a very long time, causing serious illness and death.

Truman decided to use the A-bomb. On August 6, 1945, an American bomber dropped an atomic bomb on the city of Hiroshima (hir-uh-**shee**-muh). Most of the city was destroyed. At least 75,000 people were killed instantly. Many thousands of others died soon after. Yet Japan did not surrender. The United States dropped another bomb on Nagasaki (nah-guh-**sah**-kee). Finally, on August 14, 1945, the Japanese surrendered. World War II was over.

Rebuilding Europe

The war had ended, but the suffering continued. During the years of the war, Hitler had built many more concentration camps. The Nazis planned to kill all the people of the world whom they considered enemies. By the end of the war, they had killed about 6 million Jews and millions of others. Tens of thousands of concentration camp prisoners were freed when Germany was defeated. There were also hundreds of thousands of other people left homeless and in need of aid.

After the war, much of Europe's farmland and industry was in ruins. Europe needed to be rebuilt. General George Marshall, President Truman's secretary of state, developed a plan for rebuilding Europe. The United States would give money to European countries so that they could help themselves. The money was to be used to rebuild factories and farms. Congress approved the Marshall Plan. It voted to spend at least $5 billion to rebuild Europe. In 10 years, most of Europe was growing strong again.

The United Nations

In 1945, the Allies decided to set up an organization called the United Nations to work for world peace. The idea for the United Nations, or the UN, was a lot like Woodrow Wilson's League of Nations. The Allies had two reasons for thinking the UN would be stronger than the League. First, all the world powers agreed to join. Second, the UN had the power to enforce its decisions with troops. Member countries would supply soldiers to be part of the UN's peace-keeping forces.

The UN has not accomplished all its goals. But it has prevented war in some trouble spots. It also has helped sick and needy people all over the world.

The United Nations building in New York City

Section Review

Write your answers on a sheet of paper.
1. What was Harry Truman's tough decision?
2. How did the Marshall Plan help rebuild Europe?
3. Why did the founders of the UN think that their organization would be stronger than the League of Nations?
4. At the end of World War II, the United States joined the UN. In what way did this show that the United States had changed since the end of World War I? Why was this change important?

4 The War at Home

When Hitler went to war against the United States, he thought it would take several years before Americans could produce enough to help the Allied side. By that time, the Nazi leader reasoned, Germany and the Axis would have won the war. But Adolf Hitler had made a big mistake. He did not know how hard Americans could work and how well they could use the rich resources of the United States.

Americans Help

During the depression, many people had been without jobs. In wartime, however, there were not enough workers to do all the work. As in World War I, the entire industrial strength of the nation was used to fight the enemy. Peacetime industries geared up for war. American factories made weapons for all the Allied countries, not just the United States. Car factories made planes, tanks, trucks, and jeeps. Factories that usually made refrigerators began producing rifles, machine guns, and bombs. Factories were open around the clock. Planes, guns, ships, and trucks came out of American factories and shipyards faster than anyone thought possible. By 1943, the United States was making five new ocean-going ships every day.

For the first time, women went off to work in great numbers. Thousands of women worked in the factories doing work that only men had done before. Women working in the factories changed people's ideas about what women could do. Women made planes and guns. They did hard, dirty, heavy work. Women also joined the armed forces.

United States War Production			
Airplanes	Tanks	Ships	Machine Guns
296,429	86,333	11,000	2,679,799

Women working in a defense plant during World War II

They drove trucks and fixed tanks. Women pilots flew new planes from the factories to the war zones.

Black Americans also served in the United States armed forces. About one million black men were in the army, navy, and marines. Most served in all-black units. But it was in this war that the United States took an important step. For the first time, some blacks and whites served together in the same unit.

The United States needed great amounts of food to feed the soldiers as well as the people in the Allied countries. American farmers raised record amounts of crops. At home, people planted gardens in their backyards and called them Victory Gardens. Victory Gardens produced about half the nation's vegetables during the war.

Children were involved in the war effort too. They helped collect scrap metal and rubber tires. These could be used again to make parts for planes and tanks.

Clothing styles changed because of the war. Boy's and men's pants were made without cuffs. Women's skirts were shorter. These styles used less material. The extra material was needed for uniforms and bandages.

Gasoline, tires, coffee, sugar, meat, and other goods were in short supply because of the war. To deal with the shortages, the government set up a system called **ration-ing.** People received stamps that entitled them to buy a

rationing

a system used for distributing goods that are in short supply

Children in Chicago, Illinois, collecting scrap to help in the war effort at home

Poster designed by Norman Rockwell showing an American soldier's welcome home

certain amount of the goods in short supply. To buy goods, a customer had to pay money and turn in the correct amount of stamps.

Rationing meant that Americans could not travel as much or always eat what they wanted to. But most Americans made sacrifices willingly to help the war effort.

The war cost a huge amount of money. Americans paid for part of the expenses with their taxes. But they also helped by buying government **bonds.** A bond is like a loan that the government agrees to pay back with interest in the future. Americans bought millions of dollars' worth of special wartime bonds called Victory Bonds.

The Sad Mistake

After the attack at Pearl Harbor, some people feared that the Japanese would invade the United States mainland. Thousands of Japanese Americans lived on the west coast, mostly in California. There was no reason to suspect that Japanese Americans would not be loyal to the United States during the war. But many people did suspect them. So Japanese Americans were forced to give up their homes and businesses. Then they were moved to camps that were far from the coast.

Camp for Japanese Americans during World War II

In spite of this treatment, Japanese American leaders appealed to the government for a chance to show their loyalty. Army units of Japanese Americans were formed. One of these units, the 442nd Regimental Combat Team, became one of the most famous units in the United States Army.

The 442nd first saw action in Italy. American forces were having trouble advancing against the German army. The 442nd attacked a German unit. Despite heavy fire, they advanced. Soldiers in the 442nd won many honors and medals.

After the war, Americans realized that Japanese Americans had been treated unfairly. It was indeed the United States' sad mistake.

Members of the 442nd Regimental Combat Team in France during World War II

Section Review

Write your answers on a sheet of paper.

1. What changes occurred in American industries during the war?
2. How did women help the war effort?
3. What important step took place in World War II that affected black servicemen?
4. What happened to Japanese Americans during the war?
5. Pretend that you were your present age during part of World War II. Describe how your life would have been different from what it is now.

Close-up on

Duke Ellington

Langston Hughes

Harlem in the 1920's The time was the 1920's. The place was Harlem, a section of New York City that was, and still is, the center of black art and culture. During the 1920's, Harlem was a place of great style and excitement. Black artists, musicians, and writers lived there. They began to develop a new pride in the experience of being black Americans. They used their talents to express this pride in paintings, songs, poetry, books, and plays.

Photographer James Van DerZee and artist Aaron Douglass used their pictures to show the everyday activities and important events in the lives of black people.

Musicians such as Duke Ellington and singer Ethel Waters played and sang a new kind of music—jazz—that became one of the United States' contributions to the music of the world. The music was bright and brassy. It had rhythm and a strong beat. Sometimes the musicians made up new sounds as they played.

Black actors also performed well-

*James Van DerZee photograph
of girls in a Harlem playground*

*Detail from the Jacob Lawrence
painting, "Migration of the Negro"*

known plays. Actors Paul Robeson and Richard B. Harrison could be seen in plays by Shakespeare, as well as in new plays by young, black writers.

During the 1920's, black writers made important contributions to American literature. Writers such as Langston Hughes, Countee Cullen, and Jean Toomer wrote poetry, novels, and essays. They wrote about what it was like to be black in the United States. They wrote about the difficulties black Americans often faced finding jobs and housing and getting fair treatment from whites. These writers described the ways that blacks attempted to overcome these difficulties.

People were excited about the spirit in Harlem at this time. The art, music, and literature produced was a lesson to all Americans. White Americans began to enjoy and appreciate black contributions to American life. Many of the works that came out of Harlem in the 1920's became an important part of the nation's culture.

UNIT REVIEW

Word Work

Write the sentences below on a sheet of paper. Fill in the blanks with the correct words from the list.

rationing   blitzkrieg   depression   suffrage   stocks

1. In 1869, women began a movement to gain _____.
2. In World War II, the Germans used a new type of battle attack called a _____.
3. During the _____, many people were out of work.
4. In the 1920's, many Americans bought _____ in different companies.
5. To keep meat supplies from running out during World War II, the United States government used _____.

Knowing the Facts

Write your answers on a sheet of paper.

1. What were the causes of the Spanish-American War?
2. What were the two causes of the depression?
3. Explain two goals of the New Deal.
4. How did the United States get involved in World War II?
5. How did Americans at home help in the war effort?

Using What You Know

Choose one of the following activities. Follow the directions given here.

1. Use research materials in the library and an outline map of the world to prepare a battle map of either World War I or World War II.
2. Write a two-page report about the changes that took place in the United States during the 1920's. Discuss different groups, such as women and blacks, and give examples of changes that affected them in particular. Also describe some of the business methods that changed the way Americans acquired goods.

Skills Practice

Use both maps to answer the questions below. Write your answers on a sheet of paper.

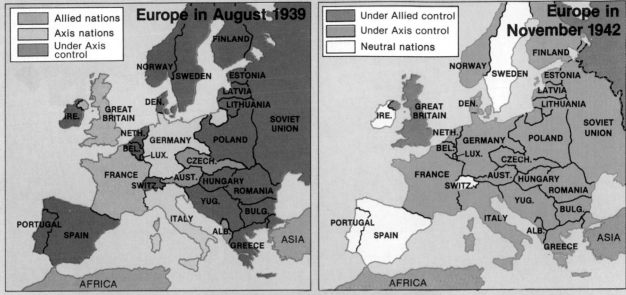

Europe in August 1939

- Allied nations
- Axis nations
- Under Axis control

FINLAND
NORWAY
SWEDEN
ESTONIA
LATVIA
LITHUANIA
DEN.
GREAT BRITAIN
IRE.
SOVIET UNION
NETH.
GERMANY
POLAND
BEL.
LUX.
CZECH.
FRANCE
AUST.
HUNGARY
SWITZ.
ROMANIA
YUG.
ITALY
BULG.
PORTUGAL
SPAIN
ALB.
GREECE
ASIA
AFRICA

Europe in November 1942

- Under Allied control
- Under Axis control
- Neutral nations

FINLAND
NORWAY
SWEDEN
ESTONIA
LATVIA
LITHUANIA
IRE.
GREAT BRITAIN
DEN.
SOVIET UNION
NETH.
GERMANY
POLAND
BEL.
LUX.
CZECH.
FRANCE
AUST.
HUNGARY
SWITZ.
ROMANIA
YUG.
ITALY
BULG.
PORTUGAL
SPAIN
ALB.
GREECE
ASIA
AFRICA

1. In 1939, which were the Axis nations? Which were the Allied nations?
2. Which nations were controlled by Axis powers in 1942? How many of these nations had been Allied powers before 1942?
3. Which power seemed to be winning the war in 1942? Why?

Your Heritage

Many people who were alive during the 1920's, 1930's, and World War II are still alive today. Ask people who were alive during those years to tell you what the times were like. Ask them what they were doing during certain times, such as the 1920's, the depression, and the war. Take notes during your interviews and report what you find out to the class.

UNIT 8

The United States Today: Challenge and Hope

The United States changed rapidly after World War II. Suburbs grew. Superhighways changed the way the nation looked. Television and computers changed home life and businesses. Scientists conquered many diseases and made space travel a reality.

Americans faced other challenges in the fifties, sixties, seventies, and eighties. Peace was threatened by the Soviet Union's desire to control more and more land. At home, blacks, women, and other groups demanded fairer treatment. People grew concerned about dirty air and water.

In this unit, you will read about changes in the United States since World War II. You will learn how Americans have worked to meet their nation's challenges.

CHAPTER 20 The United States After World War II

People celebrating the end of World War II in New York City

People shouted with joy. They leaned on their car horns and cheered. World War II was over. Americans welcomed their soldiers home from all over the globe.

People hoped the world would be at peace. Instead, the United States was soon facing a new rival—its wartime ally, the Soviet Union. This rivalry and other developments at home helped shape American life after World War II.

At the end of this chapter, you should be able to:

○ Identify the causes of the Cold War and describe Cold War actions of the 1940's, 1950's, and 1960's.

● Compare and use maps drawn to different scales.

○ Describe changes in American life after World War II.

○ Summarize the achievements of Presidents of the United States since 1952.

370

1 The Search for Peace

During World War II, the Soviet Union and the United States fought side by side. After the war, the two countries were on opposite sides in a new conflict. Americans believed that the Soviet way of life and Soviet efforts to control other countries robbed people of their freedom. They saw the Soviet Union as a threat to peace. So the two wartime allies became rivals.

The Soviet government and way of life is called **communism.** Under communism, all land, buildings, and businesses are owned by everyone together. The leaders of the communist government decide how these things will be used and who will use them. They decide where people live, work, and go to school. They decide what information gets printed in books and newspapers and what television shows people see.

The Soviet Union is run by the Communist party. Only certain people are allowed to belong to it. It is also the only political party in the Soviet Union.

After World War II, Soviet leaders tried to spread communism to other countries. The United States government opposed the spread of communism outside the Soviet Union.

communism
a system in which all property, including industry, is owned by all the people and managed by the government

The Cold War

The struggle between the United States and communist countries after World War II was called the **Cold War.** The war was "cold" because it was fought mainly without guns or bombs. The "weapons" in the Cold War were words, ideas, and economic and military aid.

The Cold War began when World War II ended. Soviet soldiers who had fought in Eastern Europe continued to occupy countries in that area. Within a few years, there

Cold War
the struggle between communist and democratic nations, using ideas and aid rather than weapons

Berlin airlift

airlift

the transporting of goods by airplane when ground routes are blocked

were communist governments in Poland, Hungary, and Czechoslovakia. These new governments took their orders from the Soviet Union.

After the war, the Soviets also occupied part of Germany. The United States, Great Britain, France, and the Soviet Union each governed a part of Germany. The first three countries wanted to create a new, democratic Germany. The Soviet Union wanted the new Germany to be communist. So Germany remained divided. West Germany became a democratic nation. East Germany—the area held by the Soviet Union—became communist.

Like Germany, the city of Berlin was also divided. The former German capital city lay 176 kilometers (110 miles) inside East Germany. East Berlin was communist. West Berlin was like an island of democracy inside communist territory.

In 1948, the communists tried to force West Berlin to become part of East Germany. They blocked all roads and railroads that led to the city. This action cut off all supplies of food and fuel to West Berlin.

The United States took quick action to protect West Berlin. President Harry Truman began an **airlift**—a project that sent supplies into West Berlin by airplane. Thousands

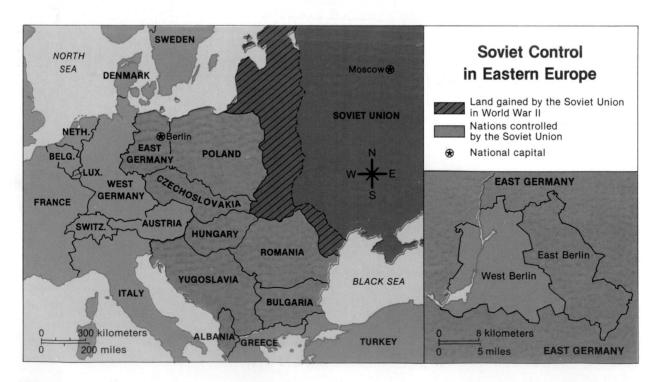

372

of American planes flew supplies to West Berlin. The Berlin Airlift went on for almost a year. Finally, the Soviet Union realized its blockade was not working. The Soviets reopened transportation routes to West Berlin.

The situation in Berlin remained tense though. Many East Germans escaped from their communist government by sneaking into West Berlin. This angered and embarrassed the East Germans and the Soviets. In 1961, the East Germans built the Berlin Wall. This concrete and wire wall stretches all along the West Berlin–East Berlin border and is guarded by soldiers. It makes it very difficult for East Germans to leave their country.

Berlin Wall

The War in Korea

World War II produced a divided Germany in Europe. In Asia, Korea was also divided at the end of the war. Soviet troops occupied the northern part of Korea. American troops were in the South. A communist government was set up in North Korea. South Korea had an anti-communist government. In 1950, the Cold War in Korea became "hot." Soviet-trained North Koreans invaded the South. In a few weeks, they overran most of South Korea.

The United Nations voted to send in troops to help South Korea fight back. The war lasted more than three years. Soldiers from the United States and from 15 other nations joined the South Koreans. The Chinese joined the North Koreans. In the end, UN forces succeeded. They forced the North Koreans and Chinese back across the border that had been established before the Korean War began.

Trouble in Cuba and Vietnam

Americans had long been worried about the worldwide growth of communism. The take-over of Cuba by Fidel (fee-**dell**) Castro in 1959 added to those fears. Castro's government had been receiving help from the Soviet Union. The small island of Cuba lies only 145 kilometers (90 miles) from Florida. Many Americans thought that the Soviets could easily attack the United States from Cuba if there were a war.

In 1962, the United States learned that the Soviets were

American soldier in Vietnam

planning to install missiles in Cuba. Soviet ships were making deliveries of missile-building equipment to Cuba. American leaders decided that the Soviets had to be stopped. American ships surrounded Cuba. They prevented the deliveries from getting through.

This blockade worked. Soviet ships heading for Cuba turned back. The missiles in Cuba were removed. The crisis, or time of danger, was over quickly. But it made Americans feel they had to be on constant guard against the Soviet Union.

In the 1950's and 1960's, the Cold War also became "hot" in Southeast Asia. Soldiers from communist North Vietnam attacked cities in noncommunist South Vietnam. The South Vietnamese asked the United States for help. At first, Americans were sent to train South Vietnamese soldiers. Then, in 1964, the United States Congress voted to send American soldiers to Vietnam. By 1968, about 500,000 American soldiers were in Vietnam. The Soviet Union and China gave supplies to the North Vietnamese. The fighting went on and thousands of Americans and Vietnamese died.

As the death and destruction continued, people looked for ways to end the fighting. In 1973, a cease-fire was agreed upon. All sides agreed to stop fighting. The United States withdrew its troops from Vietnam. But the fighting did not stop for long. By 1975, South Vietnam had surrendered to North Vietnam.

Section Review

Write your answers on a sheet of paper.
1. What was the Cold War? Why did it begin?
2. Who came to help South Korea fight off North Korean troops?
3. Why were many Americans frightened when they learned there were Soviet missiles in Cuba?
4. The Cold War began in the 1940's. Based on what you have seen in newspapers or on television, explain whether you think the Cold War is still going on today.

Comparing Map Scales

When comparing one map to another, it is important to notice the scale used to draw the map. The scale indicates how many kilometers or miles are represented by each centimeter or inch on the map.

Each of the two maps below has a different scale. On the map of East and West Germany, one centimeter equals 143 kilometers. The other map shows only one part of Germany, the area around Berlin. On this inset map, one centimeter equals only 30 kilometers. The map was made on a small scale in order to show the Berlin area in greater detail. Notice that the Berlin area is outlined on the map of Germany to help you make comparisons.

Practice Your Skills

1. What is the distance in kilometers from West Berlin to Munich? Which map did you consult for the answer?
2. Name four towns or cities that appear only on the inset map. Why do you suppose these places do not appear on the larger map?
3. What is the distance in kilometers from East Berlin to Dessau? Which map did you consult for the answer?

2 Life After World War II

During the 1950's, almost all Americans were worried about the Cold War. But in everyday life, it seemed that Americans were better off than ever. Business was booming. There were plenty of goods to buy, and most Americans could afford to buy them. New industries, new products, and new neighborhoods appeared during those years.

Boom Times

In the 1950's, the United States enjoyed the greatest economic growth of its history. In a little over one decade, the number of employed people jumped from 54 million to 70 million. By 1960, 94 percent of Americans who wanted a job had one. The average worker's pay rose steadily. The country's **gross national product,** or GNP, went up too. The GNP is the total dollar value of all goods and services a country produces in any one year. The GNP of the United States rose from $286 billion in 1950 to $506 billion in 1960.

The reason for the booming economy was clear. It was a result of the shift from wartime to peace. During World War II, most Americans had jobs but there was little to buy. The United States was using its resources to win a war. Instead of cars, the country made tanks and planes. Instead of

gross national product (GNP)

the total value in dollars of all goods and services produced by a country in one year

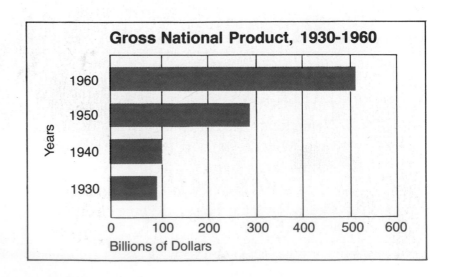

clothing for civilians, the United States made uniforms.

After the war, Americans went on a shopping spree. People needed new houses, cars, furniture, appliances, and clothing. Factory owners needed more workers to meet the demand. That created more jobs. The new workers added to the boom, too, by using their salaries to buy the goods they needed.

Completely new industries also added to the boom. Many of these centered around electronics and computers. New words such as "hi-fi," "TV," and "transistor" became part of the American vocabulary.

Like the economy, the **birth rate** in the United States boomed in the fifties. The birth rate is the number of babies born each year per 1,000 people. Before the war, the birth rate was 19 per 1,000. By 1947, just after the end of the war, the birth rate had gone up to 27 per 1,000. The increased birth rate, or "baby boom," took place as the war ended and people settled down to raise families. Many parents believed that the world would be at peace. And they felt they could support their children in a growing economy.

birth rate
the number of births per 1,000 people in a year

People shopping for appliances after World War II

The Rise of the Suburbs

To care for their growing families, Americans needed houses. Builders quickly supplied them. Housing developments, or large groups of similar houses, were built in towns outside the nation's cities. These towns, called **suburbs,** grew rapidly.

Americans moved to the suburbs for several reasons. Many wanted to live in one-family houses with yards. This type of house was more cheaply built in the suburbs where there were large amounts of open land.

People also liked the fact that suburbs were usually cleaner and quieter than most cities. Suburban schools were thought to be better than city schools. Suburbs were said to have less crime too.

Cars and new highways made travel between cities and suburbs easy. Many people worked in the city and lived in the suburbs. As time passed, new stores and businesses also moved to the suburbs. Many suburban residents started to shop and work closer to home. By the 1960's, cities were losing people and business to the suburbs.

suburb

a town that is close to a city

View of a suburban housing development built in the 1950's

"I Love Lucy," starring Lucille Ball, was a popular television comedy show in television's early years.

The Growth of Television

During the 1950's, more and more people began to watch television. In 1948, there were only 17,000 television sets in the United States. By 1960, the number was up to 46 million. Ninety percent of American families had sets. And people were spending more and more time watching them.

Television's early viewers saw comedies, quiz shows, musical shows, and westerns. Many of the shows were not filmed before broadcast. They were performed live in front of the television cameras.

Television brought many interesting and entertaining shows into American living rooms. Americans could watch some of the world's best actors without leaving their homes. They had front-row seats for important speeches and events. The evening news was like a living newspaper. People could see headline-making events on television as they happened.

Sports fans enjoyed games broadcast from all over the nation. Sports such as football and basketball grew in popularity because of television.

Viewers also tuned in to operas, concerts, and plays. In 1953, more people watched one of Shakespeare's plays on television than had seen it performed on the stage in 350 years!

Howdy Doody was the star of a popular children's television show during the 1950's.

The Youth Culture

As a result of the "baby boom," young people made up a large part of the American population in the 1950's and 1960's. Many of these young people had a lot in common. They all grew up during the Cold War. Fear and the threat of war were part of their childhood memories. This was the first generation that had grown up watching television shows. Almost all of them liked rock music. Because of their common experiences, they felt that they were a group apart from the older generation.

In the 1960's, many young people began to question some basic American values. Many young Americans thought their parents' way of life was not the one they wanted for themselves. Some left their parents' homes in the suburbs. They moved in with other young people in the cities or they moved to the country. They left behind their television sets and other possessions—the products of the fifties.

Young people developed their own way of life—a youth culture. Instead of wealth and power, young people valued peace, love, and the freedom to do as they chose.

The youth culture was also shaped by the events of the time. Many young people questioned American involvement in other countries' affairs. They held protests against the Vietnamese War. The struggle by blacks and women for equal rights that was taking place in the 1960's also affected the way young people looked at their society.

Young woman at a rally supporting equal rights for blacks

Section Review

Write your answers on a sheet of paper.
1. What was the main cause of the economic boom that started in the 1950's?
2. Name three reasons why people moved to the suburbs.
3. List three ways in which you think television affects your life. Tell whether you think the effect is good or bad.

3 Recent Presidents

Americans depend on the President to work for peace, economic growth, and equal rights for all Americans. Since World War II, many problems have faced the Presidents as they tried to achieve these goals.

Dwight D. Eisenhower (1953–1961)

World War II was still on the minds of many Americans when they voted for Dwight D. Eisenhower, the Republican candidate for President in 1952. During the war, General Eisenhower had led the Allies to victory over Germany. Now Americans wanted him to lead the United States during the Cold War.

As President, Eisenhower set up few new programs. Instead he tried to cut the size and responsibilities of the federal government. This policy pleased many American voters. With a booming economy, most Americans needed little help from the government. In 1956, Eisenhower was reelected by a wide margin.

One of President Eisenhower's achievements was the construction of an interstate highway system, highways that go from one state to another. The number of cars and trucks in the United States had greatly increased during the 1950's. Under Eisenhower, the federal government began a huge program of highway building. These better roads helped move industrial and agricultural products to markets more quickly. The new highways also made travel between states easier.

Dwight D. Eisenhower at the 1952 Republican National Convention

John F. Kennedy (1961–1963)

By 1960, Americans were ready for a change. The Democratic candidate, John F. Kennedy, won the election by a small percentage of votes. At 43, he was the youngest President ever elected. Kennedy believed the American space program was very important. During his presidency, the United States sent its first astronaut into space. Kennedy also wanted to improve medical care and education in the

John F. Kennedy and his wife, Jacqueline Kennedy, campaigning in New York City in 1960

Peace Corps

a program of the United States government in which Americans teach needed skills to people around the world

civil rights

the rights guaranteed to every American by the Constitution and by laws passed by Congress

United States. And he supported equal rights for all Americans.

President Kennedy was also interested in improving conditions around the world. He set up the **Peace Corps.** It is a program that helps people in poor nations. Peace Corps volunteers train people in modern methods of farming, building, education, and health care.

The Peace Corps was a big success. But Kennedy did not have a chance to succeed in achieving his other goals. He was assassinated in 1963. Vice-President Lyndon Johnson became the new President.

Lyndon B. Johnson (1963–1969)

Before he was Vice-President, President Johnson had been a successful senator from Texas. He knew Congress well. Johnson was able to convince its members to pass the laws Kennedy had supported. One such law was the Civil Rights Act of 1964. **Civil rights** are the rights guaranteed to every American by the Constitution and by laws passed by Congress. The Civil Rights Act made job discrimination against blacks and other minorities illegal.

President Johnson did much to help the poor. His War on Poverty improved many people's lives. Laws were passed to provide food, jobs, and medical care for Americans in need.

In another war—the Vietnamese War—Johnson was not so successful. Many Americans were angry that American soldiers were fighting in Vietnam. Johnson himself was disappointed at his failure to win the war. So he decided not to run for reelection in 1968.

Richard M. Nixon (1969–1974)

Richard M. Nixon was elected President in 1968. As the Republican candidate, Nixon had promised to end the Vietnamese War. But before the war ended, it spread to Vietnam's neighbors, Cambodia and Laos (**louss**). It was not until 1973 that the last American troops were withdrawn from Vietnam.

Nixon took some important steps toward world peace. He visited the communist leaders of the People's Republic of China and the Soviet Union. Nixon's visits helped reduce the tensions of the Cold War.

After he was reelected in 1972, a **scandal** destroyed Nixon's ability to govern. A scandal is a situation that shocks and offends people. The scandal began during the 1972 presidential election campaign. Men were caught breaking into the offices of the Democratic Party. They were looking for information they could use against the Democrats in the election. These offices were at the Watergate Apartments in Washington, D.C.

It became clear that Republican officials from the White House had organized the break-in. President Nixon had tried to cover up this illegal act by holding back evidence from investigators. In order to avoid being impeached by Congress, Richard Nixon left office on August 9, 1974. He was the first President to resign.

Gerald R. Ford (1974–1977)

Vice-President Gerald Ford was the first person to become President because of a resignation. Unemployment and inflation were high when Ford took office. During his presidency, the economy improved slightly. The nation also celebrated its two-hundredth birthday while Ford was President.

Lyndon B. Johnson being sworn in as President on November 22, 1963, the day President Kennedy was killed

scandal
a public disgrace

President Richard M. Nixon and his wife, Patricia Nixon, at the Great Wall in China

From left to right, Anwar Sadat of Egypt, President Jimmy Carter, and Menachem Begin of Israel, shaking hands after signing the Camp David Agreement

Jimmy Carter (1977–1981)

In 1976, Americans elected a Democrat—Jimmy Carter. His greatest success was his work for peace between Egypt and Israel (**iz**-ree-ul). Carter and the leaders of Egypt and Israel worked out a peace treaty. The treaty was called the Camp David Agreement. It was an important step toward ending the violence in the troubled Middle East.

The Middle East also produced the greatest problem of Carter's presidency. In 1979, a revolution took place in Iran. Supporters of the new government took control of the American embassy in Iran on November 4, 1979. Americans there became prisoners, or **hostages.**

President Carter worked to find a peaceful way to get the hostages back. The hostages were finally freed in 1981 as a new President, Ronald Reagan, took office.

hostage

a person who is taken prisoner and not released until certain promises or conditions are met

Section Review

Write your answers on a sheet of paper.
1. Name an important accomplishment of the Eisenhower and Kennedy presidencies.
2. What was President Johnson's War on Poverty?
3. Why did President Nixon resign from the presidency?
4. Why would an American President try to bring peace to two nations far from the United States?

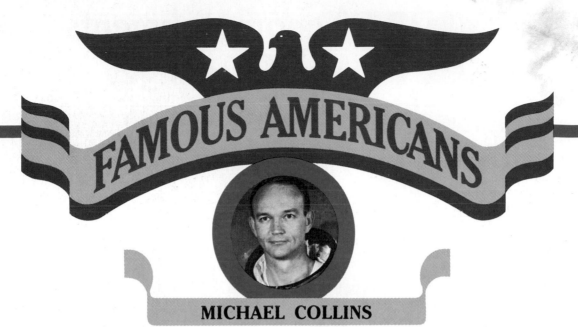

FAMOUS AMERICANS

MICHAEL COLLINS

Throughout his life, Michael Collins has held many different jobs. But he is best known for the job he did in 1969. Collins was a pilot for *Apollo 11*. That was the first space mission to land people on the moon.

Michael Collins was born on October 31, 1930, in Rome, Italy. His father was in the United States military, and the family moved often as Collins was growing up. His best subject in school was mathematics, but he majored in science at West Point Military Academy. He graduated from West Point in 1952.

In 1960, Collins became a test pilot. He tested new airplanes to see how well they worked. When he learned about the nation's space program, Collins applied to be an astronaut. He was chosen to be a pilot for the Gemini program, which sent two astronauts at a time into orbit around the earth. In July 1966, Collins and astronaut John Young circled, or orbited, the earth for three days in *Gemini 10*.

When the crew of the moon mission, *Apollo 11,* was chosen, Collins was included. He was to be the pilot of the *Columbia*, the craft that would remain in space, above the moon's surface. Neil Armstrong and Edwin E. Aldrin, Jr., would land on the moon.

Apollo 11 blasted off on July 16, 1969. Four days later, Armstrong and Aldrin became the first men to land on the moon. Meanwhile, Collins stayed in the main spaceship and orbited the moon 30 times.

After the *Apollo 11* mission, Collins left the space program to try other jobs and to spend more time with his family. In 1971, he became director of the National Air and Space Museum of the Smithsonian Institution in Washington.

Through his many jobs, Collins has shown his courage, his love of adventure, and his excitement about the worlds beyond the earth.

CHAPTER 21 Accomplishments and Challenges

Two-hundredth birthday celebration in New York City, July 4, 1976

As the United States entered its third century as a nation, many Americans were filled with pride and hope. They had pride in the achievements of the past. They had hope for greater accomplishments in the future.

In this chapter, you will read about progress made in science. You will learn about efforts to achieve equal rights for all Americans. You will also read about the challenges that Americans hope to meet in the future.

At the end of this chapter, you should be able to:

○ List American achievements in space and medicine.
○ Tell how Americans worked for greater equality at home.
● Explain how a graph can be used to make a point.
○ Describe the challenges faced by Americans today.

1 Science and Progress

Television was just one invention that changed American life after World War II. In the 1940's and 1950's, scientists started experimenting with new ideas and inventions in many areas.

The Race to Space

In October 1957, a strange object streaked through the night sky. It was *Sputnik I*—the first **satellite** ever launched from the earth. This humanmade object orbited the earth and sent back information about outer space. Many Americans were worried when they heard about it. *Sputnik I* seemed to prove that the Soviet Union was ahead of the United States in the fields of science and technology.

Throughout the early 1960's, the Soviet Union kept the lead in space exploration. But President Kennedy was determined to see the United States catch up. In 1961, Kennedy had set a goal for the country: Americans would land a spaceship on the moon by 1970. The nation's moon program was called Project Apollo.

Each year, astronauts on Apollo missions made more progress in space. Finally, on July 20, 1969, the *Apollo 11* mission achieved the historic goal. The American spacecraft *Eagle* landed on the moon. Neil Armstrong, commander of the mission, became the first person ever to walk on the moon's surface. His first step on the moon, he said, was "one small step for man" but "one giant leap for mankind."

After exploring the moon, the United States sent up spaceships without crews that reached farther into space. In the 1970's, United States spaceships sent back information from the planets Mars, Venus, Mercury, and Jupiter. Later spaceships moved on to Saturn.

satellite

a humanmade object that orbits around the earth, moon, or other bodies in space to gather and send information

Rocket launch at Cape Canaveral, Florida

In 1973, the United States launched *Skylab,* an orbiting space station. Crews of scientists could stay aboard *Skylab* for more than two months at a time. *Skylab* was used for many important experiments. Telescopes on board the station were used for studying objects deep in space. The *Skylab* telescopes could reveal much more about the universe than telescopes on earth. There is no atmosphere in space to dim the view of the telescopes on board *Skylab.*

The space shuttle *Columbia* was launched by the United States in 1981. The *Columbia* was our first reusable spaceship. It could take off like a rocket and land like an airplane. Each space shuttle could be used for more than 100 missions. The space shuttle was used to transport people and equipment back and forth from space to earth. The *Columbia* carried many American satellites into orbit. It also launched satellites for other countries and for private companies.

The second space shuttle, *Challenger,* made its first flight in 1983. Sally K. Ride, a member of the *Challenger's* second crew, became the first American woman to travel in space. Lieutenant Colonel Guy Bluford became the first black American to travel in space on the Challenger's third flight. In 1984, the *Challenger* successfully repaired a damaged satellite and returned it to orbit.

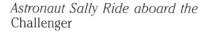
Astronaut Sally Ride aboard the Challenger

The War Against Disease

In the field of medicine, new scientific knowledge has helped people to live longer and healthier lives. Penicillin, an antibiotic, or germ killer, saved thousands of lives during World War II. Many new antibiotics have been developed since the war. Vaccines, or substances that prevent diseases, have also been developed. As a result, there are far fewer cases of diseases such as polio and measles.

Medical scientists have made advances in the operating room too. Microsurgery, the use of microscopes in operations, is becoming more common. Microsurgery allows doctors to rejoin very small nerves and blood vessels that have been cut or torn.

Microsurgery is also used to replace diseased organs, such as kidneys, livers, or hearts. These replacements, or transplants, allow some patients to live longer. At first doctors were unable to solve the problem of organ rejection. The bodies of patients often rejected transplanted organs. Further research helped to solve this problem. Today organ transplants are a common medical practice.

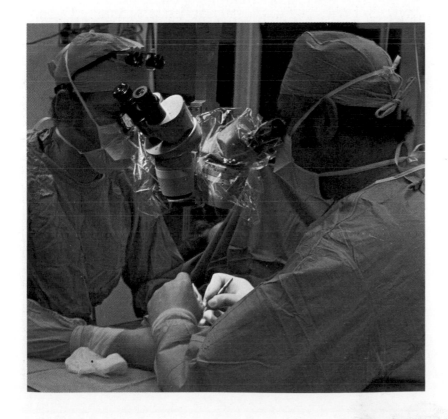

Microsurgery being performed

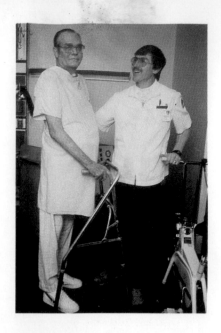

Barney Clark after his heart transplant operation

Scientists have also developed artificial organs to replace damaged or diseased ones. Kidney dialysis (die-**al**-uh-sis) machines help keep people alive whose natural kidneys are no longer healthy. The dialysis machine removes harmful wastes from the patient's blood. An artificial heart, containing two pumps, was designed by an American doctor in 1982. It was placed in a patient whose own heart was diseased. The patient was Barney Clark, a retired dentist from Washington State.

Americans are becoming healthier for other reasons too. They are exercising more and developing healthful eating habits. Physically fit people develop fewer diseases. They also recover from illnesses more quickly.

Speedy Machines

In 1946, the first electronic computer was put to work in the United States. Thirty-five years later, over one million were in use in the United States. Today computers play an important role in science, business, industry, agriculture, education, and everyday life.

Computers can perform thousands of calculations every second. They also store millions of bits of information in a tiny space. As a result, businesses can keep better records. Scientists can solve problems more quickly. Cities can run their transportation systems more safely. The federal government uses computers to help collect taxes. Police departments use computers to store and to organize millions

ENIAC, the first computer

of fingerprints. Computers can even be used to compose music, write poems, and make drawings.

In the late 1970's, many Americans began to use computers at home. Computer games became a popular source of entertainment. Some families bought small computers to help them keep family records.

Scientists in the 1980's are working to build computers with artificial intelligence, or AI. A computer with AI would be able to reason or think like a human being. Creating AI has turned out to be very difficult. American scientists, however, are making great progress toward building a computer that is truly intelligent.

Schoolchildren at work on classroom computer

Section Review

Write your answers on a sheet of paper.
1. What was *Sputnik I?* Why did it worry Americans?
2. Describe three advances in the war against disease.
3. What are some of the ways computers can help people in business, science, and city government?
4. What are two ways that computers make your life different from the way you would have lived 60 years ago?

2 Advances in Democracy

During the 1960's, the United States made great advances in space. Closer to home, however, we were making different types of progress. While doctors were curing long-feared diseases, other people were looking at the problems of society. Discrimination and poverty needed solutions too.

The Struggle for Civil Rights

More than a million blacks served in the United States armed forces during World War II. They fought bravely for freedom around the world. Yet at home they were denied many freedoms. They were not allowed to live in certain neighborhoods or go to certain schools. Many could not get jobs or even exercise their right to vote.

After the war, some states still practiced segregation. Many people felt that setting aside schools or restaurants for whites only was unfair. So many blacks and whites looked for ways to end segregation.

In 1954, an elementary school student from Kansas won an important battle in the fight against segregation. Linda Brown wanted to go to a school near her home. But a law said the school was for whites only. Linda Brown, who was black, would have to go elsewhere.

Linda Brown and her parents decided to fight this law in court. In 1954, their case reached the Supreme Court, the highest court in the United States. The famous court decision is known as *Brown* v. *Board of Education.*

The Supreme Court justices agreed with Linda Brown. They said having separate schools for black and white students was unconstitutional. All states had to **integrate** their schools. To integrate is to do away with segregation by bringing people of different races together.

After the Supreme Court decision, other public places were integrated as well. Some cities had laws saying blacks could only take seats at the back end of buses. In 1955, a black woman named Rosa Parks sat down in the

integrate
to bring people of different races together

392

front of a bus in Montgomery, Alabama. Parks refused to get up from the seat so that a white person could sit down. As a result, she was arrested.

Angry about the arrest, Montgomery's blacks refused to ride city buses. This boycott lasted close to 13 months. At last, the law was changed, and Montgomery's buses were integrated.

The bus boycott was led by Dr. Martin Luther King, Jr., a 26-year-old black minister. Dr. King had deep religious beliefs, as well as a strong desire to win blacks their civil rights.

King believed in nonviolent, or peaceful, protest when blacks were denied their rights. Blacks followed Dr. King's advice. They held "sit-ins" at segregated restaurants. At a sit-in, blacks would sit at a restaurant table or counter and demand the same service as white customers. They would stay in their seats until they were served. In other peaceful protests, black and white freedom riders rode buses from state to state. They tried to integrate buses, bus terminals, and other public places along the bus routes.

Many of the blacks who worked for integration were arrested. Newspapers and television news programs showed pictures of black protestors being beaten by police. These shocking scenes upset both blacks and whites. Many more people joined the movement for civil rights.

Rosa Parks sitting in the front of a bus in Montgomery, Alabama, after the city's segregation laws were changed

Sit-in demonstration at a lunch counter in Little Rock, Arkansas, in 1963

Dr. Martin Luther King, Jr. speaking at a civil rights march in Washington, D.C., in 1963

Rev. Jesse Jackson, Dr. Martin Luther King Jr., and Rev. Ralph Abernathy on the balcony in Memphis where Dr. King was killed a day later

The 1960's were a time of change for blacks in the United States. In August 1963, 250,000 Americans marched in Washington, D.C. They demanded equal rights for black Americans. Congress later responded by passing the Civil Rights Act of 1964 and other laws that guarantee equal rights to blacks. Also in 1964, Dr. Martin Luther King, Jr., won the Nobel Peace Prize for his civil rights work. In 1967, Thurgood Marshall became the first black Supreme Court justice.

However, for most blacks, conditions were slow to improve. Many blacks continued to live in poor housing. Often they could not find jobs. In the mid-1960's, riots broke out in some of the black neighborhoods of American cities. Then, in 1968, Dr. King was assassinated by a white man. Blacks grew angrier, and there were more violent protests.

The violence drew attention to the problems blacks faced. Working together, blacks and whites have been looking for solutions during the 1970's and 1980's. Much progress has been made, but there is still a great deal left to do.

In recent years, blacks have also gained important new political power. Black mayors head 30 of the nation's largest cities. Among the most important black leaders today are Mayor Thomas Bradley of Los Angeles, Mayor Andrew Young of Atlanta, Mayor Coleman Young of Detroit, Mayor W. Wilson Goode of Philadelphia, and Mayor Harold Washington of Chicago. Reverend Jesse Jackson was a candidate for the Democratic nomination for President in 1984. Jackson did well in several states, but he failed to win the nomination.

Democratic candidate Jesse Jackson campaigning for the Presidential nomination, 1984

One of the keys to black progress has been education. The number of black students attending college in 1975 was nearly four times as large as in 1965. By the early 1980's, the percentage of black high-school graduates going on to college was about the same as that of white graduates.

(left) College graduates at commencement

(right) Lt. Colonel Guy Bluford, a Vietnam veteran, is an aerospace engineer and was the first black American in space.

Women Fight for Equal Rights

The Nineteenth Amendment, which gave women the right to vote, was passed in 1920. Laws passed in the late 1800's and early 1900's had also helped women gain more rights. Women could own property and run businesses. Many colleges began accepting female students. A few women were elected to political office. But women still did not have the same rights as men.

In the 1960's, a movement was begun to gain equal rights for women in all aspects of life. It was called the **women's liberation movement.** Women's liberation supporters were called **feminists.** They said women should have the same opportunities as men to participate in sports, education, business, and other career areas.

Feminists also worked to have certain laws passed. These laws say that women cannot be treated unfairly just because they are women. For example, many states used to deny women credit so that women could not borrow money on their own. Many women supported the equal rights amendment, or ERA. This amendment to the United States Constitution would guarantee that all laws be applied equally to men and women. The ERA in 1982 failed to be ratified, or approved, by enough states. It did not become a part of the Constitution.

women's liberation movement
a campaign by women to achieve equal rights with men in all aspects of life

feminist
a person who supports equal rights for women

In the 1960's, women began to pursue careers in all kinds of fields. At the left is a mayor and at the right is a telephone company worker.

MAYOR
CAROLE KEETON McCLELLAN

Supreme Court Justice Sandra Day O'Connor taking the oath of office given by Chief Justice Warren Burger

Women have made important gains in entering new careers. In 1950, only about 30 percent of American women worked outside the home. By 1980, more than 50 percent were part of the paid labor force. Many women have entered such fields as law, medicine, engineering, and government service. Nearly 1,000 women hold offices in state legislatures. More than 20 women serve in the House of Representatives. In 1981, Sandra Day O'Connor became the first woman Justice of the United States Supreme Court.

Equal Rights for All

Other groups have also joined the effort to end discrimination in the United States. During the 1960's and 1970's, many American Indians protested. They wanted to end the unfair treatment they received from other Americans and the United States government. They demanded an end to discrimination in housing, education, and jobs. Some wanted a part of their land back.

In 1968, a group of Indians organized the American Indian Movement (AIM). AIM demanded better opportunities for the Indian people. The leaders of AIM organized demonstrations to make other Americans aware of their demands. In 1972, nearly 1,000 demonstrators sat-in at the offices of the Bureau of Indian Affairs in Washington, D.C. At the town of Wounded Knee, South Dakota, Indian demonstrators clashed with police. One Indian was killed, and another was wounded.

American Indians also studied the treaties their tribes had signed many years before with the United States government. In some cases land had been taken from the tribes without proper payment, or without payment at all. To make up for this, United States courts ruled that the federal government owed some tribes millions of dollars. In other cases, lands once owned by some tribes have been returned to them.

American Indian protestors in front of the White House in Washington, D.C.

Cesar Chavez at a United Farm Workers rally

Mayor Henry Cisneros of San Antonio, Texas

refugee
a person who flees from her or his home country to escape discrimination for political or religious beliefs

Hispanic, or Spanish-speaking, Americans have also been working to end discrimination. Hispanic Americans are the fastest-growing minority group in the United States today. In 1970, there were about 9 million Hispanics in this country. By 1980, their number had reached about 14.6 million, or 6.4 percent of the population. The number of Hispanics in the United States is expected to rise to about 47 million by the year 2020. They would then be the largest minority group in the nation.

Hispanic Americans came to the United States from Mexico, Puerto Rico, and the nations of South and Central America. Mexican Americans are the largest group of Spanish-speaking Americans. They have lived in the American Southwest for hundreds of years, often working as ranchers, farmers, and craftspeople. They have contributed much to American life.

Hispanic Americans also face severe problems. About one in four Hispanic families lives in poverty. Many Hispanic workers are unskilled. Most are unable to find high-paying jobs. Many Hispanic children must drop out of school to help support their families.

In the 1960's, Mexican-American farm workers joined together to try to improve their working conditions. Led by Cesar Chavez (**say**-zahr **shah**-vez), they formed a labor union—the United Farm Workers. By the early 1970's, many farmers had signed agreements with the union.

As with other minority groups, Hispanic Americans have increased their political power in recent years. In the early 1980's, Hispanics were elected mayors of several large American cities. Henry Cisneros became mayor of San Antonio, Texas. The voters of Denver elected Frederico Peña as their leader. Nine Hispanics were elected to the House of Representatives. New Mexico elected a Hispanic governor, Toney Anaya.

A Home for the Homeless

In the past the United States has usually welcomed **refugees.** Refugees are people who leave their home countries because they are attacked for their political or religious beliefs.

Some refugees have fled communist-controlled countries. When the North Vietnamese took control of South Vietnam after the Vietnamese War, many people fled that country in overcrowded, unsafe boats and ships. Some of these "boat people" came to the United States. By 1980, there were over 260,000 Vietnamese refugees living in the United States. Many Americans helped the refugees by sponsoring individual families.

Other refugees have come to our country to escape the communist government in Cuba. Soviet Jews have come to the United States so that they can have religious freedom. Some Americans say that the United States will become too crowded if we continue to welcome refugees. But others say the United States must remain open to these homeless people. Our country is working to find a solution to this difficult problem.

Vietnamese refugee children playing at Fort Indiantown Gap, Pennsylvania

Section Review

Write your answers on a sheet of paper.
1. How did Linda Brown help fight segregation?
2. What type of protest did Dr. Martin Luther King, Jr., believe in? Give an example of this kind of protest.
3. What is the aim of the women's liberation movement?
4. How might the struggle by blacks for civil rights have encouraged other groups to work for their rights too?

Understanding How Line Graphs Can Make a Point

A line graph can show at a glance how numbers or amounts have changed over a period of time. A line graph can also be used to make, or emphasize, a point about such changes.

Study the population graphs on these two pages. Both show how much the black population of the United States increased between 1880 and 1980. Yet at a quick glance, you might think that graph A shows a greater population increase than graph B. Why?

The answer is in how the two graphs are drawn. On both graphs the numbers along the left side—the vertical axis—stand for numbers of people. The numbers along the bottom line—the horizontal axis—stand for years. However, these numbers are spaced differently on the two graphs. On graph A, the numbers along the vertical axis are spaced far apart. This gives graph A a tall, vertical look. And it makes the increase in population seem very dramatic, more dramatic even than it really was. On graph B, the numbers along the vertical axis

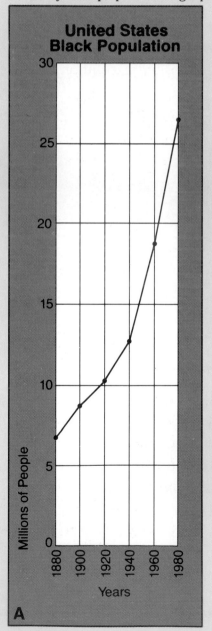

United States Black Population

A

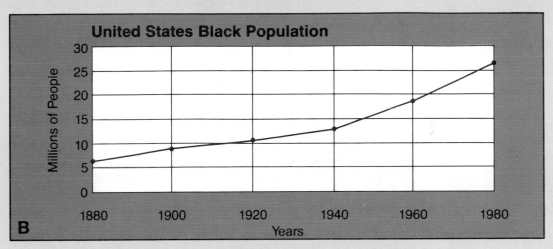

United States Black Population

B

are close together. The years are stretched far apart. This gives graph B a wide, horizontal look. And it makes the population increase seem much more gradual than it really was.

When you are reading a graph, it is sometimes important to pay attention to how it is drawn. Only then can you be sure that what the graph seems to be showing is an accurate picture of the facts.

Practice Your Skills

1. Look at either graph. What was the black population in the United States in 1880? in 1940? Was this difference a doubling or tripling of the population? Which graph makes the point most clearly?
2. Imagine that the spaces between the years on graph B could be stretched out even farther. What would happen to the line connecting the points on the graph?
3. Explain in your own words the differences between the two graphs in this exercise.

Price of a gallon of gasoline in the winter of 1974

Price of a gallon of gasoline in the summer of 1984

3 Future Challenges

By the 1980's, several problems were troubling American life. Rising prices were hurting both businesses and people. Dirty air and water were endangering our health.

Still, Americans did not lose hope. Instead they worked harder to meet the challenges of the future.

The Energy Crisis

Edwin Drake drilled the first oil well in the United States in 1859. Since then, the nation's wells have pumped out millions of barrels of oil. Without oil, most cars, trucks, ships, and planes could not run. Oil powers factories, heats homes, and is used to make electricity. It is used in manufacturing plastics, drugs, and fertilizer.

After World War II, oil became harder to find in the United States. So the country turned to foreign sources. At first, the price of foreign oil was low. Then, in 1960, the oil-producing countries banded together. They formed OPEC, the Organization of Petroleum Exporting Countries. OPEC nations explained that they had only limited supplies of oil. Some day their oil would run out. For this and other reasons, OPEC began to raise oil prices rapidly in the 1970's. In 1972, our country spent $5 billion on imported oil. By 1979, imported oil cost us $60 billion!

Oil's rapid price rise caused many problems. High oil prices pushed up the prices of other goods. This happened because oil is used in the machines that make or transport almost everything Americans buy. Manufacturers and store owners faced higher production and transportation costs. So they raised the prices of their goods. Rising oil prices hurt everyone.

Many Americans tried to find ways to reduce their use of oil. They bought smaller cars that would use less fuel. They kept their homes cooler in winter and warmer in summer.

Scientists also looked for new energy sources closer to home and for sources that would never run out. One such source is energy from the sun, or solar energy. Solar energy can be used easily to heat homes and offices. In the early 1980's, many American families put solar water heaters in their homes. Another source of energy that will never run out is the wind. In many communities large windmills have been built. The windmills are used to generate electricity. Elsewhere **geothermal energy** is drawn from the heat of the earth. Hot water or steam near the earth's surface is used to run electric generators.

geothermal energy
energy from hot water or steam near the earth's surface.

Solar, wind, and geothermal energy are important new sources of energy. Scientists predict that sources such as these can provide 25 percent of America's energy needs by the year 2000.

The Rising Cost of Breakfast								
Grocery Item	1967	1970	1972	1974	1976	1978	1980	1982
½ gallon of milk	$ .50	$ .58	$ .60	$ .78	$ .83	$ .86	$1.05	$1.12
one dozen eggs	$ .49	$ .61	$ .52	$ .78	$ .84	$ .79	$ .84	$ .89
one loaf of bread	$ .22	$ .24	$ .25	$ .35	$ .35	$ .42	$ .51	$ .53

The Economic Crisis and Political Action

During the 1970's, most Americans said their most serious problem was high prices. The same goods that cost $100 in 1967 cost $247 in 1980. Food, housing, clothing, services—everything Americans needed—cost more.

This rapid rise in the price of goods and services is called **inflation.** In inflationary times, people find they cannot get as many goods for their money as they once could. Rising oil prices were one cause of inflation. Other causes were increased spending by the federal government during the 1960's and the costly Vietnamese War. Workers began demanding higher salaries because they needed more money to live. So businesses raised prices even higher in order to pay workers more. Inflation got worse and worse.

inflation
a rapid rise in the prices of goods and services caused by government spending and increased demand for limited resources

In 1980, Americans elected Ronald Reagan President. Many voted for him because he promised to reduce inflation. To reach this goal, Reagan first reduced government spending. If the government spent less, he reasoned, taxes could be lowered. Because people would not be paying such high taxes, they would have more money to spend. The government hoped they would spend this money on the products of America's industries.

President Reagan also persuaded Congress to cut taxes on businesses. This left businesses with more money to buy new machines and build more factories. Then businesses could produce goods faster and more cheaply. Businesses could lower the prices they charge and hire more workers.

Not everyone agreed with Reagan's plan. Some people pointed out that it did away with government programs that aided the poor. But others claimed that poor people would be helped by lower prices and the new jobs created by business.

At first it seemed that President Reagan's plan was not working. The economy was slow to respond. Many businesses cut back on production. Workers lost their jobs. By the end of 1982, 10.7 percent of American workers did not have jobs. This was the highest **unemployment rate** since the depression of the 1930's.

Slowly the economy began to improve. President Reagan reported that prices rose less than half as fast in 1983 as they had in 1980. Businesses began to produce more goods. More workers were able to find jobs. The unemployment rate in 1984 dropped to 7.4 percent.

unemployment rate
the percentage of workers who do not have jobs

President and Mrs. Reagan with Vice-President and Mrs. Bush at Republican Convention in Dallas, Texas

In the election of 1984, President Ronald Reagan and Vice-President George Bush were nominated by the Republican Party for a second term. Former Vice-President Walter Mondale defeated the Reverend Jesse Jackson and Colorado Senator Gary Hart to win the Democratic nomination for President. Mondale chose Representative Geraldine Ferraro as his Vice-Presidential candidate. Ferraro was the first woman to be chosen by a major party to run for such high office. Mondale ran a strong campaign. President Reagan, however, received wide support for his economic policies. President Reagan's popularity was too much for Mondale to overcome. In November 1984, Ronald Reagan was re-elected President. The President plans to continue his efforts to reduce government spending, support a strong defense, and help American business growth.

Representative Geraldine Ferraro

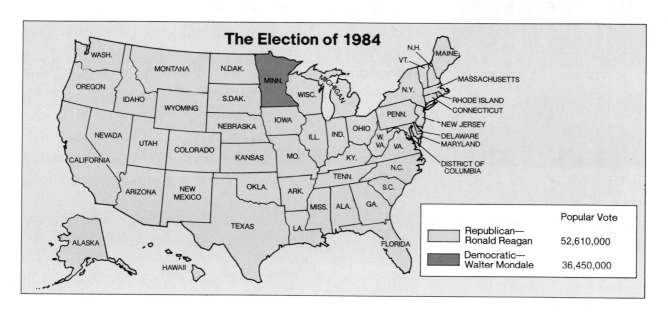

Foreign Crises

The United States became deeply involved in foreign crises during the early 1980's. In Central America, the United States increased its aid to the government of El Salvador. Communist-led rebels in El Salvador were trying to overthrow the government. American military advisers helped train Salvadoran soldiers to fight the rebels. Meanwhile, the United States was also involved in the nearby

405

country of Nicaragua. The government of Nicaragua was supported by the Soviet Union and Cuba. The United States trained and supplied a "secret army" of Nicaraguans to overthrow their government.

In the Middle East, United States Marines were sent to Lebanon. Lebanon had long been torn by a bitter civil war. The Marines were sent to help keep the peace. In October 1983, 240 Marines were killed by a powerful bomb at their headquarters. Soon the remaining Marines were pulled out of Lebanon.

Also in October 1983, the tiny Caribbean island of Grenada was invaded by the United States. The invasion was ordered by President Reagan to protect American students on Grenada. The President also said that the Soviet Union and Cuba were using Grenada to extend their influence in the Caribbean. Some Americans felt the use of force was unnecessary. Many, however, supported the successful action of the President.

Tensions between the United States and the Soviet Union increased during the early 1980's. In 1983, the Soviet Union shot down a civilian Korean airliner. There were 60 Americans aboard the plane. The airliner had flown into Soviet air space by mistake. In 1984, the Soviet Union refused to send its athletes to the Summer Olympics in Los Angeles.

Cleaning Up Our Nation

Some problems caused by the rapid industrial and population growth of the 1950's became obvious in the 1960's. Smog from traffic filled the air, making it unhealthy to breathe. Factories drained wastes into lakes and rivers, dirtying our water supplies. Chemicals used on farm crops to control insects poisoned our food. Dangerous atomic wastes started building up. No one knew what to do with the wastes.

Pollution—whatever makes land, water, and air impure or contaminated—was a national problem. To solve the problem, people became more aware of the **environment.** The environment is everything that surrounds us, including our air, land, and water.

The federal and state governments worked with communities to clean up pollution. In 1970, Congress created the

President Ronald Reagan

pollution
anything that makes air, water, or land impure or contaminated

environment
everything that surrounds us, especially our air, land, and water

406

Environmental Protection Agency. It set standards for clean air and water. This agency tried to make sure people and factories did not pollute. In addition, people were encouraged to practice **conservation,** the careful use and protection of natural resources. As a result of these efforts, much progress has been made. Americans are working to clean up the environment and to make wise use of our natural resources.

conservation
the careful use and protection of natural resources

Future Improvements

While people clean up the earth's environment, scientists are looking for new ways to meet our needs for food and shelter. They have found ways to raise larger crops and healthier farm animals. They have also started to develop underwater ocean farms. In the future, fish and plants from these farms will become valuable food sources.

Scientists also say future Americans might spend time living in colonies in space. At the same time, more and more people on the earth will probably work at home instead of in offices. Satellites that beam television messages to every home will help co-workers keep in touch with each other. So will computers. People will save time by not traveling to and from work. That will also help them save energy.

Our society is changing rapidly. Throughout history, Americans have adjusted to society's changes and met its challenges. The challenges that we face today will shape the United States of tomorrow.

Design for a space colony of the future

Section Review

Write your answers on a sheet of paper.
1. Why did oil prices rise rapidly in the 1970's?
2. What did President Reagan do to reduce inflation?
3. How have Americans tried to clean up the environment?
4. Choose one crisis discussed in this section and explain how it is shaping our future.

Computer Art   For thousands of years, artists have used tools such as brushes, pencils, paints, and blocks of wood to make pictures. A very modern tool used by some artists is the computer.

Certain kinds of computers are able to draw pictures and show, or display, them on a screen or picture tube. They can also print the pictures. The computers work very fast. They can make pictures or change parts of the pictures much faster than an artist could working with paper and pencil.

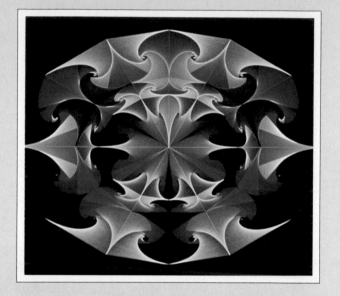

America

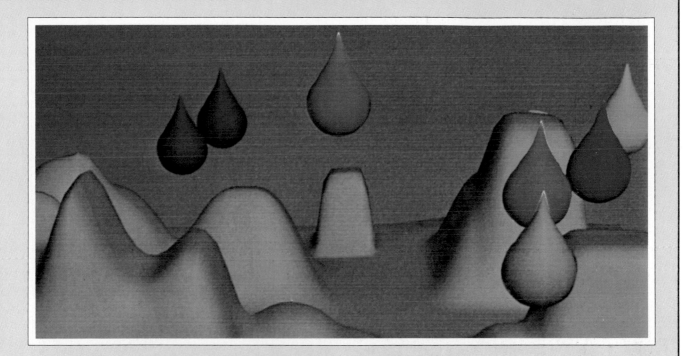

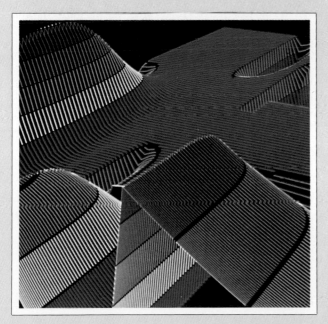

How is a computer able to do what the artist wants? The artist types instructions into the computer using a keyboard that looks like a typewriter. These instructions are called a program. Some programs are very complicated. There may be thousands of instructions a computer has to carry out in order to create a picture.

In the future, people are likely to see more examples of computer art. As Americans continue to buy their own home computers, they can experiment with computer drawings themselves.

UNIT REVIEW

Word Work

Write the sentences below on a sheet of paper. Fill in the blanks with the correct words from the list.

airlift   hostages   integration   suburbs   refugees

1. The bringing together of blacks and whites in schools and neighborhoods is called _____.
2. _____ are towns located close to cities.
3. People held as prisoners for political reasons are _____.
4. People who flee their home countries because they are discriminated against for their beliefs are _____.
5. An _____ of supplies by plane may be used when ground routes are blocked.

Knowing the Facts

Write your answers on a sheet of paper.
1. Why did the United States and the Soviet Union get involved in the Cold War?
2. Name three ways in which American life changed rapidly after World War II.
3. Describe two ways in which black Americans protested against segregation.

Using What You Know

Choose one of the following activities. Follow the instructions given here.
1. Write a one-page description of life in the computer age using the information in Chapter 21 and whatever else you may know about computers. Explain how computers have changed the way Americans work, play, learn, and run their homes.
2. On an outline map of the world, indicate those nations controlled by communist governments today. Where

possible, indicate the date when the country became communist. You may use a modern historical atlas.

Skills Practice

Use both graphs to answer the questions below. Write your answers on a separate sheet of paper.

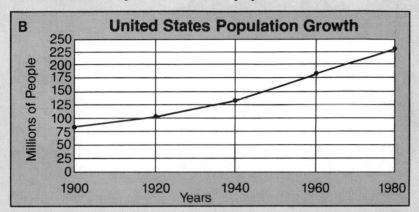

B United States Population Growth

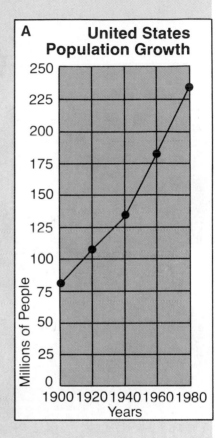

A United States Population Growth

1. During what period did the United States have the sharpest rise in population? Which graph shows this fact most dramatically?
2. In what ways are these two graphs alike? In what ways are they different?
3. If you wanted to make the line connecting the dots on either graph rise more sharply, what part of either graph would you shorten?

Your Heritage

Contact a local environmental or conservation agency. Ask about air- and water-pollution laws in your community. How well are they being enforced? Find out how garbage and sewage are treated and recycled. Get information that will let you draw a map showing sources of air and water pollution in your community. Ask what you can do to join in community conservation efforts.

Our Neighbors: Canada and Latin America

The people of the United States, Canada, and Latin America all live in the Western Hemisphere. We are all neighbors.

Mexico, the countries of Central America, the West Indies, and South America make up Latin America. The countries of Latin America are our southern neighbors. Canada is our northern neighbor.

In this unit you will read about our neighbors. You will learn about the people, land, and history of each country. And you will see the many things we have in common with our neighbors, as well as our many differences.

Niagara Falls: the Canadian, or Horseshoe, Falls are on the right, with the American Falls on the left.

Canada is our neighbor to the north. The United States and Canada share a boundary all across North America. The boundary is just over 9,000 kilometers (5,589 miles) long. There are no forts or walls along this boundary. Canada and the United States live at peace with one another. Many Canadians visit the United States each year. And many people from the United States cross the boundary to visit Canada. Canada and the United States are very good neighbors.

At the end of this chapter, you should be able to:
○ List the six land regions of Canada.
○ Identify Canada's major resources.
○ Describe the exploration and settlement of Canada.
○ Describe the ways the people of Canada are divided.
● Compare and contrast flow charts.

1 The Land and Climate

In land area Canada is the second largest country in the world. It covers about half of North America. The western border of Canada is formed by the Pacific Ocean and the state of Alaska. To the north is the Arctic Ocean. The Atlantic Ocean borders Canada on the east. The long boundary with the United States is Canada's southern border.

There are 10 provinces, or states, in Canada. Six of them are in Canada's eastern half. These are Ontario, Quebec, Newfoundland, Nova Scotia, New Brunswick, and Prince Edward Island. The four western provinces are Manitoba, Saskatchewan, Alberta, and British Columbia. North of the western provinces are two very large regions. The Northwest Territories and the Yukon Territory are vast wilderness areas where very few people live. Look at the map of Canada. Find the provinces and territories of Canada.

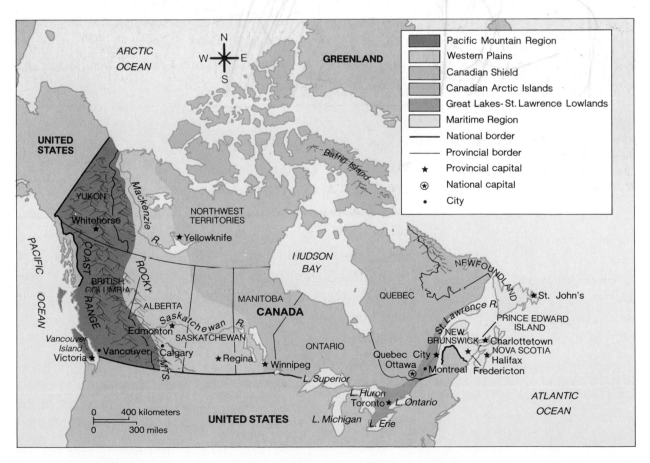

Lake Louise, Banff National Park

Land Regions

Canada can be divided into six land regions. These regions are the Pacific Mountain Region, the Western Plains, the Canadian Shield, the Canadian Arctic Islands, the Great Lakes–St. Lawrence Lowlands, and the Maritime Region. As you read about each region, find it on the map of Canada on page 415.

The Pacific Mountain Region is the most western part of Canada. It includes all of the Yukon Territory and nearly all of British Columbia. Parts of Alberta and the Northwest Territories are also in the Pacific Mountain Region. Two mountain ranges cross this region. The range farthest west is the Coast Range. To the east of this range are the Rocky Mountains. Many peaks in both ranges are covered with snow and ice all year.

The Pacific Mountain Region includes five of Canada's national parks. Many tourists visit these parks each year to go camping, hiking, or skiing.

The Western Plains of Canada are part of the Great Plains of North America. The Great Plains stretch from the Gulf of Mexico to the Arctic Ocean. The Western Plains are broad and flat. They are Canada's richest area of farmland. Vast fields of wheat cover much of the plains. Irrigated fields, orchards, and cattle ranches can also be found on the Western Plains.

The largest land region in Canada is the Canadian Shield. This region includes about half of Canada. Thousands of years ago the Canadian Shield was covered with glaciers. These thick masses of ice carried away much of the soil. The glaciers left behind rocks and boulders. Farming is possible only in the southern part of this region. The northern part of the Canadian Shield is a cold, treeless plain. It is called a **tundra.** The ground is frozen all year round beneath the surface. Few plants or animals can live in this wasteland.

The Canadian Arctic Islands are the most northern region of Canada. Nearly all of the islands are in the Arctic Circle. The seas around the islands are frozen most of the year. Some of the islands are also covered with ice. Other islands are tundras. Only very simple plants can live on

tundra
wide, treeless plain where few plants or animals live

these islands. Mosses, wildflowers, and grasses grow during the summer. Many rocks on the islands are covered with moss-like plants. These plants are called **lichens** (**ly**-kenz).

The smallest land region of Canada is the Great Lakes-St. Lawrence Lowlands. This region includes only southern parts of Ontario and Quebec. However, more than half the population of Canada lives in this region. The soils of the lowlands are very fertile. Many farms cover the rolling hills of this region. The lowlands are also the center for Canadian industry. Dams and waterfalls produce **hydroelectric power** for the region's industries.

The Maritime Region includes all of New Brunswick, Prince Edward Island, and Nova Scotia. The large island of Newfoundland and a part of Quebec are also in the Maritime Region. Much of this region is covered with low, rugged mountains. Parts of Newfoundland are level and are used for farming. Prince Edward Island has fertile farmlands of rich, red soil. There are hundreds of small bays along the coast. These bays are excellent harbors for the fishing industry.

lichen
simple moss-like plant that grows on rocks and tree trunks

hydroelectric power
energy produced by water power

New Brunswick herring boat unloading

Waterways

Canada has many lakes, rivers, and waterfalls. More than half of all the fresh water on earth is in Canada!

The largest bodies of water in Canada are the Great Lakes. The boundary between the United States and Canada passes through four of the Great Lakes. These lakes are Lake Superior, Lake Huron, Lake Erie, and Lake Ontario.

The Niagara River connects Lake Erie and Lake Ontario. Several large hydroelectric plants have been built along the Niagara River. These plants supply electric power to both Canada and the United States. About half way down the Niagara, the river plunges over Niagara Falls. Each year 10 million tourists visit these beautiful falls.

lock
a canal with gates that can change water levels

The St. Lawrence River joins Lake Ontario to the Atlantic Ocean. Lake Ontario is about 61 meters (200 feet) higher than the ocean. Many canals and **locks** have been built along the St. Lawrence River. A lock is a canal with gates. By closing or opening the gates, the level of water can be changed to raise or lower boats. The locks allow ships to travel between the Atlantic and the Great Lakes. The St. Lawrence River and this system of locks and canals form the St. Lawrence Seaway. This is one of the busiest waterways in the world.

St. Lawrence Seaway

Climate

Most of Canada has long, cold winters and short, moderate summers. There are, however, many differences in climate within Canada.

The northern parts of Canada are bitterly cold. There are only a few hours of daylight each day during the winter. North of the Arctic Circle, the sun never rises during much of the winter. Temperatures average only about 4° C (40° F) during the summer.

The Pacific Mountain Region is wet, and its coastal valleys are mild all year round. Storms drop heavy rain along the coast. The mountains of the region block the storms and keep them from going inland. In the mountains winters are cold and summers are cool.

The Western Plains and the Canadian Shield have extreme climates. Winters are very cold. Blizzards and icy winds sweep down from the north. Summers are often quite warm. Most of the rain on the Western Plains falls during the summers. The summer rainfall is ideal for farming. Crops need the most moisture during the summer growing season.

The climate of the Great Lakes-St. Lawrence Lowlands is like that of the northeastern United States. Winters are cold because of winds from the north. The winds often bring snowstorms. Summers are usually mild. Warm winds come up from the Gulf of Mexico. Average summer temperatures are around 21° C (70° F). The climate of the Maritime Region is similar to that of the lowlands. Rainfall is heavier along the coast because of storms from the Atlantic.

Horseback riding in British Columbia forest

Section Review

Write your answers on a sheet of paper.
1. Name the six land regions of Canada.
2. Describe how a lock works. Why were locks built along the St. Lawrence River?
3. In what ways is the climate of Canada like that of the United States? How is it different?

2 Resources and Industry

Like the United States, Canada is rich in natural resources. One of Canada's most valuable resources is its forestland. About one third of Canada is covered with forests. In the north there are great evergreen forests of hemlock, fir, cedar, and spruce. **Deciduous** (deh-**sihj**-oo-uhs) **forests** of maple, oak, and walnut grow in the south. Trees in deciduous forests shed their leaves each fall.

deciduous forests
forests of trees that shed their leaves each fall

Many animals live in Canada's forests. The forests also have parks for camping and hiking. Lumber from the forests is used for building and for making furniture. Much of the wood is ground up to make pulp. **Wood pulp** is used to make paper. Canada is one of the world's leading producers of wood pulp and paper.

wood pulp
ground-up wood fibers from logs

Canada also has a rich supply of minerals. Canada is among the world's leading producers of nickel, zinc, uranium, and asbestos (as-**behs**-tuhs). Uranium is used in the making of nuclear power. Asbestos is used in fireproofing, construction, insulation, and brake lining. The Canadian Shield has large deposits of silver, copper, lead, and iron ore. Oil and natural gas have been discovered on the Arctic Islands and on the Western Plains.

The mineral resources of Canada are used by Canadian industries. Iron ore and nickel are used to make steel. Manufacturing plants in Ontario and Quebec make automobiles, buses, and railroad cars. Other factories produce textiles.

A limestone plant in Alberta. Limestone is used for iron extraction and in cement and building stones.

The soils of Canada are another important resource. The richest soils are on the Western Plains. Huge fields of wheat cover much of southern Alberta, Saskatchewan, and Manitoba. Farther north are fields of barley, oats, and rye. Farmers on the Western Plains also raise cattle and hogs. There are many dairy farms around the Great Lakes and in the Maritime Provinces. Prince Edward Island and New Brunswick are famous for their potatoes. Farmers in British Columbia raise dairy cattle and poultry. Fruit ranchers in British Columbia grow delicious apples, pears, and peaches.

Canada has some of the world's richest fishing grounds. Millions of salmon are caught each year along the west coast. Along the east coast, great numbers of mackerel, herring, cod, and lobster are caught. Fresh-water fish are caught in the Great Lakes.

Section Review

Write your answers on a sheet of paper.
1. Why are the forestlands of Canada a valuable resource?
2. What mineral resources does Canada have?
3. Which region of Canada has the richest soils? What crops are grown in this region?
4. Why are Canada's mineral resources important to Canadian industries?

3 Exploration and Settlement

No one knows when or how the first people arrived in what is now Canada. Many scientists believe that the first people arrived more than 20,000 years ago. These people may have crossed the land bridge from Asia. They are the ancestors of the Indians of Canada.

Most early Canadian Indian tribes lived in small bands. They hunted elk, deer, caribou, and buffalo. They gathered wild plants. The rivers and lakes of Canada provided the Indians with a rich supply of fish. The Indians built wooden frames for their homes. They covered the frames with bark or animal skins. Two of the largest tribes lived in eastern Canada. These tribes were the Iroquois and the Huron.

Eskimo stone sculpture

Some scientists believe that 5,000 years ago another group of people settled in Canada. These people also came from Asia. Most of them settled near the sea in northern Canada. They hunted seals and whales. They lived in snow or ice shelters during the winter. In the summer, they lived in tents made of animal skins. These people ate their food raw. They were called Eskimos by the Indians of Canada. The word Eskimo means "eaters of raw meat." The Eskimos called themselves Inuit, which means "people."

The first Europeans to reach Canada were the Vikings. About 500 years after the Vikings, other Europeans came to Canada. You read about the voyages of Leif Erikson, John Cabot, Jacques Cartier, and many other explorers in Chapter 2. You learned how explorers for England and France claimed what is now Canada for those two countries. Cabot and Henry Hudson claimed it for England. Cartier, Samuel de Champlain, and others claimed it for France.

Cabot also discovered the Grand Banks, one of the world's best fishing areas. The Grand Banks is off the southern coast of Newfoundland. Fish there were so plentiful they could be caught just by lowering baskets into the sea!

During the late 1500's, fishing boats from France and England often came to the waters off Newfoundland. Some of the French began to trade with the local Indians. They traded kettles, blankets, knives, and other goods for beaver pelts. The pelts were taken back to Europe. Beaver hats became very popular in France and elsewhere in Europe.

Statue of Samuel de Champlain

Rival fur traders racing to Indian camp to trade

The first permanent French settlement in Canada was Quebec. Champlain founded Quebec in 1608 as a fur-trading post. After Quebec's first winter, only 8 of the 24 settlers were still alive.

Soon, however, more fur-trading posts were begun along the St. Lawrence River. French fur traders also built forts along the Mississippi River. The French called their land in Canada "New France." Soon New France stretched from the mouth of the St. Lawrence River south to the Gulf of Mexico.

The French worked hard to keep peaceful relations with the Indians of New France. Indian help was needed for further French exploration. And Indian cooperation was needed for success in the growing fur trade.

The success of the fur trade attracted more French settlers to New France. Some settlers came to join the trade for furs. Others went into the forest as trappers, collecting furs and living in the wilderness.

Missionaries and farmers also came to New France. The missionaries were Roman Catholic. They converted many of the Indians to Christianity. Missionaries founded the settlement of Montreal as an Indian mission in 1642. Farmers settled in New France to raise crops and livestock. Their main crops were wheat and oats. Life for these pioneer farmers was very hard. Many of the pioneers lived in crude log cabins. They had to make their own tools and clothing.

Quebec settlement, 1758

Meanwhile, settlers from Great Britain were also arriving in North America. English fur traders moved into the area around Hudson Bay. English colonists arrived in Newfoundland. Further south 13 English colonies were set up along the Atlantic Coast. The English colonists and the French colonists soon became rivals. The French and English fought over control of the fur trade. They also fought over control of the land.

British General James Wolfe lies dying as his troops defeat the French at Quebec.

In Chapter 5 you learned that the French and English fought four wars between 1689 and 1763. During the last of these wars, the British captured Quebec and Montreal. The wars ended with the Treaty of Paris in 1763. In this treaty France agreed to give to Great Britain all the lands of New France.

Under British rule, Canada was divided into two colonies. The two colonies were called Upper Canada and Lower Canada. Upper Canada was the land nearest the

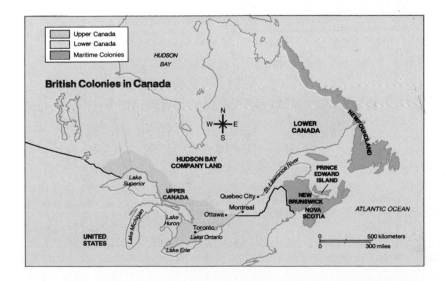

Great Lakes. Most of the people in this colony spoke English. Lower Canada included the land from Newfoundland to the St. Lawrence River. Many of the colonists in Lower Canada were French-speaking people.

The British government created a united Canadian colony in 1867. The name of the new colony was the Dominion of Canada. The colony included four provinces. Its two largest provinces were Quebec and Ontario. Quebec included the old colony of Lower Canada. Ontario included the lands of Upper Canada.

The people of Canada were now united in one colony. The years of warfare and rivalry between the English and French, however, left many bitter feelings.

French and British Canadians had many differences. They spoke different languages and lived under different laws and customs. Most French Canadians were Catholic. Most British Canadians were Protestant. Few French Canadians owned businesses; most were farmers. Laws to help business or the Protestant church angered French Canadians. Laws to protect French customs and language angered British Canadians.

Keeping Canada united was a big challenge. It is a challenge Canada still faces today.

Section Review

Write your answers on a sheet of paper.
1. In what ways are the Indians of Canada and the Eskimos different from one another? How are they alike?
2. What was the first permanent French settlement in Canada?
3. Why did the French settlers want to keep peaceful relations with the Indians?
4. When did Great Britain gain control over New France?
5. Based on your reading of this section, why do you think the English and French people of Canada had bitter feelings toward each other?

FARLEY MOWAT

FAMOUS CANADIAN

One of Canada's most popular writers is Farley Mowat. His stories and books are enjoyed by people around the world.

Farley Mowat was born in the small town of Belleville, Ontario, in 1921. His family moved often, from one town to another on the plains of Ontario and Saskatchewan. Every time the family moved, they took with them a large collection of pets. Farley Mowat later described these early adventures of his family. In *The Dog Who Wouldn't Be*, he wrote about a dog named Mutt. Mutt could climb ladders, walk on fences, and dive for crayfish. Mutt refused to believe he was merely a dog. Farley Mowat's pet collection also included two very unusual pets. Wol and Weeps were pet great-horned owls. Their funny adventures are described in *Owls in the Family*.

When Farley Mowat was 14, his uncle took him on a trip to the Arctic region of Canada. This trip sparked a lifelong interest in the far north. Farley Mowat returned to the Arctic as a young man and lived for two years among a tribe of Eskimos. He was angered at how the Eskimos had often been mistreated. He described the life of the Eskimos in two powerful books called *People of the Deer* and *The Desperate People*. Both books were very popular in Canada and helped gain support for Canada's Eskimos.

Later Farley Mowat returned to the far north. This time he was dropped alone onto the frozen tundra. Farley Mowat's job was to live near a family of wolves and to carefully study their behavior. He came to know the wolves well and to have a great respect for them. His book, *Never Cry Wolf*, describes his experiences among the wolves. *Never Cry Wolf* became a best seller in Canada and the United States. It was also made into a movie.

4 Canada Today

Canada gained full independence from Great Britain in 1931. At that time Canada became a member of the **Commonwealth of Nations**. The Commonwealth is a group of nations that includes Great Britain and many former British colonies. Commonwealth nations help each other with trade and defense agreements.

Since independence Canada has remained close to Great Britain. The official head of the Canadian government is Queen Elizabeth of Great Britain. The queen, however, has little power in Canada. She is permitted to choose a governor general to represent her in Canada. The governor general's powers, though, are mostly ceremonial.

Canada, like the United States, is a democracy. Parliament makes the laws for Canada. Parliament, like our Congress, has two houses, a House of Commons and a Senate. The House of Commons is the more important house. Members of the House of Commons are elected by the people of Canada. Any Canadian over the age of 18 may vote in national elections. Members of the Senate are chosen by the governor general.

After each national election the leader of the party that wins the most seats in the House of Commons is called upon to form a government. The leader of the winning party becomes prime minister. The prime minister of Canada is like our President. He or she is the executive of the government. To form a government the prime minister chooses a cabinet of advisers from Parliament, usually the House of Commons. Cabinet ministers help Parliament write and pass Canada's laws. If an important law does not pass Parliament, the prime minister may have to either resign or call for new elections.

The two largest political parties in Canada are the Liberal party and the Progressive Conservative party. Like the Democratic party and the Republican party in the United States, Canadian parties name candidates to run for office. The Liberal party has been the strongest party in Canada for most of the past 20 years. Liberal party leader Pierre

Commonwealth of Nations

a group of nations that includes Britain and many former British colonies

Queen Elizabeth II, Prince Philip, and former prime minister Pierre Trudeau

Elliot Trudeau (troo-**doh**) served as Canada's prime minister from 1968 to 1979. Joe Clark replaced Trudeau as prime minister in 1979 when the Progressive Conservative party gained control of Parliament. Nine months later the Liberal party regained control of Parliament and Trudeau was once again prime minister.

Parliamentary elections were held in 1984, and the Progressive Conservative party gained control of Parliament. Party leader Brian Mulroney became the new prime minister.

Each of Canada's provinces has a government of its own, much like the state governments in the United States. Provincial leaders are called premiers. The provincial law-making body is the Legislative Assembly. The party that wins the most seats in the Legislative Assembly names its leader premier.

Government of the Yukon Territory and the Northwest Territories is more fully under the direct control of Canada's national government.

The governor general presides at a meeting of the Senate.

Bilingual sign on school bus

bilingual
able to speak two
languages

The People of Canada

Canada is a land of many different kinds of people. The largest group of Canadians is made up of people whose ancestors came from Great Britain. About 45 percent of all Canadians have British ancestors. Nearly all British Canadians speak English. The English-speaking Canadians have been the most powerful group in Canada for many years. They usually have held the most important offices in the Canadian government. They have also owned many of the country's largest businesses. British Canadians live in all parts of Canada. In some provinces practically everyone speaks English.

The second largest group of Canadians is made up of those whose ancestors came from France. About 29 percent of Canada's people have French ancestors. Most French Canadians speak only French. Others speak English. Some Canadians are able to speak both French and English. They are **bilingual**. Both French and English are now official languages in Canada.

French Canadians live mostly in the province of Quebec. More than 80 percent of Quebec's people have French ancestors. They call themselves *Québécois* (kay-bey-**kwah**). Many French Canadians also live in the province of New Brunswick. The French Canadians of New Brunswick are sometimes called Acadians (uh-**kay**-dee-uhnz). The early French settlement in New Brunswick was known as Acadia.

French village in Quebec

Canada's third largest group is made up of people whose ancestors came from European countries other than Great Britain or France. These people make up about 23 percent of Canada's population. Their ancestors came from Germany, Italy, and other nations. Many Europeans began to arrive in Canada in the late 1800's. A large number also came after World War II. Most of these people live on the Western Plains of Canada. The provinces of Alberta, Saskatchewan, and Manitoba have large numbers of Canadians whose ancestors came from countries other than Great Britain or France.

About 2 percent of the Canadian people are Indians or Eskimos. Most of the Indians live on reservations. Canada has more than 2,000 Indian reservations. The Eskimos live in the far northern parts of Canada. About two thirds of the Eskimos live in the Yukon and Northwest Territories.

Some Indians and Eskimos still live much as their ancestors did. They hunt and fish for food. They trap beavers and sell their pelts. Most Eskimos and Indians, however, live as other Canadians do. They buy their food and clothing in stores. They work on farms or in factories and shops. Many, however, are not able to find good jobs. They have had little education. Many Eskimos and Indians today are very poor.

Canada also has a small population of Asians. People have come to Canada from China, Japan, and other Asian nations. Most of the Asians in Canada live along the west coast. About 3 percent of the population of British Columbia is Asian.

Young Eskimo with drying fish

Asian-Canadians at work in Vancouver's salmon industry

Toronto, Canada

Montreal, Canada

Cities

Canada has many large and beautiful cities. The capital of Canada is Ottawa. It is located on the Ottawa River in southeastern Ontario. The largest city in Ontario is Toronto. Toronto lies on the northwestern shore of Lake Ontario. It is the main center of Canadian industry. The capital of the nearby province of Quebec is Quebec City. This is the oldest city in Canada. It lies along the northern bank of the St. Lawrence River. One of the largest cities in western Canada is Winnipeg. It is located in southern Manitoba province. Winnipeg is called the "Gateway to the West."

Montreal is Canada's biggest city. Today about two thirds of the people of Montreal are French Canadians. Montreal is the second largest French-speaking city in the world. Only Paris, France, has a larger French-speaking population. Montreal lies along the main route of the St. Lawrence Seaway. Its location makes it the center of transportation in Canada. Ships traveling between the Atlantic Ocean and the Great Lakes often stop in Montreal. Each year 4,000 ships visit Montreal's harbor.

The waterways of Montreal are also an important source of hydroelectric power. This plentiful supply of electric power has attracted many industries to Montreal. There are more than 7,000 factories in the city. The leading industries are oil refining and food processing. Among the many food products of Montreal are canned fruits and vegetables. Montreal is also a major steel-making city. Factories produce airplanes, railroad cars, and other transportation equipment.

Downtown Montreal has some of Canada's tallest buildings. Many of the nation's finest stores line Montreal's busy streets. Beneath the streets is a subway system called the "Metro." The Metro connects downtown Montreal with the rest of the city. It runs on rubber tires. The Metro is one of the quietest trains in the world.

Vancouver is the largest city on the west coast of Canada. It is the busiest port on the Pacific Coast of North America. Much of Vancouver's trade is with Asia. Lumber and wood products are shipped from Vancouver to many Asian ports. Manufactured goods, such as automobiles from Japan, arrive daily in Vancouver's harbor. Two railroad lines carry goods between Vancouver and the rest of Canada.

Vancouver has a variety of people. The largest group is made up of British Canadians. There are also groups whose ancestors came from Germany, Italy, and other European countries. Vancouver has the second largest Chinese community in North America. The ancestors of many Chinese Canadians came to build the nation's railroads.

Vancouver attracts many tourists each year. The city has a mild climate. Vancouver's Stanley Park Zoo is one of the best in North America. It is famous for its polar bears and other arctic animals.

Vancouver, Canada's Stanley Park Zoo

Section Review

Write your answers on a sheet of paper.
1. What is the Commonwealth of Nations?
2. What are the two largest groups in the Canadian population today?
3. Name the capital of Canada. What is Canada's oldest city? What is its largest city?
4. Compare a Canadian city to a city in your state. How are the two cities alike? How are they different?

Comparing and Contrasting Flow Charts

approval
acceptance, agreement, or saying yes to

veto
to turn down, or say no to

Look at the flow charts showing how a bill becomes a law in Canada and in the United States. The chart on the left side shows the steps needed for a bill to become a law in Canada. To read the chart begin at the top and follow the arrows. The first step is the reading of the bill in either the House of Commons or the Senate. Most important bills in Canada are introduced by a member of the cabinet. The last step is the **approval** of the bill by the governor general. By tradition the governor general approves bills passed by both houses of Parliament.

The chart on the right side of the page shows how a bill becomes a law in the United States. All bills are introduced by a member of Congress, either in the House of Representatives or the Senate. If Congress approves the bill, the President may approve or **veto** it. If the President vetoes the bill, it may still become law if it is passed again by two-thirds of the members of both houses. If the President takes no action on the bill, the bill becomes a law after 10 days.

Compare one chart with the other. Many steps in the two charts are similar. The main differences are at the beginning and at the end of each chart.

Practice Your Skills

1. Who introduces bills in the Canadian Parliament? Who introduces bills in the United States Congress?
2. After Congress passes a bill, what choices does the President have?
3. What are the main differences between the two charts? Tell which steps are different.

HOW A BILL BECOMES A LAW IN CANADA

Introduction of Bill
by Cabinet Member
↓
Readings of Bill in
House of Commons
↓
Study and Vote by
House Committee
↓
Vote by House
↓
Readings of Bill
in Senate
↓
Study and Vote by
Senate Committee
↓
Vote by Senate
↓
Approval by Governor
General
↓
Law

HOW A BILL BECOMES A LAW IN THE UNITED STATES

Introduction of Bill
by Member of Congress
↓
Readings of Bill in
House of Representatives
↓
Study and Vote by
House Committee
↓
Vote by House
↓
Readings of Bill
in Senate
↓
Study and Vote by
Senate Committee
↓
Vote by Senate
↓

Approval by President	Veto by President	No Action by President
	↓	↓
	Passed by Two-thirds of Both Houses	Passage of 10 Days
	↓	

→ Law ←

CHAPTER 23 Latin America

Mexico City

Our neighbors to the south are the countries of Latin America. This enormous region includes all of the continent of South America and the southern part of North America. Altogether, Latin America covers over 20 million square kilometers (8 million square miles). Latin America is more than twice as large as the United States.

At the end of this chapter, you should be able to:

○ List the seven climate zones of Latin America.
○ Describe the resources and industries of Mexico.
○ Discuss the problem of poverty in Central America.
○ Identify the three main population groups of South America.

1 The Land and Climate

Many different countries make up Latin America. Mexico is the largest Latin American country in North America. South of Mexico is a narrow bridge of land called Central America. There are seven countries in Central America. Look at the map of Latin America. What are the names of the seven countries of Central America?

The continent of South America forms the largest part of Latin America. This vast area includes 12 independent countries. Find these countries on the map of Latin America.

Latin America also includes the West Indies. The West Indies are a group of islands in the Caribbean Sea. There are three main groups of islands in the West Indies. The largest group is known as the Greater Antilles (an-**tih**-leez). This group includes Hispaniola, Cuba, Jamaica, and Puerto Rico. Southeast of Puerto Rico are the many small islands of the Lesser Antilles. Northeast of Cuba are the Bahamas. The Bahamas are a chain of about 3,000 islands and **reefs.** A reef is a ridge of sand, rock, or coral near the surface of the sea.

reef
a ridge of sand, rock, or coral near the surface of the sea

Diver exploring a coral reef

Latin America

SONORAN DESERT

SIERRA MADRE OCCIDENTAL

CENTRAL PLATEAU

Rio Bravo del Norte

Rio Grande

SIERRA MADRE ORIENTAL

MEXICO
⊛ Mexico City

GULF OF MEXICO

TROPIC OF CANCER

Havana ⊛

CUBA

BAHAMAS
⊛ Nassau

DOMINICAN REPUBLIC

HAITI
Port-au-Prince ⊛

Santo Domingo ⊛

WEST INDIES

PUERTO RICO
⊛ San Juan

ATLANTIC OCEAN

JAMAICA
Kingston ⊛

GREATER ANTILLES

LESSER ANTILLES

Belmopan ⊛

GUATEMALA
Guatemala City ⊛

BELIZE

HONDURAS
⊛ Tegucigalpa

San Salvador ⊛

EL SALVADOR

NICARAGUA
Managua ⊛

CARIBBEAN SEA

CENTRAL AMERICA

San José ⊛

COSTA RICA

Panama City ⊛

PANAMA

Caracas ⊛

Orinoco R.

VENEZUELA

GUYANA
Georgetown ⊛

SURINAME
Paramaribo ⊛

⊛ Cayenne

FRENCH GUIANA

Magdalena R.

⊛ Bogotá

COLOMBIA

EQUATOR

Quito ⊛

ECUADOR

Negro R. *Amazon River*

CENTRAL PLAINS

SOUTH AMERICA

BRAZIL

São Francisco R.

Brasília ⊛

PERU
⊛ Lima

• Cuzco

BOLIVIA
⊛ La Paz

⊛ Sucre

PACIFIC OCEAN

N
W   E
S

Paraguay R.

PARAGUAY
⊛ Asunción

Rio de Janeiro •

São Paulo •

TROPIC OF CAPRICORN

ANDES   MOUNTAINS

Paraná R.

Uruguay R.

CHILE

URUGUAY

Santiago ⊛

Buenos Aires ⊛

⊛ Montevideo

Rio de la Plata

Latin America

⊛	Capital city
•	City

ARGENTINA

PAMPAS

Concepción •

0 ———— 800 kilometers
0 ———— 600 miles

FALKLAND ISLANDS
⊛ Stanley

438

Land Regions

The land surface of Latin America is similar to that of the United States. Along the coast of North and South America are low, flat areas. These **lowlands** include hot and dry lands such as the Sonoran Desert of northwestern Mexico. The lowlands of Colombia and Ecuador (ehk-**wuh**-dawr) are swampy and covered with forests. Along the Pacific Coast of South America, the lowlands are often less than 80 kilometers (50 miles) wide. In Central America the lowlands are even narrower. Much of the West Indies is also considered lowlands.

Two great mountain ranges extend through Latin America. These mountains actually begin all the way north in Alaska. The range in western Mexico is the Sierra Madre (see-**ayr**-uh **mah**-dray) Occidental. The Sierra Madre Oriental is in eastern Mexico. Occidental means west. Oriental means east. These two ranges narrow and join before they reach Central America. In South America the ranges divide again. Along the entire western coast of South America are the rugged Andes Mountains. To the east is an area of hills or mountains known as the Eastern Highlands.

Between these two great mountain ranges in North and South America is a region of plateaus and plains. The Central Plateau of Mexico is part of a plateau that extends north to Arizona, New Mexico, and Texas. In South America the area between the two ranges is called the Central Plains.

lowland
low, flat land area

Highland farmers in the Ecuadoran Andes

Port market on the Amazon River

The longest river in Latin America is the Amazon. The Amazon begins high in the Andes Mountains. It flows eastward down to the Atlantic Ocean. The Amazon is very deep and wide. At one point, it is more than 80 kilometers (50 miles) wide. The Amazon River carries more water than any other river in the world.

The most important inland waterway in Latin America is the Rio de la Plata (**ree**-oh day lah **plah**-tah). This water system serves Argentina, Bolivia, Brazil, Paraguay, and Uruguay. The Orinoco (ohr-uh-**no**-koh) River is the major waterway of northern South America. It forms the border between Colombia and Venezuela. The Rio Grande flows along the border between Mexico and Texas. It begins more than 3,000 kilometers (1,863 miles) away from its mouth on the Gulf of Mexico.

Climate

Most of Latin America is in the tropics. The Tropic of Cancer and the Tropic of Capricorn are imaginary lines drawn north and south of the equator. The lands between these two lines are called the tropics. The tropics are usually hot all year because the sun's rays are more direct near the equator.

There are seven climate zones in Latin America. Find these zones on the map of Latin America. The wet tropical climate zone has hot summers and warm winters. There is little change in the seasons. Plant and animal life is plentiful, but farming is hard. Crops need minerals in the soil to grow well. The heavy rainfall in the tropics washes minerals from the soil. This process is called **leaching.** The rain also breaks down the humus in the soil. **Humus** is the decayed leaves and other vegetable matter in the soil.

The wet and dry tropical climate zone has heavy rains in the summer months. It is dry in the winter. Much of the land is covered with grass. Cattle ranches can be found in many parts of this zone.

The warm humid climate zone is far enough from the equator to have clear changes of season. Summers are

leaching
the washing of minerals out of the soil by heavy rains
humus
decayed leaves and other vegetable matter in the soil

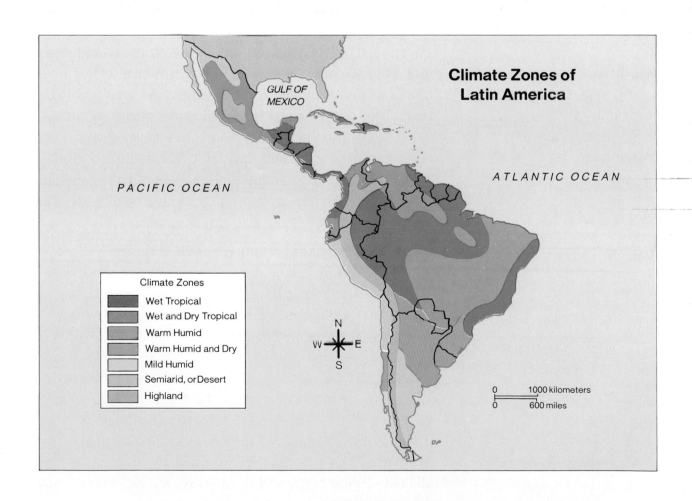

Climate Zones of Latin America

GULF OF MEXICO

PACIFIC OCEAN

ATLANTIC OCEAN

Climate Zones
- Wet Tropical
- Wet and Dry Tropical
- Warm Humid
- Warm Humid and Dry
- Mild Humid
- Semiarid, or Desert
- Highland

N
W — E
S

0   1000 kilometers
0   600 miles

warm to hot, and winters are cool. Rain falls in all seasons. This climate is ideal for growing cotton, sugarcane, and for raising livestock. The warm humid climate zone of Latin America is like the climate of the southeastern United States.

Perhaps the most pleasant of all climates is that of the warm humid and dry climate zone. This zone is also called the Mediterranean or California zone. Summers are warm and dry. Winters are mild and moist.

The mild humid climate zone is usually found near the sea. It is sometimes called the maritime climate zone. Moist sea winds bring rain throughout the year. The sea winds also keep the summers warm and winters mild, much like the climate of the northwest coast of the United States.

The semiarid, or desert, climate zone is very dry all year round. Parts of the southwestern United States have a semi-arid climate. Lands in this zone are sometimes in a "rain shadow." A rain shadow occurs when warm, moist winds from the sea are blocked by a mountain range. As the warm air rises to cross the mountains, it cools and moisture falls as rain or snow. The **windward** side of the mountains, facing into the blowing wind, has a wet climate. The opposite, or **leeward,** side of the mountains faces away from the blowing wind. The leeward side is in a rain shadow where little rain falls. The highland climate zone covers the most mountainous parts of Latin America. Temperatures in this zone are determined by altitude. The higher the altitude, the lower the temperature.

windward
facing into a blowing wind
leeward
facing away from a blowing wind

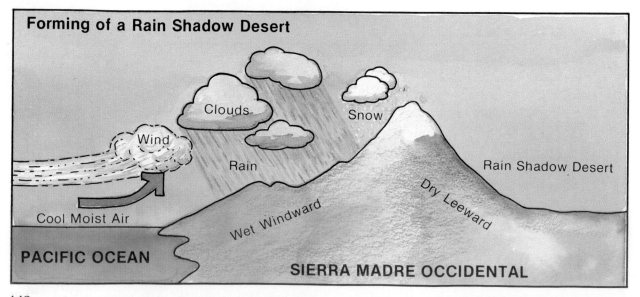

Forming of a Rain Shadow Desert

Clouds

Wind

Snow

Rain

Rain Shadow Desert

Cool Moist Air

Wet Windward

Dry Leeward

PACIFIC OCEAN

SIERRA MADRE OCCIDENTAL

Resources and Industries

One of Latin America's most valuable resources is its soil. About half the land in Latin America can be farmed. The rest is either too mountainous or too dry. The best farmland lies along the river valleys or near the coast.

Most people in Latin America are farmers. Many grow food crops such as beans and corn. Others work on large plantations or ranches that produce cash crops. Latin America's leading cash crops are coffee, cotton, sugar, bananas, and wheat.

Latin America is also rich in mineral resources. There are large deposits of iron ore in Brazil, Venezuela, and Mexico. Chile's copper deposits are among the largest in the world. Bolivia is one of the world's leading producers of tin. There are mines of gold and silver in many Latin American countries.

Today oil is Latin America's most valuable mineral resource. Venezeula and Mexico are major oil-producing nations. Colombia, Ecuador, and Peru also have large oil reserves.

Many of the food crops and minerals of Latin America are sent out of the country for sale. Most Latin American **exports** are sold in the United States or Europe. Latin America's minerals are also used by local industries. There are large manufacturing industries in Mexico, Argentina, Brazil, Chile, Colombia, Peru, Uruguay, and Venezuela.

Bolivian tin miners

export
a product that is sent out of a country for sale; to send a product to another country for sale

Section Review

Write your answers on a sheet of paper.
1. What are the main land regions of Latin America?
2. Name and describe the seven climate zones of Latin America.
3. What is an export?
4. Describe briefly the climate of the area where you live. Choose one of the climate zones of Latin America. Tell how your climate is different from this zone. Tell how it is the same.

2 Mexico, a Nation in Latin America

Mexico is the most northern country in Latin America. It borders the United States for more than 2,880 kilometers (1,800 miles). Its closest neighbors in the United States are Texas, New Mexico, Arizona, and California. To the west of Mexico is the Pacific Ocean. The Gulf of Mexico lies to the east. The Central American countries of Guatemala and Belize form Mexico's southeastern border.

Land and Climate

There are five land regions in Mexico. The Peninsula of Baja (**bah**-hah) California is in far western Mexico. *Baja* means "lower" in Spanish. This long and narrow peninsula is mostly desert land.

The Coastal Plains lie along the Pacific and Gulf coasts of Mexico. Some of Mexico's richest farmland is in this region. Along the Gulf Coastal Plain are plantations of sugarcane and rice.

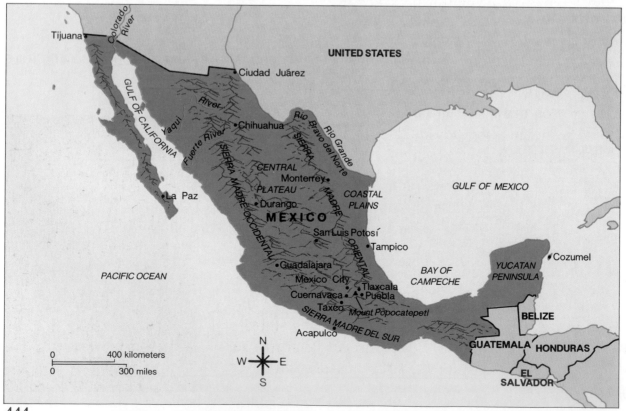

The third land region of Mexico is the Sierra Madre mountain ranges. The Sierra Madre Occidental range is high and very rugged. The Sierra Madre Oriental range is somewhat lower. At the southern end of the Sierra Madre are several volcanoes. One of the largest is Mount Popocatepetl (poh-poh-kah-**tay**-pet′l). Clouds of smoke and gas often rise from the crater of this volcano. Its name means "smoking mountain."

Mount Popocatepetl

Mexico's largest land region is the Central Plateau. The plateau lies between the two ranges of the Sierra Madre. The northern part of the plateau is very flat. Rolling hills, rivers, and lakes are found in the south. About two thirds of the Mexican people live on the Central Plateau.

The Yucatan (yoo-kuh-**tan**) Peninsula is a low plain. Parts of the peninsula are covered with hilly woodlands and marshy swamps.

Mexico has few large rivers. The longest river is the Rio Grande. This river is known in Mexico as the Rio Bravo del Norte (**ree**-oh **brah**-voh del **nor**-tay), which means "bold river of the north." The Rio Grande is an important source of water for irrigation and hydroelectric power.

Desert cactus

The climate of Mexico is varied. Most of northern Mexico is hot and very dry. It has a semiarid climate. Some areas, such as Baja California, receive almost no rainfall. The southern part of the Central Plateau has a highland climate. At altitudes of 610 to 1,830 meters (2,000 to 6,000 feet), temperatures are usually between 21° and 24° C (70° and 75° F). Annual rainfall on much of the plateau is between 30 and 50 centimeters (12 and 20 inches). Rainfall is heaviest in southern Mexico. The Yucatan Peninsula receives more than 100 centimeters (39 inches) of rain each year.

Mexican oil worker

Resources and Industries

Mexico has many valuable resources. Its soil is used for growing many different crops. Corn, beans, wheat, cotton, sugarcane, and coffee are grown in Mexico. Mexican farmers grow other vegetables and many kinds of fruits. Ranchers on the Central Plateau raise beef cattle. Dairy cattle are raised in southern Mexico.

Mexico is rich in mineral resources. Southern Mexico has large deposits of sulfur. Sulfur is used to make matches and gunpowder. Mexico is the world's leading producer of fluorite, a mineral used in making steel. Mexico is also among the world leaders in silver mining. Other minerals found in Mexico are iron ore, gold, copper, lead, and zinc. In recent years oil and natural gas have been discovered along Mexico's Gulf coast.

The industries of Mexico are growing rapidly. The most important industries are chemicals, clothing, and processed foods. Mexico's textile mills use more factory workers than any other industry. The textile mills make clothing from cotton grown in Mexico. The mills also produce clothing made from synthetics, or human-made materials. Huge factories in Mexico produce steel, railroad equipment, and automobiles.

Conquest and Independence

People have lived in the land that is now Mexico for thousands of years. About 1,000 years ago the Maya Indians ruled the Yucatan Peninsula. The Mayas were talented artists and pottery makers. They built homes and pyramids of stone. The Mayas developed a form of writing.

In Chapter 2 you read about the powerful Indian empire of the Aztecs. You also read about the Spanish conquistador, Hernando Cortés. Cortés and his army defeated the Aztecs in 1521. The Spanish took over the Aztec Empire with its fine cities and great wealth.

For the next 300 years, Mexico was the Spanish colony of New Spain. Spaniards came to the colony as soldiers, missionaries, and settlers. They brought to New Spain many new kinds of crops, tools, and livestock. The Indians taught the Spaniards to grow corn, tomatoes, tobacco, and cacao (kuh-**kay**-oh). The seeds of the cacao plant are used to make chocolate and cocoa.

The rulers of New Spain were **peninsulares** (peh-nin-soo-**lah**-rays). A *peninsulare* was a person born in Spain who lived in the New World. The *peninsulares* owned the best lands in the colony of New Spain. They were very wealthy and powerful. Spaniards who were born in the colony were called **criollos** (kree-**oh**-yose). The *criollos* were also wealthy. They had little power, however. The *criollos* were not allowed to serve in important posts in the colonial government.

Mayan architecture in Yucatan

peninsulare
a person born in Spain who lived in the New World

criollo
a Spaniard born in a Spanish colony

(left) Spanish painting of fighting at Tenochtitlan; (right) Aztec painting of fighting at Tenochtitlan.

mestizo

a person who has Spanish and Indian ancestors

The two largest groups in New Spain were the **mestizos** (meh-**stee**-zohs) and the Indians. The *mestizos* were people who had Indian and European ancestors. Many *mestizos* were soldiers, small farmers, or workers. They had no power in the colonial government. The Indians also had no power. Many of the Indians lived in poverty.

On September 15, 1810, the Mexican War of Independence began. The war was led by the *criollos.* The *criollos* wanted to gain more power for themselves and to be independent of Spain. Many *mestizos* also supported the war, hoping that change would improve their conditions.

The leader of the Mexican forces in the war was a priest named Miguel Hidalgo y Costilla (ee-**dahl**-goh ee koh-**stee**-yah). Hidalgo's soldiers were armed only with clubs, axes, and knives. They were soon defeated, and Hidalgo was killed. The war continued under new leaders.

Finally, in 1821, the Spanish forces were defeated. Mexico had won its independence.

Mural of Father Hidalgo, hero of Mexico's War for Independence

The People of Mexico

Today Mexico is a country of more than 75 million people. It is the largest Spanish-speaking nation in the world. Most of the people of Mexico are *mestizos.* They are proud of their Spanish and Indian heritage.

About one million of Mexico's people speak only an Indian language. Many Indians still speak the languages of the ancient Mayas and Aztecs. Aztec words have entered our own language. When we say "tomato," "avocado," or "chocolate," we are using words from the Aztecs. Even the word "Mexico" is from the Aztec language.

One of Mexico's biggest problems is providing education for its people. Mexican law requires all children between the ages of 6 and 14 to go to school. Yet there are not enough schools or teachers. About one out of three Mexican children do not attend school. In the countryside few schools offer classes beyond the fourth grade.

Mexico is working hard to solve its education problem. The National University of Mexico and other colleges are training new teachers. Each year Mexico builds many new schools. In 1900, less than 25 percent of the Mexican people were **literate.** Now 74 percent of the people of Mexico are literate, or able to read and write.

literate
able to read and write

Cities

About two thirds of Mexico's people live in cities and towns. There are 47 cities in Mexico with more than 100,000 people in each.

The capital and largest city of Mexico is Mexico City. It is the second largest city in the world. Mexico City was built by the Spaniards in the 1500's on the site of the Aztec capital. The city is surrounded on all sides by mountains. It lies in a high valley 2,309 meters (7,575 feet) above sea level.

The Basilica of Our Lady of Guadalupe in Mexico City

449

Mexico City slum

Mexico City is the industrial and commercial center of Mexico. There are about 25,000 factories in the city. Each year thousands of workers come to the city in search of jobs. Many cannot find work. They live in crowded apartments or shacks in the poorest parts of the city.

Like our own national capital, Mexico City has many well-known landmarks. The National Palace was built as the home of the Spanish governor of New Spain. Today it houses the offices of Mexico's president. Over the main entrance of the palace hangs Mexico's Liberty Bell. The bell is rung each year on September 15 to celebrate Mexican independence.

One of the most interesting sites in Mexico City is the Plaza of the Three Cultures. This plaza honors the Indian and Spanish heritage of the Mexican people. Ruins of an ancient Aztec temple stand in the plaza next to a Spanish church built in 1524. Modern apartment buildings have been built around the plaza. These buildings represent both Mexico's past and Mexico today.

Section Review

Write your answers on a sheet of paper.
1. Describe briefly the five land regions of Mexico.
2. List three mineral resources and three industries of Mexico.
3. What words from the Aztec language have entered our own language?
4. How is Mexico City like Washington, D.C.? How is it different?

FAMOUS MEXICAN

ROSARIO CASTELLANOS

Rosario Castellanos (kah-stay-**yahn**-ohs) was born in 1925 in Mexico City. She grew up in Comitan, a small town near the border between Mexico and Guatemala. Many Indians live in the area around Comitan. They are descendants of the ancient Mayas. As a young girl Rosario Castellanos was cared for by an Indian nurse. From her nurse she learned many of the legends and beliefs of the Indian people.

When Rosario Castellanos was sixteen, she moved back to Mexico City. She went to college at the University of Mexico. Later she traveled to Spain and studied at the University of Madrid.

Rosario Castellanos wanted to write about the people of Mexico. She especially wanted to tell about the Indians and their way of life. As a young woman, she went to work for the Indian Bureau in southern Mexico. She began writing poems and stories about the Indian people.

In 1957, Rosario Castellanos published her first novel, *Balún Canán*. The title of the novel was taken from the old Indian name for the site where the town of Comitan now stands. The novel is told from the point of view of a seven-year-old girl. It describes the conflict between Indians and whites on a sugar plantation near Comitan. *Balún Canán* was voted the best Mexican novel of 1957.

Rosario Castellanos wrote many other novels and stories. *Family Album* is a book of short stories about women. One of them, called "Cooking Lesson," tells of the troubles of a Mexican housewife. Another, "Little White-Head," is a moving story of a lonely and aging widow. Rosario Castellanos wrote with great power and feeling about her people. She was one of Mexico's best writers. In addition to the many awards for her writing, she was chosen in 1971 to serve as her nation's ambassador to Israel. Rosario Castellanos died in 1974 while serving in Israel.

3 Central America

At the southern end of North America is the narrow bridge of land called Central America. To the west of Central America is the Pacific Ocean. The Caribbean Sea lies to the east. The seven countries of Central America are Guatemala, Belize, El Salvador, Honduras, Nicaragua, Costa Rica, and Panama. Altogether, the countries of Central America cover an area smaller than that of Texas.

More than 1,000 years ago, the Maya Indians built limestone palaces, temples, and pyramids in Central America. They dug great canals to irrigate their fields. The Maya studied **astronomy** and developed a calendar system. Astronomy is the study of the sun, moon, planets, and stars. The Maya recorded their history on carved blocks of stone.

In 1502, Christopher Columbus sailed along the coast of Central America. He claimed the land for Spain. Spanish conquistadors conquered all of Central America by 1540. The region became a Spanish colony for the next 300 years. In the early 1800's, the people of Central America won their independence from Spain.

The United States has been very involved in Central America for many years. From 1904 to 1979, our nation owned a strip of land across Panama. This land was called the Panama Canal Zone. The United States finished building the Panama Canal in 1914. The canal linked the Atlantic and the Pacific oceans. The United States returned the Canal Zone to Panama in 1979.

astronomy
the study of the sun, moon, planets, and stars

American soldiers in Honduras

452

Land and Climate

Central America has two main land regions, the highlands and the coastal lowlands. The highlands are formed by rugged mountains. Many of the mountains are volcanoes. There is at least one volcano in each Central American country. Guatemala has 27 volcanoes! Most people in Central America live in the highlands. They live in areas of rich farmland in mountain valleys and plateaus.

The coastal lowlands run along both coasts of Central America. Parts of the lowlands are covered with swamps and jungles. Other areas have large plantations.

The lowlands have a tropical climate. They are hot and damp. Average temperatures along the coast are usually above 27° C (80° F) each day. Rain falls during the rainy season from May to November. Rainfall is heaviest along the east coast. The climate of the highlands is mild. Daytime temperatures vary from about 19° to 27° C (66° to 80° F). Rainfall is heavy enough for farming in much of the highlands.

Resources and Industries

The most valuable resource of Central America is its soil. Ash from the volcanoes makes the soil very fertile. Farmers use the soil to grow corn, beans, rice, and wheat. These crops are grown for use by the farmers. Large plantations also produce cash crops. Most of the cash crops are exported, or sold to other countries. The United States buys much of the cash crops of Central America.

Guatemalan farm

Coffee being prepared for export

The main cash crop in the highlands is coffee. Central America produces about 10 percent of the world's supply of coffee. It is the major export of Guatemala and El Salvador. There are many plantations of bananas, cotton, and sugarcane in the coastal lowlands. About 10 percent of the world's bananas are grown in Central America. Bananas are the chief export of Honduras, Panama, and Costa Rica. The main export of Nicaragua is cotton. Belize's leading export is sugarcane.

Central America's forestland is another important natural resource. Lumber from the forests is used for building and for making furniture. Mineral resources in Central America include gold, silver, copper, lead, nickel, and zinc.

developing nation

a country that has not yet made full use of its resources and has little or no heavy industry

The countries of Central America are **developing nations**. They have not yet made full use of their resources, and they have little or no heavy industry. The major industries in Central America are processed foods, clothing, and textiles. The people of Central America must buy most of their manufactured goods from other countries. The United States is the main source of manufactured goods for the developing nations of Central America.

The People of Central America

As in Mexico, most of the people of Central America are *mestizos.* They have both Indian and Spanish ancestors. Spanish is the official language in all of Central America except Belize. In Belize the official language is English. Many Indians in Central America speak their own native languages.

Poverty is widespread in Central America. A few Central Americans are wealthy. Most are very poor. Many people live on small farms. Their homes are made of sun-dried clay bricks called **adobe.** Others live in **wattle huts** made of woven branches covered with mud. Their tools are often limited to a digging stick and a hoe. They plow their fields with a mule or an ox. A large number of Central Americans also work on plantations. They earn low wages, and most live in poverty.

In recent years many Central Americans have come to the cities seeking a better life. But there are not enough jobs for the people in the cities. Many must live in shacks or in crowded slums. Poverty remains one of Central America's biggest problems.

adobe
bricks made out of clay and then dried in the sun
wattle hut
a house made of woven branches covered with mud

Urban slum in Guatemala

Cities

One of the largest cities in Central America is Managua (mah-**nah**-gwah), the capital of Nicaragua. The city was built in the 1850's on the southern shore of Lake Managua. It is the center for business and industry in Nicaragua. Much of the nation's coffee and cotton crop is brought to Managua for sale. Industries in the city include cement plants, textile mills, and shoe factories.

Managua has often been heavily damaged by earthquakes. An earthquake in 1931 destroyed many buildings. The city, however, was soon rebuilt. The entire downtown area was again destroyed by an earthquake in 1972. About 10,000 people were killed. The old downtown area has not yet recovered from the 1972 earthquake. Much of the city's center is empty fields where buildings once stood.

San Salvador is the capital and largest city of El Salvador. It has many modern office buildings. Well-to-do Salvadorans live in comfortable apartments or homes in the city. San Salvador also has large slums where the city's poor live.

Visitors to San Salvador often enjoy visiting the outdoor markets along the city's busy streets. Colorful baskets, pottery, and fresh fruits are sold by Salvadoran merchants.

El Salvadoran marketplace

Section Review

Write your answers on a sheet of paper.
1. Name the seven countries of Central America.
2. What is Central America's most valuable resource?
3. What is a developing nation?
4. Describe the problem of poverty in Central America.
5. Which do you think would help end poverty in Central America: a) more jobs, b) better education, c) more help from other countries. Why?

4 South America

South America is the fourth largest continent. There are 12 independent countries and two territories in South America. The largest country is Brazil. It covers nearly half the continent. The two territories in South America are French Guiana (ghee-**an**-uh) and the Falkland Islands. Find these territories on the map on page 438. French Guiana is governed by France. The Falkland Islands are ruled by Great Britain.

Land and Climate

South America is shaped roughly like a huge triangle. Near its northern edge is the equator. The southern tip of the continent is only 970 kilometers (600 miles) from the continent of Antarctica.

There are four major land regions in South America. The most western region is the Pacific Lowlands. This narrow region includes swamps and tropical forests in the north. Farther south are desert lands. The southern coast of Chile is cut by many **fiords** (fee-**ordz**). A fiord is a narrow arm of the sea. The second region of South America is the Andes Mountains. The Andes is the longest mountain range in the world. Only the Himalaya Mountains of northern India are taller than the Andes. The Andes' tallest peaks are covered with ice and snow.

fiord
a narrow inlet of the sea between high, rocky banks

The Chilean Andes

Cattle ranch

pampa
a treeless, grassy plain in South America

tributary
a river or stream that flows into a larger body of water

South America's third region is the great Central Plains. Much of this area is covered with grassy fields or tropical forests. The treeless, grassy plains of Argentina are called **pampas** (**pam**-pahs). The pampas provide excellent grazing land for cattle and sheep.

The Eastern Highlands form the fourth region of South America. The highlands include most of the northern and eastern part of South America. This region of rolling hills and plateaus is much lower than the Andes.

Many large rivers flow across South America. The Amazon River is the second longest river in the world. It begins high in the Andes Mountains of Peru. More than 200 rivers or streams flow into the Amazon as it moves through Brazil to the Atlantic Ocean. The Rio de la Plata water system drains much of the southern part of the continent. Its **tributaries** are the major transportation routes in the south. A tributary is a river or stream that flows into a larger body of water.

South America has almost every type of climate. Look at the climate map of Latin America on page 441. Find the major climate zones of South America. Most of the continent is warm all year round. Near the equator it is always hot and humid. Farther south the summers are cool and the winters are mild. It gets cold only in the high Andes Mountains and at the southern tip of the continent. Most of South America lies south of the equator. Its seasons are opposite those of North America. Summers in South America are from December to March. Winters last from June to September.

Resources and Industries

Only about 5 percent of South America's land is used for farming. Much of the land is either too wet or too dry for farming. Other areas are too mountainous. The most important cash crops are coffee and sugar. Brazil and Colombia are the world's leading producers of coffee. Sugar is a major export of Ecuador and Venezuela. The pampas of Argentina are one of the richest farming areas in the world. Wheat from Argentina is sold to many countries. Cattle ranching is a major activity in Argentina, Uruguay, Brazil, Venezuela, and Colombia.

South America has many valuable mineral resources. Its most important resource is oil. Venezuela is one of the world's leading oil-producing nations. Most of the oil from Venezuela is exported to the United States. There are also large oil deposits in Colombia, Ecuador, and Peru. Chile is the world's leading exporter of copper. Brazil has about one third of the world's supply of iron ore. Most of the world's emeralds come from Colombia. Gold and silver are mined in Peru, Colombia, and Chile.

Industries in South America have grown rapidly in recent years. Steel production has tripled in Brazil in the past 30 years. Chile has built some of South America's largest steel mills and cement plants. The leading industries of South America are textiles and processed foods. Factories also build airplanes, cars, furniture, and many other goods. In spite of this rapid growth, South America must still import many of its manufactured goods.

Chilean copper mine

Terraced fields of the Incas

Discovery and Conquest

Long before Europeans discovered the New World,
South America was the home of many Indian tribes. The
highlands of the Andes were the home of the Inca Indians.
The Incas ruled an empire that ran from southern Colombia to central Chile. They built roads and bridges. They
farmed by cutting **terraced fields** into the steep hillsides
of the Andes. The Incas made jewelry and tools of gold,
silver, and copper.

Christopher Columbus was the first European to reach
South America. He landed at the mouth of the Orinoco
River in 1498. He claimed the land for Spain. Explorers
from Portugal also soon arrived in South America. In 1500,
Pedro Cabral (kah-**brahl**) claimed large areas of Brazil for
Portugal.

Francisco Pizarro (pih-**sah**-roh) led the Spanish conquest of the Incas. Pizarro captured the king of the Incas
and held him for **ransom.** The ransom was paid, but the
Inca king was killed anyway. By 1540, most of South America had been conquered by the Europeans.

South America was divided into European colonies. Brazil became a colony of Portugal. Most of the rest of South
America was controlled by Spain. The Indians of South

America were put to work on plantations and in mines. Blacks from Africa were brought as slaves to South America.

South America remained under European control for about 300 years. In the early 1800's, the colonies of South America fought for, and won, their independence. One of the great leaders of the fight for independence was Simón Bolívar (boh-**lee**-vahr). His victories led to independence for Bolivia, Colombia, Ecuador, Peru, and Venezuela. Simón Bolívar is called the "George Washington of South America."

The People of South America

South America is a land of varied people. Its three main population groups are whites, *mestizos,* and Indians. The ancestors of the whites came to South America from Europe. Most people in Argentina, Brazil, and Uruguay are white. Most Brazilians have Portuguese, Italian, or German ancestors. Brazil has a larger population than all of the other countries of South America put together.

Mestizos are the largest group in Colombia, Venezuela, Chile, and Paraguay. Indians form the largest group in Bolivia, Ecuador, and Peru. There are small groups of blacks in many South American countries.

Most people in South America speak Spanish or Portuguese. Spanish is the official language in nearly every country. The official language of Brazil is Portuguese. In Peru both Spanish and the language of the Incas are official languages. Many Indians in South America still speak their native language.

All of the countries of South America have free public elementary schools. The high schools are either public or church-owned. There are also many fine colleges and universities in South America. Yet many South American children are not able to go to school. They live in villages far from the nearest school. They must work all day in the fields with their parents. They have no time to go to school. As a result many South Americans are **illiterate,** that is, unable to read or write. In Bolivia and Peru more than half the people are illiterate.

Statue of Simón Bolívar

illiterate
not able to read or

463

Several South American countries have developed a new kind of school for their people. Teachers travel from village to village to meet with their students. They teach their classes after the children and their parents have finished working. These new schools are bringing education to many parts of South America for the first time.

Cities

The largest city in South America is São Paulo (sow **pow**-loh). More than 7 million people live in São Paulo. It is almost as large as New York City, the largest city in the United States. The busy downtown area of São Paulo has wide avenues and tall skyscrapers. São Paulo is the business and industrial center of Brazil. It is also a center for education and the arts. Many of Brazil's poor people have moved to São Paulo in the hope of finding work. The poor of São Paulo live in crowded slums.

The capital and largest city of Chile is Santiago (sahn-tee-**ah**-goh). Santiago is Chile's business and political cen-

Apprentice jewelers in São Paulo industrial school

Santiago, Chile

ter. It houses one third of Chile's total population. Wealthy Chileans live in large homes with beautiful courtyards. Like São Paulo, Santiago has received many of its nation's poor people who come to the city in search of jobs. About one fourth of the people of Santiago live in poverty.

Section Review

Write your answers on a sheet of paper.

1. Name and describe the four major land regions of South America.
2. What is the most valuable mineral resource found in South America?
3. Why is Simón Bolivar known as the "George Washington of South America?"
4. Why are many South American children not able to go to school?
5. In what ways do you think the people of South America would be helped by a better education?

UNIT REVIEW

Word Work

Write the sentences below on a sheet of paper. Fill in the blanks with the correct words from the list.

bilingual   literate   pampa
            developing nation   hydroelectric power

1. A _____ is a treeless, grassy plain in South America.
2. _____ is energy produced by water power.
3. People who are _____ are able to speak two languages.
4. A _____ is a country that has not yet made full use of its resources and has little or no heavy industry.
5. To be _____ means to be able to read and write.

Knowing the Facts

Write your answers on a sheet of paper.
1. Describe briefly the climate of three of the land regions of Canada.
2. Why are Canada's forests a valuable natural resource?
3. Who led the Mexican War of Independence?
4. What are some of the major accomplishments of the Maya Indians of Central America?
5. What are the three main population groups of South America?

Using What You Know

Choose one of the following activities. Follow the instructions given here.
1. Prepare a pie graph showing the different population groups of Canada. Have each section of your graph stand for one of the population groups described in Section 4 of Chapter 22.

2. Prepare a chart comparing the six land regions of Canada and the five land regions of Mexico. Include information about each land region.

Skills Practice

Use the flow charts on page 435 to answer the questions below. Write your answers on a sheet of paper.

1. How many different steps are there between the introduction of a bill and its approval by the Canadian governor general?
2. How many steps are there between the introduction of a bill and its approval by the President of the United States?
3. According to these two charts, does the governor general or the President have more power in the law-making process?

Your Heritage

The United States is a nation of immigrants. People have come from many other lands. Some have come from our neighbors Canada and Latin America. Are there any students in your school who were born in other countries? Ask them what they remember about their other countries. Ask them what things surprised them most when they came to the United States. Report to the class on what you have found out.

GLOSSARY

abolitionist a person who wanted to do away with slavery

adapt to change in order to fit new conditions

adobe bricks made out of clay and then dried in the sun

airlift the transporting of goods by airplane when ground routes are blocked

alliance a group of nations that agrees to help each other

ally a person, nation, or group that promises support to another

almanac a book of facts that is published every year, containing information about the stars and weather and often other information as well

amendment a change or addition, especially a change or an addition to the United States Constitution

amnesty a pardon for a crime, especially a crime against a government

approval acceptance, agreement, saying yes to

assembly line a method of producing goods in which workers put together a product as it goes past them on a moving belt

astronomy the study of the sun, moon, planets, and stars

atlas a book of maps or the map section of a book

band a group formed of different American Indian families that traveled and worked together

barter to trade by exchanging goods or services instead of money

bilingual able to speak two languages

birth rate the number of births per 1,000 people in a year

blitzkrieg lightning war; a fast-moving attack of tanks and aircraft focused on one area

blockade the blocking off of a place so that no one can enter or exit without permission

bond a paper that states that a citizen has lent money to the government; the government agrees to pay back the loan with interest, at a later date

boycott to refuse to deal with a person, country, or business as a means of protest

bribe an illegal payment given in return for expected favors

burgess a landowner who could vote in colonial Virginia

cabinet a group of advisers or assistants to a nation's leader

carpetbagger the name given to a Northerner who moved to the South to take part in Reconstruction governments

cash crop a crop raised to be sold, rather than used, by the farmer

charter a document that gave the right to establish a colony

checks and balances a political system in which different branches of government limit, or check, the power of the other branches

circumnavigate to sail completely around

civil rights the rights guaranteed to every American by the Constitution or by laws passed by Congress

civil war a war fought between people of the same nation

clan a group of families in which all members have a common ancestor

climate regions map a map showing the kind of weather, such as temperature and rainfall, in a particular area

Cold War the struggle between communist nations and the United States and its allies, using ideas and aid rather than weapons

colony a place that is governed by people from another country

communism a system in which all property, including industry, is owned by the people and managed by the government

compass an instrument that shows directions with a needle of magnetized iron ore

compass rose a drawing on a map of a compass showing the main directions of north, south, east, and west

compromise an agreement reached when each side gives in a little

concentration camp a prison for those the government says are its enemies

confederation the joining together of states in order to achieve common goals

conquistador a Spanish leader who led the conquest of the Americas

conservation the careful use and protection of natural resources

consolidate to combine or unite

constitutional in agreement with the laws set down in the United States Constitution

coordinate a number or letter used to help pinpoint a location

criollo a Spaniard born in a Spanish colony

currency the money in general use in a country

deciduous forest forest of trees that shed their leaves each fall

democracy a type of government where all adult citizens have the right to vote in elections

depression a time when the economy fails to grow and many people are out of work

developing nation a country that has not yet made full use of its resources and has little or no heavy industry

distance scale a measuring line on a map that helps the reader figure the actual distance from one place to another

economy the method of producing and distributing wealth

elevation map a map showing the height of the landforms of a particular area, such as mountains, plateaus, and plains

Emancipation Proclamation President Lincoln's order that granted freedom to the slaves in the Confederate states

environment everything that surrounds us, especially the air, land, and water

equator a line of latitude, or parallel, that marks the middle of the earth, halfway between the North and South poles

ethnic having to do with people who share the same customs, language, and culture

executive having to do with directing a government and enforcing its laws

expedition a journey for a special purpose

export a product that is sent out of a country for sale; to send a product to another country for sale

factory a place where goods are made by machine

federal a form of government that divides power between individual states and the national government

feminist a person who supports equal rights for women

fiord a narrow inlet of the sea between high, rocky banks

forge to work into shape by heating or hammering

frontier an area at the very edge of a settled region that borders on an unsettled area

geothermal energy energy from hot water or steam near the earth's surface

glacier a huge sheet of slowly moving ice

globe a round model of the earth

grid a pattern formed when vertical and horizontal lines cross; on a globe, the parallels and meridians form a grid used to measure distances and locates places

gross national product (GNP) the total value in dollars of all goods and services produced by a country in one year

hemisphere half of a sphere; on a globe, a hemisphere represents one half of the earth

Hessian a German soldier who fought for the British during the American Revolution

homesteader a person who settled on government land and owned it after five years

hostage a person who is taken prisoner and not released until certain promises or conditions are met

humus decayed leaves and other vegetable matter in the soil

hydroelectric power energy produced by water power

Ice Age a period of time, starting almost 2 million years ago and ending 10,000 years ago, when much of North America was covered by glaciers

illiterate not able to read or write

immigrant a foreign-born settler

impeachment the process by which the House of Representatives brings charges against a government official

inaugurate to install in office with a formal ceremony

indentured servant a person who agreed to work for someone for a certain amount of time to pay off the cost of passage to the United States

indigo a plant from which a blue dye is made

inflation a rapid rise in the prices of goods and services caused by government spending and increased demand for limited resources

installment buying paying part of the purchase price of an item and making regular payments plus interest for the rest of the amount

integrate to bring people of different races together

interest a charge for borrowing money

irrigation a way of supplying water to land

judicial having to do with examining laws in a court of law

labor union an organization of workers that tries to improve its members' wages and working conditions

leaching the washing of minerals out of the soil by heavy rains

leeward facing away from a blowing wind

legislative having to do with the making of laws

legislature a group of persons chosen to make the laws of a nation or a state

liberate to make free

lichen simple moss-like plant that grows on rocks and tree trunks

literate able to read and write

lock a canal with gates that can change water levels

longhouse a long, wooden house shared by many families of Iroquois Indians

lowland low, flat land area

map key a section of a map that explains the symbols used on a map

mass production the use of machines to manufacture goods cheaply and quickly

meridian a vertical line circling a globe, passing through the North Pole and the South Pole, used to indicate distances and to locate places on the earth

mestizo a person who has Spanish and Indian ancestors

minuteman a colonial soldier who could be ready to fight at a minute's notice

mission a church settlement built by priests who teach people about religion

missionary a person who tries to convert people to his or her religion

monopoly a company that has complete control of an industry

mouth the place where a stream or river empties into a larger body of water

muckraker a person who looks for wrongdoing and lets others know about it; muckrakers were usually newspaper or magazine reporters

navigate to direct the course of a ship or airplane

neutral not supporting one side or another in a conflict

Northwest Passage an imaginary water passage that early explorers believed would lead through North America to Asia

ordinance an order or law made by a government

overseer a boss who watched over the slaves for a plantation owner

pampa a treeless, grassy plain in South America

parallel a horizontal line circling a globe, used to indicate distances and to locate places on the earth

parliament the lawmaking body of some nations, including Great Britain

patent a government document that gives to the inventor alone the right to make and sell a new invention for a certain number of years

patriot an American colonist who wanted independence from Great Britain

Peace Corps a program of the United States government in which Americans teach needed skills to people around the World

peninsulare a person born in Spain who lived in the New World

pillory a wooden frame with holes for head and arms, used by the Puritans to punish people

pioneer one of the first settlers in a new area who opens the way for others

plantation a large farm on which many workers are needed to raise crops

political map a map showing how people have divided an area into nations, states, counties, or townships with boundaries

pollution anything that makes air, water, or land impure or contaminated

potlatch a Northwest Indian ceremony in which the host gives away valuables to prove her or his wealth

Prime Meridian the line of longitude circling a globe from the North Pole through England and western Africa to the South Pole

proclamation an official announcement

quarter to provide housing for soldiers

radical extreme

range a large area of land where cattle graze

ransom a price paid to free someone who has been captured

ratify to approve officially

rationing a system used for distributing goods that are in short supply

reef a ridge of sand, rock, or coral near the surface of the sea

refining making finer or purer

reform to improve living conditions, government, health care, and working conditions

refugee a person who flees from her or his home country to escape discrimination for political or religious beliefs

religious toleration the willingness to allow people to worship according to their own beliefs

repeal to do away with; take back

republic a country that is governed by elected representatives

reservation an area of land set aside by the government as a home for American Indians

revolution the overthrow of a government by force

road map a map showing the roads for automobile travel in a particular area

saga a story of the adventures and heroic deeds of a family

satellite a humanmade object that orbits around the earth, moon, or other bodies in space, often used to gather and send information

scalawag the name given to a white Southerner who took part in Reconstruction governments

scandal a public disgrace

secede to leave or withdraw from

secretary a head of a United States government department and an adviser to the President

segregation the separation of people on the basis of race

settlement house a center that offers community members social, educational, and recreational activities

sharecropping a system of farming in which farmers rent land from landowners and pay their rent with a share of the crops they grow

slum a run-down area of a city where housing is poor and crowded

smuggler a person who brings things into, or takes things out of, a country illegally

stock a share in a business or company

stock market a place where shares in companies are bought and sold

strait a narrow waterway that connects two larger bodies of water

strike a refusal to work until workers can reach an agreement with their employer

suburb a town that is close to a city

suffrage the right to vote

surplus an extra supply

symbol something that stands for something else

tariff the money charged for permission to bring goods into a state

tenement an apartment house that is run-down, very crowded, or poorly built

tepee a cone-shaped tent made of animal skins

terraced field a level strip of farmland cut into the side of a hill

territory the land and waters that belong to an area, region, state, or nation

Tory an American colonist who supported the British during the War for Independence

transcontinental going from one side of the continent to the other

treaty a formal agreement between nations, signed by each

tributary a river or stream that flows into a larger body of water

trust a group of businesses that unites in order to control the production and price of certain goods

tundra wide, treeless plain where few plants or animals live

unemployment rate the percentage of workers who do not have jobs

urban having to do with a city or cities

veto to turn down, or say no to

voyageur a person who traveled by canoe in North America, buying and trading furs

wattle hut a house made of woven branches covered with mud

welfare the condition of being well and having enough money

wigwam an Eastern Woodlands Indian dwelling with an arched frame and a bark or hide covering

windward facing into a blowing wind

women's liberation movement a campaign by women to achieve equal rights with men in all aspects of life

wood pulp ground-up wood fibers from logs

INDEX

ART CREDITS

Wendy Biggins p. 262
Lauren Simeone p. 93
Bryn Thomas p. 159
Randi Wasserman p. 442
MAPS: General Cartography, Inc.
Fine Line Illustrations, Inc. pp. 16–17, 18–19

PHOTO CREDITS

Sources are abbreviated as follows:
AMNH American Museum of Natural History
BA Bettmann Archive
CP Culver Pictures
LC Library of Congress
MMA Metropolitan Museum of Art, New York City
NYHS New York Historical Society, New York City
NYPL New York Public Library
UPI United Press International
WW Wide World Photos

UNIT 1: pp. 22–23 Eric Kroll/Taurus Photos; p. 23(t) Granger Collection; p. 23(b) Detail from Sebastiano del Piombo's *Christopher Columbus,* MMA. Gift of J. Pierpont Morgan, 1900; p. 24 Field Museum of Natural History; pp. 26, 28 Courtesy of AMNH; p. 32 Richard Erdoes; p. 33 The Seatte Art Museum, Eugene Fuller Memorial Collection, 59.105; p. 34(l) Museum of the American Indian, Heye Foundation; p. 34(r) Denver Art Museum; p. 35 Courtesy of AMNH; p. 37 National Maritime Museum, England; p. 37 Ted Spiegel/Black Star; p. 40(l) Granger Collection; p. 40(r) Bodlein Library; pp. 42, 43 NYPL, Rare Book Division; p. 45 Duque del Infantado/Foto MAS; p. 46(t) Courtesy of AMNH; p. 46(b) Irmgard Groth, Mexico City; p. 47 Granger Collection; p. 48 Harvard University; p. 54(l) © David Barnes/Photo Researchers; p. 54(m) © Russ Kinne 1976/Photo Researchers, p. 54(r) HRW Photo by John King; p. 55 Courtesy of AMNH.
UNIT 2: pp. 58–59 The Society of California Pioneers; p. 59(t) Henry Francis Dupont Winterthur Museum, Winterthur, Delaware; p. 59(b) By Courtesy of the National Portrait Gallery, London; p. 60 John Lewis Stage/The Image Bank; p. 62 Richard Erdoes; p. 63 Museo Naval, Madrid; p. 64 David Muench; p. 65 LC; p. 66 Walters Art Gallery; p. 67 Culver Pictures; p. 70 NYPL, Rare Book Division; p. 71(t) Folger Shakespeare Library, Washington, D.C.: p. 71(b) John Lewis Stage/The Image Bank; p. 72 Colonial Williamsburg Foundation; p. 73 Culver Pictures; p. 74(t,b) Barbara Kirk; p. 75 Worcester Art Museum; p. 76 CP; p. 77 Detail, Courtesy, National Portrait Gallery; p. 78 Maryland Historical Society; p. 80 Historical Picture Service; p. 81 The Art Museum, Princeton University, Edward Duff Balkan Collection of American Folk Art; p. 82 Massachusetts Historical Society; p. 83 Granger Collection; p. 85 Thomas Gilcrease Institute, Tulsa, Oklahoma; p. 86 NYPL, Prints Division; p. 87 Historical Society of Pennsylvania; p. 88(t) Courtesy of the Franklin Institute Science Museum,

City; p. 257(b) George Eastman House; p. 258 Smithsonian Institution; p. 260(t) Bella C. Landauer Collection, NYHS; p. 260(b) Minnesota Historical Society; p. 261 Nebraska State Historical Society; p. 263 © Charles J. Belden; p. 264 California Historical Society; p. 265 Denver Public Library; p. 266 Minnesota Historical Society; p. 267 National Archives; p. 268 U.S. Signal Corps; p. 269 LC; p. 270(t) © Anheuser-Busch, Inc., NYHS, New York City; p. 270(b) Smithsonian Institution; p. 271 U.S. Signal Corps; p. 272 Chicago Historical Society; p. 274 Union Pacific Railroad; p. 276 BA; p. 277 Bethlehem Steel Corporation; p. 278 LC; p. 281 BA; p. 282 C; pp. 283, 284 BA; p. 285 LC; p. 286 Edison Historic Site; p. 288(t) Tuskegee Institute; p. 288(b) Museum of Modern Art, New York City; p. 289 BA; p. 290 The Brooklyn Museum, Dick S. Ramsay Fund; pp. 291, 292, 293 Museum of the City of New York; p. 294 Brown Brothers; p. 295 Granger Collection; p. 299(t) LC; p. 299(b) BA; p. 300 CP; p. 301 Bancroft Library, University of California, Berkeley, California; p. 303(l) © 1978 Tom McHugh/ Photo Researchers; p. 303(r) CP; p. 306(l) Detail, MMA, Gift of Frederick H. Hatch; p. 306(r) Museum of the City of New York; pp. 307, 308 CP; p. 309 Culver Pictures; p. 310 (detail) Collection of Mrs. John Steuart Curry; p. 311 Collection of Harry T. Peters, Jr. **UNIT 7:** pp. 314–315, p. 315(t) CP; p. 315(b), p. 316 LC; p. 317 Chicago Historical Society; p. 318(t) Granger Collection; p. 318(b) Photo Courtesy of Remington Art Museum, Ogdensburg, N.Y.; p. 319 LC; p. 322 Granger Collection; p. 323 HRW Photo File; pp. 324, 325 Imperial War Museum, London; pp. 328, 329 CP; p. 330 Brown Brothers; pp. 331, 332 CP; p. 333 FPG; p. 334 Brown Brothers; p. 335 Granger Collection; p. 336 CP; p. 337(t) BA; p. 338(b) CP; p. 338 Granger Collection; p. 339 WW; p. 340 Franklin D. Roosevelt Library p. 341(t) The Oakland Museum; p. 341(b) NYPL; p. 342(t) Harris and Ewing; p. 342(b), pp. 343, 344 CP; p. 345 Franklin D. Roosevelt

Library; p. 348 Combat Art Division, U.S. Navy Department; pp. 349, 350(t) WW; p. 350(b) HRW Photo File; pp. 351, 352 WW; p. 353 UPI; p. 354 BA; p. 355 WW; p. 356 Official U.S. Coast Guard Photo; p. 357 UPI; p. 358 United States Atomic Energy Commission; p. 359 UPI; p. 361(t) U.S. Office of War Information; p. 361(b), p. 362 LC; p. 363(t) HRW Photo File; p. 363(b) U.S. Army Photograph; p. 364(l) Brown Brothers; p. 364(r) LC; p. 365(l) James Van Derzee; p. 365(r) Detail from the Phillips Collection. Photo by Henry Belville. **UNIT 8:** p. 368 NASA; p. 369(l) Hank Morgan; p. 369(tr) R. Eyerman/Black Star; p. 369(br) © Richard Hutchings/Photo Researchers; p. 370 UPI; p. 372 Ferno Jacobs/Black Star; p. 373 Robert Lackenback/Black Star; p. 374 Robert Ellison/Empire News/ Black Star; p. 377 WW; p. 378 Messerschmidt/Alpha Photos; p. 379(t) WW; p. 379(b) UPI; p. 380 John Messina/Black Star; p. 381 UPI; p. 382 Manfred Kreiner/Black Star; p. 383(t) Cecil Stoughton/ Lyndon Baines Johnson Library; p. 383(b) WW; p. 384 Dirk Halstead/Gamma-Liaison; p. 385 NASA; p. 386 R. Steedman/The Image Bank; p. 387 NASA; p. 388 Shelley Katz/Black Star; p. 389 Leonard Freed/Magnum Photos; p. 390(t) Brad Nelson/University of Utah Medical Center; p. 390(b) UPI; p. 391 Robert Knowles/Black Star; p. 393(t,b) U.P.I.; p. 394(t) U.P.I.; p. 394(b) AP/Wide World Photos; p. 395(t) Allan Tannenbaum/Sygma p. 395(bl) Jan Halaska/Photo Researchers, p. 395(br) Bob Dickerson/ Black Star; p. 396(l) Michal Heron/Woodfin Camp, p. 396(r) Bill Cadge/Image Bank; p. 397(t) White House Photo/Black Star; p. 397(b) Frank Johnson/Black Star; p. 398(t) Bob Fitch/Black Star; p. 398(b) Herman Kokojan/Black Star; p. 399 Leonard Freed/Magnum; p. 402(t) Terence Moore/Black Star; p. 402(b) Maggie Berkvist; p. 404 Gamma Liaison; p. 405 Joe Traver/Gamma Liaison; p. 406 Walker/Gamma Liaison; p. 407 NASA; pp. 408–409 Dr. Melvin L. Prueitt, Los Alamos National Laboratory. Work performed under the auspices of the Department of Energy.

UNIT 9: pp. 412–413 David Madison/Stock Market; p. 413(t) Freeman Patterson/Masterfile; p. 413(b) Bill Stanton/Stock Market; p. 414 Steve Vidler/Leo de Wys; p. 416 Tom Tracy/Stock Shop; p. 417 Bill Brooks/Masterfile; p. 418 Fred Ward/Black Star; p. 419 Earl Roberge/Photo Researchers; p. 420 Chris Bruun/Masterfile; p. 421 Ted Grant/Masterfile; p. 422 Mark Tomalty/Masterfile; p. 423(t) Michael Phillip Manheim/Photo Researchers; p. 423(b) Frederic Remington painting/Granger Collection; p. 424 Granger Collection; p. 425 National Gallery of Canada, Ottawa; p. 427 Masterfile; p. 428 Jonathon Wenk/ Black Star; p. 429 Bob Anderson/ Masterfile; p. 430(t) Ida Wyman/Int'l Stock Photo; p. 430(b) Porterfield Chickering/Photo Researchers; p. 431(t) R. Semeniuk/Stock Market; p. 431(b) Bill Stanton/Int'l Stock Photo; p. 432(t) Frank Grant/Int'l Stock Photo; p. 432(b) Derek Carey/Masterfile; p. 433 Leo de Wys; p. 436 K. Benser/Leo de Wys; p. 437 Alese and Mort Rechter/The Stock Market; p. 439 Victor Englebert/Black Star; p. 440 Claus Meyer/Black Star; p. 443 Leo de Wys; p. 445(t) Keith Gunnar; p. 445(b) John Running/Black Star; p. 446 Sergio Dorantes/Gamma Liaison; p. 447(t) Robert Frerck/ Woodfin Camp; p. 447(l) Miguel Gonzalez painting, Museo de America, Madrid; p. 447(r) American Museum of Natural History; p. 448 Robert Frerck/ Woodfin Camp; p. 449 J. Messerschmidt/Stock Shop; p. 450 Sergio Dorantes/Gamma Liaison; p. 452 M. Naythons/Gamma Liaison; p. 453 Carl Frank/Photo Researchers; p. 454 Antonio Gusmao/Black Star; p. 455 Chas. Henneghien/Bruce Coleman; p. 456 Luis Villota/Stock Market; p. 457 F. Goltier/Photo Researchers; p. 458 Arturo A. Wesley/Black Star; p. 459 M.P. Kahl/Photo Researchers; p. 460 Fred Ward/Black Star; p. 461 Norman Tomalin/Bruce Coleman; p. 462 Wm. A. Graham/Photo Researchers; p. 463 Arnim Walker/ Shostal.